REPRESENTATION AND RESISTANCE

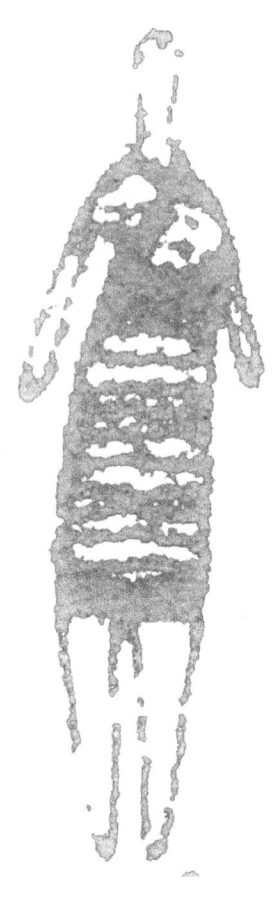

UNIVERSITY OF
CALGARY
PRESS

REPRESENTATION AND RESISTANCE
South Asian and African Women's Texts at Home and in the Diaspora

JASPAL KAUR SINGH

© 2008 Jaspal Kaur Singh

University of Calgary Press
2500 University Drive NW
Calgary, Alberta
Canada T2N 1N4
www.uofcpress.com

No part of this publication may be reproduced, stored in a retrieval system or transmitted, in any form or by any means, without the prior written consent of the publisher or a license from The Canadian Copyright Licensing Agency (Access Copyright). For an Access Copyright license, visit www.accesscopyright.ca or call toll free 1-800-893-5777.

LIBRARY AND ARCHIVES CANADA CATALOGUING IN PUBLICATION

Singh, Jaspal Kaur, 1951-
    Representation and resistance : South Asian and African women's texts at home and in the diaspora / Jaspal Kaur Singh.

Includes bibliographical references and index.
ISBN 978-1-55238-245-5

    1. South Asian literature (English)–Women authors–History and criticism.
2. African literature (English)–Women authors–History and criticism. 3. Women in literature. 4. Feminism and literature. 5. Sex role in literature. 6. South Asian diaspora in literature. 7. African diaspora in literature. 8. Postcolonialism in literature. I. Title.

PN56.5.W64S563 2008   820.9'9287   C2008-905794-5

The University of Calgary Press acknowledges the support of the Alberta Foundation for the Arts for our publications. We acknowledge the financial support of the Government of Canada through the Book Publishing Industry Development Program (BPIDP) for our publishing activities. We acknowledge the financial support of the Canada Council for the Arts for our publishing program.

Cover design, page design, and typesetting by Melina Cusano

TABLE OF CONTENTS

Preface	vii
Acknowledgments	xiii
1: Postcolonial Women Writers and Their Cultural Productions	1
2: Dominant Epistemologies and Alternative Readings: Gender and Globalization	29
3: The Indian Diasopra and Cultural Alienation in Bharati Mukherjee's Texts	61
4: Postcoloniality and Indian Female Sexuality in Aparna Sen's Film *Parama*	89
5: Educational Debates and the Postcolonial Female Imagination in Mariama Bâ's *So Long a Letter*	103
6: The Diasporic Search for Cultural Belonging in Myriam Warner-Vieyra's *Juletane*	115
7: Maddening Inscriptions and Contradictory Subjectivities in Tsitsi Dangarembga's *Nervous Conditions*	125
8: Globalism and Transnationalism: Cultural Politics in the Texts of Mira Nair, Gurinder Chadha, Agnes Sam, and Farida Karodia	135
9: Queering Diaspora in Shani Mootoo's *Cereus Blooms at Night*, Nisha Ganatra's *Chutney Popcorn*, and Deepa Mehta's *Fire*	163
10: Transnationalism and the Politics of Representation in the Texts of Meena Alexander, Gurinder Chadha, Zainab Ali, and Samina Ali	177
Conclusion: The Politics of Location and Postcolonial/Transnational Feminst Critical Practices	197
Notes	201
Bibliography	205
Index	217

Preface

My name is Jaspal Kaur Singh. I was born in Taunggyi, Burma. When I was eleven years old, I went to a priest at the St. Joseph Catholic church and said, "Father, I want to become a Catholic." As I stood hesitating, my friend Maria, tall and lanky, with long, greasy plaits hanging down on both sides of her dark, brown Indian face, nudged me forward a bit and I repeated the request.

Maria had told me that Christian children could write a long wish list, that Santa would come down the chimney (although we didn't have chimneys, I was assured he was smart enough to find other means of entry), and that if one had been good, one's wishes would come true. Maria had asked me solemnly, "Are you a good girl?"

Feeling a slight tightening in my chest, for I did not believe I was a good girl, I fibbed, "Yes."

The priest, in his beautiful white habit, smiled kindly at me. "Why?"

"Because I want Santa Claus to come to my house."

"Bring your parents next Sunday to me, and we will take care of that," he smiled kindly at me.

I couldn't imagine my Sikh parents allowing me to convert. Sorely disappointed at not having Santa come to my house, I left the church with Maria, who was still talking about Santa and his sleigh.

I, too, was tall and lanky like Maria, and also equally brown with greasy plaits hanging down my back. My school uniform, a navy tunic with a white short-sleeved shirt, was rumpled from playing in the schoolyard after school.

Maria was a year older than me and got to be the class monitor sometimes. Our school's name was Saint Anne's Convent High School, run by Roman Catholic Nuns from Ireland and Italy, and other Anglo-Burmese or biracial nuns.

Every morning, we children gathered in the schoolyard for hymn singing. Our voices lusty, we would sing, "Comboly Gos send down those beams! Comboly Gos send down dose beams! Whis seefly flow in, in silent steem, from thy bight thone above! Oh, come thy father of thy but the bather!" The nuns made sure our fingers were clean and our shoes polished.

Oh, but the ones the nuns loved best were the boarders, with names like Daisy, and Rosy, and Margaret! We were merely tolerated. In fact, when my father, turbaned and bearded, took my oldest sister for admission, he was turned away. However, when my maternal uncle, a clean-shaven Sikh who worked in the British administration as a clerk, took my sister for admission, she was accepted. Subsequently, all of my five siblings and I attended the convent. My father said, "You are lucky to be in the convent school. Learn to become like the nuns. They are good women. They will teach you how to become successful in life."

One day, I said to Mother Christine, the Anglo-Burmese supervisor of the kindergarten, "Maria told me all about Holy Communion. Can I too dress up in a beautiful dress and come to church on Sunday?"

"If you can bring your parents, you may."

Maria later said to me that she didn't think I could go for Holy Communion.

"Why not? My mother can sew a beautiful dress for me."

"If you do Communion, you have to confess."

"Confess what?"

"Everything. All your sinful thoughts in your head. Do you hate your parents?"

"Sometimes." I thought about my simple mother with her *salwar kameez* and Punjabi-speaking habits, always working hard, and knew I wanted to be … Christian and English-speaking.

"Well, you must tell the father about those thoughts as well. You have to be a good girl, you know. Because, if you lie and you take the wafer, you will vomit blood right then and there."

I thought about all the blood covering my beautiful dress and decided that the time had not yet come for me to be a Christian.

Every Christmas, all the school-children lined up and waited for hours to get a handful of candies from England. The candies looked beautiful, like colourful jewels. The nuns, in their crisp habits, spooned the candies and dropped them in our waiting palms. They seemed like angels to us. The Anglo-Burmese teachers – Teacher Haig, Teacher Judy, Teacher Jasper – were all so special. They showed us worlds we did not know existed. I wished I could go Christmas carol singing with my friends. They sounded so melodious, singing "Silent Night," playing the guitar, and carrying a glowing lantern. My sisters and I could only peek surreptitiously from behind the curtains. Father wouldn't let us join them. He said, "You are not Christians!" We hated being left out.

Teacher Maggie, whom I used to adore because she could speak such good English, was quite astringent in her way of speaking to us children. One day, as we were gathered around her looking at some pictures of Indians in the English Reader, she mentioned that the Indians were quite dirty and lived like rats. In my thirteen-year-old brashness, I said, "Teacher, if the Indians are dirty, why do you call all the beautiful furniture and curtains Indian-chair, or table, or curtain?" The term for them was *kalaga*, for curtain and *kala htaing*, for chair. *Kala*, I thought, meant Indian. Her eyes behind her thick glasses gleaming, she said, "Oh, those are not named after you Indians – *kala mai*. They are named after the English – *kala phew*." *Mai* means black and *phew* means white. *Kala* are the ones who crossed the waters and came to Burma. It could also mean black. I looked down at my skin and realized it was quite dark and greasy. I smiled, foolishly.

It was a sunny day in May. We all went on a picnic with my fourth grade class. Teacher Betty, a Muslim Burmese, cooked coconut chicken noodles for us. The picnic was at the dam built by the Russians. After a whole day of playing games, such as passing the parcel and catch-catch, we were walking back home. My Sikh friend Amarjeet, looking really worried and pale, said, "Jaspal, I think the chicken was *halal*."

"What are you saying! It is against Sikhism to eat that, isn't it?"

"Yes."

I went up to Gurdeep, another Sikh friend.

"Gurdeep, did you eat the chicken noodles? The chicken was *halal*!"

We walked all the way home, worried sick to our stomachs that something ominous would befall us soon. Only Muslims ate *halal* meat.

As soon as we reached town, Gurdeep, Amarjeet, and I ran to my house and walked upstairs to my grandmother's room. She had an altar with the *Gurugranth Sahib*, the Sikh holy book, where she always kept some *amrit*, the holy water.

"Here, let me drink some first."

Taking a large gulp, I passed around the bottle. We all drank the entire bottle of holy water, asked *Waheguru* to forgive us, and, then, looked at each other with fear.

"Do you think we are forgiven?" asked Gurdeep.

"I think we might be thrown in purgatory for all eternity," I answered.

"You think?" said Amarjeet.

"Well, it is better than hell. At least, there will be no hellfire and brimstones there," I said.

Then, when I was fifteen, I cut my hair. While it was just a tiny bit of hair right in the middle of forehead that I had snipped, I was terrified that I would be discovered and punished by my parents. Not to mention the fear of hell that started to plague me as soon as I did that. I took my father's *fixxo*, the glue that he used to keep his beard in place, and stuck the hair back to my forehead. That night, I dreamed of eternal hell.

The next morning, we had to go and get passport pictures as we were contemplating "returning" to our "motherland." The Ne Win military regime was becoming increasingly brutal, particularly to Chinese and Indians. I still remember the passport picture with the hair sticking up on my forehead!

My grandmother, who accompanied us to the photo studio, noticed my hair, and smacked me on my head. "*Badmash kuri,*" she said. Bad girl.

Rubbing my head, I asked, "Why is it that the Burmese are not punished and sent to hell when they cut their hair?"

"They are *junglees*. They don't have religion."

"Where do they go when they die?"

"*Shaitaan*, you ask too many questions! You will go to *Narak!*"

"But why must the Sikhs never cut their hair? Didn't Guru Nanak say we must not believe in blind faith?"

"*Htair ja!* Just you wait!"

And as she lumbered to her feet to come get me, I ran all the way to Khin Mala's house. She was my best friend, and I specially loved her for trying to help me turn into a Burmese girl.

"Khin Mala, I wish I could have a nose like you, flat and Burmese."

"Sit down and close your eyes," Khin Mala would say with a twinkle in her eyes. "Now, wish hard." Then she would bring out the mortar and pestle, pound it seven times, and touch it lightly to my nose. "Tomorrow, when you wake up, your nose will be flatter and you will be one of us." That I never turned Burmese was somehow my fault, I used to think. I was not good enough.

As I reached Mala's house, I asked her mother, Ah Daw Gyi, "Daw Daw, what happens when the Burmese people die?"

"They attain Nibana."
Nibana. Nirvana. Moksha.
"How?"

Ever since then, I have been seeking. My search has led me to many parts of the world. Navigating various cosmologies, ideologies, and economies, first in Burma, then in India, Iraq, and now in the United States, I am mindful of words, meanings, and truths.

What I learned most from the search is that due to the many cultural influences and border crossings, and the various ideological underpinnings that I was exposed to in my childhood, I don't know which answers are right. Or are there things that fall into categories of neither right nor wrong but something else? This book is the culmination of my inquires and sensibilities, where I try to uncover similar pitfalls of language and consciousness in postcolonial writers so that we may all, readers and writers, critics and students, know that there are other realities and truths, as well as other universalisms, that are equally valid.

This book, then, examines how certain postcolonial female Indian and African voices are fragmented and conflicted, formed as they are by oppositional discourses of modernity and tradition, East and West, local and global, and how their representational subjects, too, show their ambiguous and conflicted stances in relation to modernity and tradition.

The collection of mad female voices in this book reveals the ambiguities embedded in their psyches, and more importantly perhaps, their treacherous co-optation by vested interests of globalization and other elite institutions in order to further dangerous strategies. The continued use of the idioms of modernism by many postcolonial female writers and artists writing resistance to gender identity constructions is troubling and, indeed, dangerous in the present global climate. Some of the representational mad subjects of these female-authored texts, who continue to speak in the language of modernity and globalization, when co-opted, contribute to the continued violence against and brutalization of many men and women in the Global South.

One need only examine the situation in Afghanistan and Iraq, where U.S. imperialism's deployment of the rhetoric of civilization – "white men saving brown women from brown men" (Spivak, "Can the Subaltern Speak?" 120) – is redolent of colonialist ideals. See, for example, the December 3, 2001, issue of *Time* magazine featuring an Afghani woman on the cover with the caption: "Lifting the Veil: The shocking story of how the Taliban brutalized the women of Afghanistan. How much better will their lives be now?" Thus, the *burqa*, *purdah*, and the veil are once again seen as the markers of uncivilized nation-states, whose borders need to become more porous for the penetrative need of globalization, the rhetoric of which is then couched in terms of liberation and freedom.

Ultimately, I will posit a methodology of criticism for these female-authored texts representing madness which will encompass the legacy of modernity and globalization and their inter-connections to gender relations in postcolonial nation-states and their ideological and representational spaces.

Acknowledgments

As I think of writing this acknowledgment page, I think of hands, old hands, young hands, hands that held mine in encouragement, soothed my forehead, patted my back, wrote critical comments, cooked, folded in prayers, and, today, I shall name them, as they are not separate from the persons who helped me along in writing the book.

First and foremost, I wish to thank my mentor and friend, Mona Fayad, who opened the door to my becoming a scholar. Her encouragement and support are always with me and I appreciate her greatly for them. Without her guidance, patience, and tolerance, I wouldn't have embarked on this project. She not only taught me postcolonial theory and literature, she lived it. Thanks also to Anita Helle, Janet Leigh, Julie Lesage, Linda Kintz, and the late Alan Woolfe for their help, encouragement, and support. I am grateful to Olakunle George for his discussions, critical feedback, ongoing support, and especially for pointing me in the right direction. Thanks also to Vinay Lal for helping me to complicate the historical analyses of the texts and for his mentorship. Thanks are due to Indrani Mitra and Sondra Hale for being there at a critical juncture. I owe a great debt to a number of friends who added significantly to the book with their discussions: Jean Amato, Rodney "Bene" Ferrao, Barbara James, and Sheila Shafer; Uzma Ahmed, Meera Prem, Narrinder Chona, and Mumtaz Bengali for endless cups of tea and talk when they were most needed.

Thanks are due to the Center for the Study of Women in Society, University of Oregon, for research support. My postdoctoral fellowship at the Institute for the Study of Gender in Africa, James S. Coleman African Studies Center, University of California, Los Angeles, provided me with the time needed to shape and write down my thoughts.

I am indebted to my colleagues at Northern Michigan University, particularly Katherine Payant, Toby Rose, and Robert Whalen, who were generous with their friendship, critical analyses, and support.

This book would not have been completed without the support, encouragement, help, and guidance of the faculty, staff, administration, and especially the students of Northern Michigan University. I would like to acknowledge and thank Northern Michigan University for a year-long sabbatical leave.

I owe a large debt to the readers of this book. Their input and suggestions were insightful and extremely helpful. I am indebted to Peter Enman, staff editor of the University of Calgary Press, for his careful reading and great patience with the ongoing editorial changes.

I would like to thank Greenwood Press for permission to reproduce parts of "Studies of Bharati Mukherjee" from *Asian American Novelists: A Bio-Bibliographical Critical Source Book* (2000), edited by Emmanuel Nelson, in Chapter 3; *Michigan Academician* (2003) for permission to reproduce large parts of my article "Globalization, Transnationalism, and Identity Politics in South Asian Women's Texts" in Chapter 8; to *South Asian Review* for permission to reproduce my articles "Representing the Poetics of Resistance in Transnational South Asian Women's Fiction and Film" (2003) in Chapter 8, and "Transnational Multicultural Feminism and the Politics of Location: Queering Diaspora in Nisha Ganatra's *Chutney Popcorn*, Deepa Mehta's *Fire,* and Shani Mootoo's *Cereus Blooms at Night*" (2005), edited by K. D. Verma, in Chapter 9.

This book is written in memory of my parents, Tej Kaur and Prabjoth Singh, who taught me love and strength through simple living, walking the true path with awareness, and journeying through various cosmologies with dignity and joyfulness. Without their encouragement, their belief in my abilities, their pride in my work, and their eternal presence, I would not have had the courage to start this project, let alone complete it. Thank you, Ma and Papaji.

I also want to thank my siblings, their significant others, my nieces and nephews for their questions and efforts in trying to understand my journey and my work.

My children Gitanjali and Gautam sustained me during the most difficult periods with their boisterous, sometimes persistent, sometimes playful, but always understanding and loving presence and support. Their passionate and intellectual interest in my ideas, their critical feedback, and their own examples in choosing the paths of their lives sustained my strength in the writing process. This book is because of you and for you. Thank you for you.

1

Postcolonial Women Writers and Their Cultural Productions

Examining middle-class female South Asian, Caribbean, and African cultural productions in contemporary postcolonial and transnational spaces, I investigate their fragmented and conflicted voices, formed as they are by oppositional discourses of modernity and tradition, East and West, local and global, and seek to understand how their representational subjects, too, show their ambiguous and conflicted stances in relation to the aforementioned discursive systems. The representations of mad female subjects suffering gender oppression by Western-educated, middle-class South Asian, Caribbean, and African women in postcolonial spaces and the West betray notions of the liberal and neo-liberal stances of these writers as they are formed by modern knowledge systems. Finally, I argue that the collection of mad female voices reveals the cosmopolitan knowledge of the writers, which leads to the continued misreading of their texts. Such misreading adds to the ongoing disempowerment of people in the Global South when their voices are co-opted to further globalization's capitalist agendas.

The continued use of the idioms of modernity by many postcolonial female writers and artists in relation to gender identity and the constructions of "Third World" subjects is troubling, and indeed dangerous, in our global climate. Some of the representational mad subjects of these female-authored texts who continue to speak in the language of modernity and globalization may be said to contribute to violence against and the continued brutalization of many people, both men and women, in the Global South, as can be seen by the examples of Afghanistan and Iraq. The *burqa*, the *purdah*, and the veil are once again seen as markers of uncivilized nation-states, whose borders need to become porous for the penetrative need of globalization, the rhetoric of which is then couched in (neo)liberal humanist terms and the coterminous espousal of liberation, freedom, and choice.

Ultimately, I will posit a methodology of criticism of these female-authored texts which will encompass the legacy of modernity and globalization on gender relations in postcolonial nation-states and their ideological and representational spaces in transnational diasporas.

In the years since independence from European colonialism, a large body of literary work in English (and other European languages), written primarily by members of the Western-educated, urban, upper- and middle-class elite, has proliferated in many parts of the world, adding to the dominant ideological construction of (postmodern and postcolonial) identity and informing social structures. As can be seen throughout the postcolonial world, the ruling classes then become responsible for the construction of cultural norms and mores in the post-independent, neo-colonial spaces. Formed as they are by colonialist ideology and through gendered oppositional discourses, the ruling classes too engage with those same constructions and discourses in their ongoing cultural relationships and formations. Many women, using the female narrative voice to investigate colonial and patriarchal constructions of identity, inhabit these privileged spaces.

It is important to locate postcolonial female narrative voices within these conflicted spaces and learn to critique them through the political and cultural conditions that produced them in the first place. For instance, if a female writer represents the "mad" female subject who is suffering brutal, patriarchal oppression, especially when she is trying to negotiate an individual identity for herself, we have to keep in mind the writer's class and her location when we examine how she addresses such complex concerns. Such concerns, no doubt, need to be raised and addressed in order for social change within existing oppressive institutions to occur, but how and where they are textualized highlights the condition of the postcolonial female writer and her representational subjects. We need to locate such writings within a particular historical and cultural context in order for a successful postcolonial/transnational/multicultural feminist methodology to occur.

What, then, are the political concerns of many postcolonial female writers? More importantly, as cultural critics, how do we critique their writings successfully? The critique of patriarchal oppression is not something new, and in fact is closely connected with nationalism and nationalist reconstruction during anticolonial movements. Much of early African literature, mostly written by men (see Elleke Boehmer, Carole B. Davies, Chiwenye Okonjo Ogunyemi, Florence Stratton, and Susheila Nasta, among others), deals with colonialism and its social and political implications, while it also emphasizes man's (not humans' or woman's) struggle within it. According to Sheila J. Petty, "The Négritude movement of the 1930s helped recover the image of 'savage' African males who were in need of 'civilizing,'" but did little for African women (22).

Here is an oft-quoted example of Négritude poetry by Léopold Sédar Senghor:

> Naked woman, black woman
>
> Clothed with your colour which is life, with your form which is beauty!
>
> In your shadow I have grown up; the gentleness of your hands was laid over my eyes.
>
> And now, high up on the sun-baked pass, at the heart of summer, at the heart of noon, I come upon you, my Promised Land.
>
> And your beauty strikes me to the heart like the flash of an eagle. (*Prose and Poetry* 105)

While the Négritude poets wrote to counter the representations of "the inherent inferiority of the black race – a myth which provided the ideological rationale for European imperialism – their re-visioning was bitterly contested" (Stratton 40) by African women writers. According to Stratton, while many other male writers since Senghor (Ousmane Sembène, Okot p'Bitek, Wole Soyinka, and Ngugi wa Thiong'o, for example)[1] revised the trope of Mother Africa, "what emerges ... is an intertext that dominates the texts, a mastertext that neutralizes the difference in their ideological projects. For underlying the trope that is embedded in all of the texts is the same old manichean allegory of gender we uncovered in Négritude poetry" (Stratton 51). This trope, finally, "elaborates a gendered theory of nationhood and of writing, one that excludes women from the creative production of the national polity or identity and of literary texts" (Stratton 51).

Essentially, Petty, along with Odile Cazenave (2000), Susheila Nasta (1992), Chikwenye Okonjo Ogunyemi (1996), Elleke Boehmer (1992), Florence Stratton (1994), Phillipa Kafka (2003), Charlotte Bruner (1993), Oyèrónké Oyêwùmí (1997), and Stephanie Newell (1997), among others, suggest that mythologizing the African woman as the Great Mother Africa keeps her in a conventional role in the domestic sphere and denies her equal participation in a national vision. Petty argues that "Women's function" in male-authored texts is to "embody the male vision of Africa as a 'nation'" (22). She adds that the Négritude poets' rendition of Africa as "Great Mother" did little for the African woman, and in fact, "the binary opposition of Mother Africa as the past or nation restored versus prostitute as the nation present degraded forcibly links woman to the male quest in the [texts] and defines the boundaries within which she is allowed to function" (22).

As can be seen from the above argument, the ideological inscription within the discourse of patriarchy that romanticizes women as the Great Mother in control of traditional cultural practices in the domestic sphere effectively closed off the public spaces for their reinscription. Therefore, the representations of women – first in colonialist and then nationalist texts, in limited terms – reinforced power relationships that became characteristic of many patriarchal cultures in colonial, postcolonial, and neocolonial spaces.

Additionally, as Carole Boyce Davies argues, colonial institutions chose males over females for education, and "then too, the sex role distinctions common to many African societies supported the notion that Western education was a barrier to a woman's role as wife and mother and an impediment to her success in these traditional modes of acquiring status" (2). In fact, with few exceptions and for a long time, girls were kept away from formal and especially higher education. Therefore, first the colonial administrators and then the nationalists used existing cultural practices to ensure secondary positions for women in (post)colonial African societies, argue many African feminists.

As Elleke Boehmer notes, "Nationalism ... found in existing social patterns the models of hierarchical authority and control, all with the blessings of earlier colonialists and indigenous patriarchy" ("Stories" 7). Women who participated in anticolonial struggles expected to benefit from the social reconstruction that took place in a post-independent era, but found that they had to wage another struggle against men – the same men alongside whom they had fought for national independence. Thus, women found that "Mother Africa may have been declared free, but the mothers of Africa remained manifestly oppressed" (7).

According to Boehmer, "The dilemma is that where male nationalists have claimed, won and ruled the 'motherland,' this same motherland may not signify 'home' and 'source' to women" ("Stories" 5). Additionally, and more importantly perhaps, Boehmer claims,

> To "Third World" women and women of colour these concerns speak with particular urgency, not only because of their need to resist the triple oppression or marginalization that the effects of colonialism, gender and male-dominated language create, but also because their own tactics of self-representation are often usefully adopted from the older and more established nationalist politics of "their men." ("Stories" 5)

In this milieu, women have felt they must rewrite their (her)stories, and to do so, they have to resist, recreate, and re-empower themselves. As Boehmer suggests, "Where women tell of their own experience, they map their own geography, scry their own history and so, necessarily, contest official representations of nationalists realities" ("Stories" 11). Or do they?

Such struggles, as well as the persistent inequalities, are represented in many postcolonial women's texts. However, the reception of these texts in the Western academy reinforces the colonial ideology that defines these cultures as backward and in need of continued civilization. Such texts persist in fostering notions, perpetuated by colonialist writing, that characterize many cultures as inferior to the West and still in need of its paternalism, which takes neocolonial forms through the rhetoric of globalism. How these texts are read and disseminated needs to be part of literary criticism, otherwise myths of enlightenment and humanist ideology continue to be fostered in the West and in Western academia.

The writers and artists from South Asia, Africa, and the Caribbean that I will examine in this book, namely Mariama Bâ, Myriam Warner-Vieyra, Tsitsi Dangarembga, Bharati Mukherjee, Aparna Sen, Agnes Sam, Gurinder Chadha, Farida Karodia, Nisha Ghanatra, Meena Alexander, Deepa Mehta, Shani Mootoo, Samina Ali (a.k.a. Zainab Ali), and Mira Nair, question social and patriarchal practices. As colonized nations have been repeatedly represented by colonialist discourse as feminine, requiring "paternal governance,"[2] nationalism too repeated the same symbolism during nationalist movements to represent woman. As women wrote to counter such representations, the ideas of *"motherlands, mothercultures, mothertongues"* (Nasta xix, original emphasis) became appropriate tropes for re-imagining. According to Nasta,

> Clearly mothers and motherlands have provided a potent symbolic force in the writings of African, Caribbean and Asian women with the need to demythologize the illusion of the colonial "motherland" or "mothercountry" and the parallel movement to rediscover, recreate and give birth to the genesis of new forms and new language of expression. (Nasta xix)

Nasta is particularly aware of women's "unwritten stories" that are "just beginning to become all that they can be" in their search for self-identity (xix).

What of the writers' class then? In examining postcolonial writers, Ania Loomba refers to Aimé Césaire's assertion that Marxist thought must be revised because the division between people was not class but race, and she relates a similar problem that exists within feminist and gender studies.

> Women's oppression was ... seriously under-theorised within Marxism... The crucial question – how does the oppression of women connect with the operations of capitalism (or other

economic systems)? – remained unanswered till feminists began to interrelate the economic and ideological aspects of women's oppression. The question of race and colonialism demanded rethinking for similar reasons. (26)

For colonized races, the focus was the interrelation between economic and the cultural, or ideological, aspects of oppression. As Partha Chatterjee asserts in his essay, "Colonialism, Nationalism, and the Colonialized Woman: The Contest in India": "Nationalism ... located its own subjectivity in the spiritual domain of culture, where it considered itself superior to the West and hence undominated and sovereign" (Chatterjee 631). This space was the spiritual or domestic realm. Thus, if women, who have been reconstructed by nationalist ideologies, resist the idea of new woman, what idiom do they use? How do they critique nationalist reconstructions?

For African postcolonial women, one aspect that complicates a necessary feminist critique is that it "presents the double challenge of critiquing the scholarship produced by African men for its gender blindness, while sharing the concerns of African male colleagues with the imperialist, colonialist and racist connotations of mainstream constructions of Africa" (Charmaine Pereira 28). Pereira adds that "considerable dilemmas for feminists arise when 'African culture and traditions' are viewed as the subjects of contestation, as is often asserted by masculinist scholars once feminists challenge hegemonic relations" (28). Thus a conflict arises, and African women writers can no longer be sure about their critical stance: should they criticize "those features of 'culture' and 'tradition' that oppress women and affirm aspects of the same 'culture' that uplift women or that have social value but have been distorted by global agendas" (Pereira 29)? Such distortions are particularly troubling, especially when they are disseminated in the Western world and the Western academy by so-called "Third World Feminists."

Nasta claims that "an entrapping cycle begins to emerge" for postcolonial female writers:

> In countries with a history of colonialism, women's quest for emancipation, self-identity and fulfillment can be seen to represent a traitorous act, a betrayal not simply of traditional codes of practice and belief but of the wider struggle for

liberation and nationalism. Does to be "feminist" therefore involve a further displacement or reflect an implicit adherence to another form of cultural imperialism? (xv)

Conflicted as they are, can postcolonial women, constructed through oppositional discourses of colonial and nationalism, of modernity and tradition, of male and female, First World and Third World, give voice to their own unique perspectives, or are they struggling to find a voice in the dominant narrative spaces through discursive strategies that still use the same trope of liberalism and emancipation bequeathed to them by colonialism? As woman becomes the metonymy of a nation, what becomes of the woman?

"Famously contradictory" and "Janus-faced," asserts Boehmer, the nation is "protean, adaptive and affiliative rather than derivative, taking on different forms at the hands of different groups and classes ... [and] continues to exert a hold on emergent geopolitical entities in quest of self-representation" (4). What of the "libratory potential" (Boehmer *Stories of Women* 4) for women? How do they rewrite in order to imagine themselves as important players and as historical actors in the formation of the nation? If the nation is Janus-faced and contradictory, what of the constructions of women as nation? And, more importantly, what of their representations?

> On the face of it, progressive, self-assertive women appear caught in a dilemma, in that the ideology that promises self-expression, liberation and transformation through political action is characterized by their simultaneous marginalization, and that nationalist resistance has often been resolved in a revivalist direction, reifying traditional gender difference. (6)

Boehmer, noting the "relative silence of the dominant postcolonial thinkers on the subject of nationalism, and of women's roles in nationalist movement," suggests that writing by women "provides diverse possibilities of self-conception for a people: not a single shining path to self-realization, but any number of symbolic fictions, as many modes of redreaming as there are dreamers in a nation" (17). Yes, it is important to dream. Many postcolonial feminists redream. As Meg Samuelson asks, "Emerging from the nightmare of apartheid, how can we not want the rainbow nation? How can we not want the miracle of national reconciliation? How can we deny that we have entered a redemptive state" (11)? Yet, and here is the important and complex question: "At the same time, in this persistent patriarchy that performs physical, psychic and discursive violence against woman, how can women not want to evoke a feminist discourse that cuts across national boundaries" (11)? So, how can women redream if that dreaming is only accessible in the dominant language, trapped as subjects within a particular ideology? Is this redreaming mostly accessible for transnational and cosmopolitan subjects? And if they dream and write, can we, as postcolonial critics, uncover their hidden and subconscious biases for a complex reading?

Let us examine Francophone African literature for a moment. In early feminist novels, "up to the 1980s, the protagonist had spoken in a biographical or semiautobiographical mode: Speech bore witness to her difficulties, particularly the suffering she experienced as part of a couple, part of a polygamous social structure, and confronted with issues of sterility" (Cazenave 4). In the second phase, "feminine speech has become more aggressive, more insistent, within an autorepresentative mode that has become more and more complex" (4). Cazenave calls the mode of the later phase the "mechanism of rebellion" (4). This mechanism has allowed women's voices a space within the dominant narrative. "Through an audacious exploration of forbidden areas of sexuality, desire, passion, love – but also mother-daughter relations and the questioning of reproduction and obligatory maternity as the qualities defining womanhood – they guaranteed themselves access to areas of language that until only recently had been exclusively the domain of men" (4). The writers in the second phase have narrative voices that are "willful, combative, and full of a new energy" and by creating characters that are "typically marginalized in African society," women writers have "created a privileged gaze and a greater space from which to freely express criticism of their society" (Cazenave 10).

By marginalizing themselves voluntarily or involuntarily from hegemonic social spaces, the women characters "find themselves in a paradoxically privileged position that allows them to be introspective and to conduct elaborate analysis of society" (Cazenave 12). They show "rejection of motherhood," and the African woman "comes out in revolt against social and familial pressures, and in particular against excessive power of the mother-in-law and the implicit obligation to bear children" (13). Finally, Cazenave's work examines "the prevalence of violence, abjection, suffering, and horror in women's texts, considering their impact and their therapeutic value within a writing that is cathartic in nature" (13).

Additionally, regarding women writers, Boehmer notes that "Postcolonial women writers have questioned, cut across, upended or refused entirely the dominant if not dominatory narrative of the independent nation. They have placed their own subjectivities, sexualities, maternal duties, private stories and intimate pleasures in tension with conventional roles transmitted by national and other traditional narratives" (*Stories of Women* 4). While these female writers write to "redream" (Boehmer 17) and recast, or write for catharsis, their reception has been variously problematic in this era of globalization. When women who, in trying to counter colonialist and nationalist misrepresentations, try to rewrite their (her)stories, certain Western or Westernized feminist criticism highlights only the oppressed condition of Third World women in domestic spaces in its misguided notions of sisterhood and common patriarchal oppression, which is then appropriated and used by certain factions in their quest for globalization and market liberalism. The idea that gender oppression will surely end if we open up the markets and spread notions of liberal democracy is resonant of imperialist, colonialist, and neocolonialist discourses. Ideas of liberation and emancipation are still ambiguous, and are used in a post–9/11 world by U.S. imperialists for their own purposes, as can be seen from the examples of Afghanistan and Iraq.

For a successful postcolonial feminist critique of these texts, however, how they question and address such concerns must depend on the cultural, social, and historical contexts, as well as on the race, class, caste, and national identity of the authors and of their representational subjects.

At this juncture, therefore, it is important to ask how postcolonial (South Asian, Caribbean, or African) feminism is different from international and transnational feminism. First, let us look at African feminism. As opposed to many other forms of feminisms, Davies argues that African feminism recognizes a common struggle with African men in anticolonial and neocolonial contexts:

> An African feminist consciousness recognizes that certain inequalities and limitations existed/exist in traditional societies

and that colonialism reinforced and introduced others. As such, it acknowledges its affinities with international feminism, but delineates a specific African feminism with certain specific needs and goals arising out of the concrete realities of women's lives in African societies. (9)

In looking at women's oppression, postcolonial feminism does not simply apply Western feminist notions of liberation and reject traditional cultural and familial practices; instead, it examines social institutions and their practices for selective acceptance or rejection.

For example, many postcolonial critics maintain that it is not necessary to completely reject all Western constructs and notions of feminism but that they must question certain concepts. Postcolonial feminists must be selective in rejecting or accepting notions of Western feminism, and they must write in order to name themselves rather than simply serve as native informants whose sole purpose is to enlighten an Other (Spivak, "Three Women's Texts" 264). Many postcolonial women writers are careful when they examine constructions of identity in relation to racism, classism, sexism, and (neo)colonialism for redefinition. Postcolonial transnational feminism tries to reconstruct the idea of what it means to be a feminist. Davies explains:

> The term "feminism" often has to be qualified when used by most African and other Third World women. The race, class and cultural allegiances that are brought to its consideration cause the most conflict. Yet, although the concept may not enter the daily existence of the average woman, and although much of what she understands as feminism is filtered through a media that is male-dominated and male-oriented, African women recognize the inequalities and, especially within the context of struggles for national liberation, are challenging entrenched male dominance. (12)

If, however, as Ogunyemi suggests, "feminism has been represented as offensive, and therefore, no respectable African woman writer openly, actively, and consistently associates herself with the ideology," why are they writing about women's oppression in monolithic ways (5)? African women writers' intent, according to Ogunyemi, is to "improve the quality of Nigerian, and not just women's lives," and since the "majority of the oppressed are women," then the idea is that they must necessarily write about women (5). Although Ogunyemi acknowledges that colonialism and neocolonialism are to be blamed for women's inferior status in Nigeria, she argues that "it would be distorting the facts ... to put all the blame on the white man's coming, for the controversy is steeped in contemporary representations of myth and is rooted in geography" (6). Such discussions invariably allow tyrannical colonizers and oppressive regimes to justify genocide or continued exploitation. It is as if to say it is justifiable to destroy a family due to sibling rivalries. Additionally, Ogunyemi sees in women's texts "power clashes that *eternally* plague gender relationships" (emphasis added, 6).

Yet, if one is to read postcolonial women's texts to uncover the *eternal* nature of the power clashes in gender relationships, what ideology are we propagating? Looking at certain African feminists, Oyèrónké Oyêwùmí suggests, "Though feminism in origin, by definition, and by practice is a universalizing discourse, the concerns and questions that have informed it are Western.... As such, feminism remains enframed by the tunnel vision and the bio-logic of other Western discourses" (*The Invention of Women* 13). In women's oppression, there is an interconnectedness of race, class, and sexual oppression, but if we look at gender oppression without looking at the oppressive structures of society in neocolonial spaces, one-sided argument will prevail and equality or change will be hard to achieve. One must look at the literary productions and the historical context that produced them in order to create a critical approach that is textual as well as contextual. As Davies suggests, such a reading will be "textual in that close reading of texts using the literary establishment's critical tools is indicated; contextual as it realizes that analyzing a text without some consideration of the world with which it has a material relationship is of little social value" (10–11). Such a methodology is particularly relevant in the postcolonial feminist criticism of Anglophone texts. Thus, for politically engaged postcolonial/transnational/multicultural feminist criticism, we have to examine why specific cultural definitions of womanhood arise, and for what purposes they are utilized at specific moments in history and by whom.

Additionally, is it useful to continue discussing female oppression in terms of colonial and patriarchal oppression as double colonization? As Oyèrónké Oyěwumí posits,

> It is not colonization that is two, but the forms of oppressions that flowed from the process for native females. It is misleading to postulate two forms of colonization because both manifestations of oppression are rooted in the hierarchical race/gender relations of the colonial situation. African females were colonized by Europeans as Africans and as African women. They were dominated, exploited, and inferiorized as Africans together with African men and then separately inferiorized and marginalized as African women. (340)

In other words, female oppression should not be seen as separate from the colonial situation. Colonialism's impact on women "cannot be separated from its impact on men because gender relations are not zero-sum – men and women in any society are inextricably bound" (Oyěwumí 341). Writers such as Zimbabwe's Tsitsi Dangarembga are particularly aware of the "boundedness" of oppression.

Therefore, postcolonial/transnational/multicultural feminism is careful in examining modernity and its deployment by certain women writers critiquing patriarchies for various audiences. Ultimately, as postcolonial academics and critics in the West, we must ask: How do we read and teach such texts as politically engaged academics and critics? For example, while looking at the "transnational cultural production and reception" of texts by postmodern and postcolonial feminists, Indrapal Grewal and Caren Kaplan critique "certain forms of feminism [that] emerge from [the feminists'] willing participation in modernity with its colonial discourse and hegemonic First World formations that wittingly or unwittingly lead to the oppression and exploitation of many women" (2). They add, "In supporting the agenda of modernity, therefore, feminists misrecognize and fail to resist Western hegemonies" (2). In her article entitled "The Politics of Location as Transnational Feminist Practice," Kaplan states that Virginia Woolf's modernist concerns with space and location in *A Room of One's Own* "intersect with Western feminists' exploration of world space for women in their shared sisterhood" (*Scattered Hegemonies* 137). Kaplan compares the articulation for this need for "physical space as a matter of material and spiritual survival with the expansion and contraction of colonial worlds," adding that "the claiming of a world space for women raises temporal questions as well as spacial considerations, questions of history as well as of place" (137). Kaplan raises the following questions: "Can such claims be imagined outside the conceptual parameters of modernity? Can worlds be claimed in the name of categories such as 'woman' in all innocence and benevolence, or do these gestures mark the revival of a form of feminist cultural imperialism?" (137). Like Kaplan, I too am interested in the politics of location for postcolonial/transnational/multicultural feminist critical practices and their various uses, and would like to examine the repercussions of such practices. For example, Phillipa Kafka, in *On the Outside Looking In(dian)*, valorizes certain Indian women writers for their attempts at finding their sexualized selves and subjectivities in purely Western terms while quoting copious so-called Indian feminist theorists to support her agenda, and suggests that critics of globalization and neocolonialism (from the left or the right) "ignore gender and sexuality issues and place priorities on resisting globalization" (10). She suggests that to critics of globalization, "gender issues are insignificant" (10). Thus, even critical texts, such as Kafka's, must be placed within a neocolonial space, and to critique them, "it is necessary to focus on the production and reception of feminist theories in transnational cultures of exchange" (Kaplan 138). The question – how are texts by transnational women theorized and received in the Western academy? – is an imperative one to address, more so than ever before. Regarding the production and reception of certain texts, Kaplan notes:

> Too often, Western feminists have ignored the politics of reception in the interpretation of texts from the so-called peripheries, calling for inclusion of "difference" by "making room" or "creating space" without historicizing the relations of exchange that govern literacy, the production and marketing of texts, the politics of editing and distribution, and so on. Most important, feminists with socioeconomic power need to investigate the grounds of their strong desire for rapport and intimacy with the "other." (Kaplan 139)

As the question – can transnational feminists remain in the West without becoming Western? (Shohat 7) – suggests, transnational feminist critical practice must analyze and contextualize the politics of location in female-authored texts to critique the commodification of ethnic cultures.

An important question to reiterate at this juncture is: Where are such texts published and consumed? How are such texts read and understood? For example, how do we read diasporic Indian women writers from Africa who deal with issues of displacement and "race redoubling" (as Indians, Asians, Africans, or Blacks) in the United Kingdom, and the United States of America, where ideas of "diversity and multiculturalism as opposed to difference prevail" (Bhabha, "The Commitment to Theory" 34)? How do we read marginal writings, with their cultural border crossings, where meanings, as Bhabha claims, are never complete or are "open to cultural translation" (162–63), especially for Indian women who are negotiating an "ambiguous" territory, all the while retaining or dragging their sense of "Indianness-in-motions" (Appadurai 10)? These questions need to be addressed for a successful postcolonial critical methodology to occur. What is this nebulous national identity, and how do women engage with ideas of nationalism in order to posit gender identity and oppression? My analysis of various feminists' texts locating violence and oppression on the female body is multipronged in that I bring in various constructions, such as gender, race, class, and sexuality, to examine the production and reception of these texts. To examine gender and violence or gender and madness, we have to reach back, far back, into the history of a culture for the analyses to be significant.

While discussing gender oppression and violence in Africa, Amina Mama points out that "The prevalence of so many pernicious forms of gendered violence demands both historical and contemporary analysis.... Imperialism is the major trope of [such] analysis because it is the common historical force that makes it possible to consider an area as large and diverse as Africa as a continent as having general features that transcend the boundaries of nation, culture, and geography" ("Sheroes and Villains" 47). However, in most critical analyses of gendered violence and oppression, this important period is either elided or negated, and African cultures are generically termed heteropatriarchalist and sexist. Yes, gender oppression and violence need to be addressed for cultural and social change to occur, but how and where they are textualized must first be investigated. Such an investigation will highlight the postcolonial condition of female writers and that of their representational subjects who are negotiating for individual identities; we need to locate such writings within a particular historical and cultural context if we are to have a successful transnational and postcolonial feminist methodology.

As Grewal and Kaplan suggest, it is the "transnational/social/cultural/economic" (*Scattered* 3) consequences of the social and historical changes within a postmodern and postcolonial framework that will engender a more complex understanding of transnational, translocal, postcolonial feminist practices.

What are the cultural, political, economic, and social consequences of postmodernity? Is the continuation of the colonizers' language one of the consequences, and one of the main ingredients in the "nervous condition"[3] of the postcolonial people, especially for those who continue to write and speak in the colonizers' language? Does it mean that the writers are somehow complicit with imperial and neocolonial ideology and continue to identify with their oppressors? What, then, are the implications for postcolonial Anglophone women writers and their texts, whose readership is obviously Western or Western-educated?

Albert Memmi, for example, suggests that due to the psychological transformation of the colonial subject, colonial aftermaths will be long-lasting: "And the day oppression ceases, the new man is supposed to emerge before our eyes immediately. Now, I do not like to say so, but I must, since decolonization has demonstrated it: this is not the way it happens. The colonized lives for a long time before we see that really new man" (88). Thus, colonization, with its knowledge systems, has lasting and ambiguous impact on the psyche of the postcolonial subject, and consequently, on their representational subjects.

Many postcolonial critics, such as Ngugi wa Thiong'o, for example, claim that schooling was imposed by the colonial administrators primarily for the dissemination of European language and culture. The result of such an education was a class of people who learned to think, speak, and write like the colonizers. Ngugi labels such writings "the literature of the petty-bourgeoisie born of the colonial schools and universities.... Its rise and development reflected the gradual accession of this class to political and even economic dominance" (20). While most of this literature was noticeably nationalistic, Ngugi suggests that its brand of nationalism closed off a majority of the people working in anticolonial struggle:

> [The literature's] greatest weakness still lay where it has always been, in the audience – the petty-bourgeoisie readership automatically assumed by the very choice of language. Because of its indeterminate economic position between the many contending classes, the petty-bourgeoisie develops a vacillating psychological make-up. Like a chameleon it takes on the colour of the main class with which it is in the closest touch and sympathy. It can be swept to activity by the masses at a time of revolutionary tide; or be driven to *silence, fear, cynicism, withdrawal into self-contemplation, existential anguish, or to collaboration with the powers-that-be* at times of reactionary tides. (emphasis added, 22)

Reactionary tides can occur in many postcolonial social spaces, whether within the Third or First World, or in transnational diasporic spaces. Ngugi adds that such literature contributed to the self-identity of this educated petty-bourgeois, which gave them a "national" tradition and literature to confront the imperialist in its anti-imperialist struggle. At the same time, however, it constructed itself as central in the dominant ideology by leaving the masses – including, of course, the majority of women – and the working classes out of this construction (26).

Putting this literature in its political context, Ngugi predicts:

> What we have created is another hybrid tradition, a tradition in transition, a minority tradition that can only be termed an Afro-European literature; that is, the literature written by Africans in European languages.... Their work belongs to an Afro-European literary tradition which is likely to last for as long as Africa is under this rule of European capital in a neo-colonial set-up. (26–27)

By situating such literature in its historical and political contexts, Ngugi helps us understand the political conditions that generated this literature and its continued proliferation in the post-independent or neocolonial spaces in the era of globalization.

As in Africa, the result of English education in India was the formation of a class of native elite, "a class of persons, Indian in blood and colour, but English in taste, in opinions, in morals, and in intellect" (Macaulay 359) to such an extent that they continue the cultural and literary practices of the West, particularly in this era of market liberalization and globalism. The continued use of European languages in postcolonial spaces suggests that European languages are, indeed, multinational commodities, supporting capitalist ideology *and* the upper and emergent middle classes in many postcolonial nations.

How are the continued uses of European languages implicated in the cultural identity of a people? What are the implications of such usage for many postcolonial people as well as writers? Ngugi calls the continued use of European language the "psychological violence of the classroom" and sees the aftermath in the continuation of the imperial ideology long after independence. He claims, "In my view language was the most important vehicle through which that power [of the colonizers] fascinated and held the soul prisoner. The bullet was the means of the physical subjugation. Language was the means of the spiritual subjugation" (9). While political and economic oppression is enforced through physical power, cultural oppression, which is imposed through language, is more subtle but has more lasting effect, and ultimately is more insidious.

Ngugi claims that the introduction of the colonizers' language is like a "cultural bomb" that changes the psyche of the victim. He states that this "cultural bomb" has the power to "annihilate a people's belief in their names, in their languages, in their environment, in their heritage of struggle, in their unity, in their capacities and ultimately in themselves" (13). The "cultural bomb" also reduces their past into a "wasteland of non-achievement" from which they wish to distance themselves while desiring to identify with "other people's language rather than their own" (13). Ultimately, "It even plants serious doubts about the moral rightness of struggle. Possibilities of triumph or victory are seen as remote, ridiculous dreams. The intended results are *despair, despondency* and a *collective death wish*" (emphasis added, 3), leading to conflicted psyches and nervous subjectivities.

To continue to speak and write in the colonizers' language indicates that the postcolonial people are not yet liberated and continue to identify with the West's universalism leading to neocolonialism. According to Immanuel Wallerstein, "The African continent was thus confronted in the process of its incorporation into the capitalist world-economy by an intrusive ideology which not only rejected the worth of the gods who had been Africans but also was pervasive in that it took on multiple clothings: Christianity, science, democracy, Marxism" (*Unthinking* 128).

What forms did resistance to these ideologies take in many postcolonial nations? Wallerstein claims that "Cultural resistance everywhere to this intrusive, insistent, newly dominant ideology took *ambiguous* forms" (emphasis added, 128). Many become complicit with this ideology while at the same time resisting it, which becomes the source of a certain form of cultural and psychological madness. "On the one hand," adds Wallerstein, "many Africans accepted, seem to accept, the new universalism, seeking to learn its secrets, seeking to tame this god, seeking to gain its favor" (128). We see such cases and such ambiguity in many literary texts (Rabindranath Tagore's *The Home and the World*, Satyajit Ray's *Devi: Goddess*, Myriam Warner-Vierya's *Juletane* for example).[4] What of resistance then? What ambiguous form does it take? "On the other hand," continues Wallerstein, "many Africans (often the same ones) rebelled against [the new universalism] ... It has long been commonplace to observe such an *ambiguous* reaction" (emphasis added, 128). The assumption, then, is that there is no escape from this "double bind" (128). What language do we use to resist neocolonial power structures and their concomitant ideological underpinnings, especially if we are to escape from this "double bind"? Wallerstein suggests that "if we are to get out of [it], we must take advantage of the contradictions of the system itself to go beyond it" (128). How do we take advantage of such a suggestion? What strategies must we use?

If we continue to engage with the language of a particular ideology, even when we are trying to resist and oppose the West's universalism and the capitalist world-economy, does it not still reinforce "the structure of cultural hierarchy and oppression internal to the system" (Wallerstein 129)? Foucault, too, argues that opposition to the dominant discourse in fact actually reinforces the very system and network of power, and that dissent is allowed to foment with the understanding that ultimately it will be incorporated within the institutions of power (*History of Sexuality* 94). Such consequences and co-optations have long been debated within Women's Studies, Ethnic Studies, Postcolonial Studies departments and programs within Western academic spaces. Initially, these programs were supposed to address resistance and change with respect to the dominant institutional power structures, but they were eventually absorbed and incorporated within the systems, thus losing any oppositional and revolutionary thrust.

This brings us back to the important question: how do we resist cultural imperialism? If nationalism in many parts of South Asia, the Caribbean and Africa used the same idioms as that of Western universalism in the creation of nation-states, are these nations still not very much part of the "modern world systems" (Wallerstein, *Unthinking* 131), created as they are by the European capitalist world economy? "The operation of the capitalist world economy," according to Wallerstein, "is premised on the existence of a political superstructure of sovereign states linked together in and legitimized by an interstate system" (131). The creation of the colonies with "their political boundaries and structures" initiated the incorporation of the colonial world into the European world economy (131), which still exists in this era of globalization with its concomitant free market rhetoric and ideology. Wallerstein states that only beyond the ideas of the nation-states can India or countries in Africa transform the past constructed by colonialism and nationalism and then "be deeply reinforced as ... enduring 'civilization[s]'" (133). Thus, only beyond nationalism, indeed, only in postnational spaces can the polities of the Global South become, once again, "enduring 'civilizations.'"

What of resistance, then? What about the present moment? In *Empire of Knowledge*, Vinay Lal states that if resistance and dissent are "couched in rational, civilized, constitutional, and adult-like language recognized by Western parliamentarian and social commentators" (11), and only then are recognized as productive and therefore, become productive, what of other forms of resistance? According to Lal, there is room for resistance within a given ideology if we use "another apparatus of dialogue and resistance," as Gandhi did when he "abandoned the placard, petition, and parliamentary speech in favor of another form of dialogue and resistance" – using another language of dissent, that of "fasting, spinning, non-cooperation, and even walking" (11). Such resistance can initially be seen as madness or deviancy; for example, Churchill's description of Gandhi as a "half naked fakir" who ought to be trampled to death is well known. At any rate, everyone can be, yes, *can be* a Gandhi and be successful; however, those potentials for self-realization and becoming interconnected and compassionate through the individual path seem to be closed off to most modern subjects.

Thus, we are back to the age-old cycle, the cycle of power and ideology. "Modernity insists that even dissenters of modernity should speak in the language of modernity" (Lal, *Empire* 13), so that, ultimately, as Wallerstein posits, we are reinforcing the structure of "cultural hierarchy and oppression internal" (129) to modernity. So to resist and dissent, "We shall have to be more attentive to critiques of modernity, more nuanced in our deliberations on the much celebrated ideas of tolerance, democracy, and freedom" (Lal, *Empire* 12). Otherwise, in the continued use of the idioms of modernity by Western and Western-educated people, "one can see the reinvention of Europe, the center of the world, to which, in Hegelian fashion, all history is fated to return" (Lal 12), leading, of course, to reinforcement of the same oppressive power structures that the formerly colonized have been resisting for decades. And while the wretched of the earth remain wretched and poor,[5] the middle class in India, according to Lal, "delighted equally at the country's new-found nuclear prowess and its enviable software successes, began to fancy as a superpower," are churning out "Indian 'billionaires' – their wealth counted not in billion of rupees … but in billion of dollars" (146), leading, once again, to the cultural and economic hegemony of this class in India. (See, for example, Tarun Khanna.) Such "Indian billionaires" proliferate in post-apartheid South Africa as well. These middle classes then continue to celebrate modernity and are very instrumental in freeing the markets. In an era of globalization and market liberalism, we are contending with literature from such middle classes in the postcolonial world, and for my purposes, particularly the *conflicted* and *ambiguous* female narrative voice from the upper and middle classes who are writing and publishing for a particular audience.

My main concern here is with postcolonial female writers representing resistance to gender identity construction. Conflicted as they are in the use of the very language of modernity which nationalism propagated, they posit even resistance to gender identity constructions in modern terms. Are their voices dissenting, or are they simply the voices of ones co-opted by the West to add "chic" (Lal, *Empire* 14) to the academic disciplines in the name of multiculturalism? For example, Bharati Mukherjee and Meena Alexander are such voices from the margins who, indeed, have become the token representative of the so-called oppressed Indian Womanhood in the Western academy. What other forms of epistemological frameworks exist besides the dominant Eurocentric ones? As the reaction in the Western world to most postcolonial texts suggests, female writers' quests for liberation and happiness are couched in Western, liberal humanist terms.

Can we uncover another epistemology? Are there other forms of dissent? Lal claims that

> the necessary oppositions are not between tradition and modernity, or between particularism and universalism; rather, the intent is to probe how one set of universalisms, associated with the trajectory of Western reason, came to establish their predominance, and what are those competing universalisms which can claim our allegiance. (14)

Modernity and individualism, seen as universal, are problematic for postcolonial spaces, particularly for those "civilizations where the ground reality and ethical thinking always inclined towards plurality" (Lal 14). Thus, we must find the disjuncture between various epistemologies to recover or reread postcolonial feminist narratives for what Lal terms the "ecological survival of plurality" (158). As postcolonial transnational feminists, we must ignore "Western civilization's desire to scientize its narrative" (Lal 161) and, instead, uncover other competing universalisms and reread ideas of "oppressive" postcolonial cultures through a thorough-going critique of "dominant frameworks of Western knowledge" (15).

This book examines the poetics of resistance to gendered identity formations in the texts of women writers of the African, Caribbean, and South Asian diasporas and their interconnections to India and Africa. How are racial and ethnic identities constructed within such spaces in an era of globalization with its transnational cultural flow? This, in turn, leads to a discussion of how such constructions impact the gender and national identity formation of the diasporic Indian or African female subject.

As Chiwenye Okonjo Ogunyemi claims, "African novels written by women, as counternarratives, fascinate with their inherent *contradictions* as they reveal strength and weakness, beauty and ugliness, *ambiguity* and clarity, in unfolding the politics of oppression" (emphasis added, 4). Additionally, how do diasporic women, who have never been to their "home" country, negotiate for gender identity and empowerment in shifting territories of the First and "Third World" diasporic spaces, when they are first displaced from their "home" cultures and alienated in another?

How are racial and ethnic identities constructed within such spaces? How do such constructions impact the gender and national identity formation of the diasporic Indian or African women?

First of all, I realize that to understand postcolonial South Asian, Caribbean, and African women and the constructions of conflicted psyches and "nervous conditions," I must examine how nationalism constructed the modern woman. Toward that end, this book delves briefly into the history of nationalism and the transformation of the colonized women into the "new" women of modernity. Following that, I focus on the South Asian, African, Caribbean, and diasporic cultural production or *"work of the imagination* as a constitutive feature of the modern subjectivity" (original emphasis, Appadurai 3). I consider films as well as fiction, as "[s]uch media transform the field of mass mediation because they offer new resources and new disciplines for the construction of imagined selves and imagined worlds" (Appadurai 3). Finally, I will examine cultural productions coming out of diasporic spaces, such as Africa, the United Kingdom, the United States of America, and Canada, where identities are negotiated and reconceptualized in ambiguous and troubled territories by postcolonial women for their self-empowerment.

At present, gender representation and construction in the West and throughout the world remain problematic. So how do postcolonial/transnational/multicultural/diasporic Indian women construct national and gender identity? How do they define gender in cross-cultural spaces where ideas of identity take on special meaning? How are hybrid identities and sexualities represented and received?

Additionally, South Asian and African women, for example, who construct a separate sexual self from that of the idealized and essentialized notion of "pure" womanhood, struggle to depict their identities in troubled First and Third World territories. Given resurgent debates on nationalism in the West since 9/11, moreover, it has also become difficult for them to negotiate identity even in First World spaces where individualism is encouraged. Offering critical thought on issues such as identity politics and representation, this book examines the comparative poetics of African, South Asian, and Caribbean women writers and filmmakers depicting gender identity representation, resistance, and identity negotiation for Indian women in India and African and their diasporas, as well as the reception of these concepts in different spaces.

In institutions of higher learning, where issues of multiculturalism, transnationalism, and feminism are taught interchangeably in efforts toward curriculum diversification, the questions posed above take on critical undertones for a politically conscious criticism. Are feminist political concerns separate from multicultural concerns? More importantly, how can we, as postcolonial/transnational/multicultural feminists, critique postcolonial texts that represent oppressed and powerless Indian women for a Westernized and Western audience? Can we refuse hierarchies of class, race, sexual, and gender-based struggles (Shohat 1)? According to Ella Shohat, "there is the mutual embeddedness between transnational and multicultural struggles, and, instead, feminists must highlight the political intersectionality ... of all these axes of stratification" (Shohat 1). In Western academic spaces, we often try to define multiculturalism and transnationalism in terms that either embrace all differences and diversity or simply become exclusionary.

According to Shohat, "even with the best of intentions, a fetishized focus on African female genital mutilation or on Asian foot-binding ends up as complicit with a Eurocentric victimology that reduces African or Asian agency and organizing" (9). Shohat suggests the "center/periphery" narratives must be disrupted by multicultural feminist critique, especially "when talking 'about' the 'Third World,' [and the] feminist resistant practices within a conflictual community, where opposition to such practices does not perpetuate the false dichotomy of savagery versus civilization or tradition versus modernity" (9).

Many in the Western academy continue to critique postcolonial feminist texts in a reductive, Eurocentric manner to which I am an ongoing witness. As there are so many so-called postcolonial feminist texts that are proliferating in the West in the past few decades, their ongoing examination in simple binaries of East/West, or colonialism and nationalism, abounds. Chetty quotes Shashi Deshpande, who comments that "Indian Literature suffers from a feeling of instability because of the tendency to inflate, ethnicise, exoticise, 'present,' 'explain,' or package India for foreign audiences" (*Indias Abroad* 8). Why or how did it come about that certain writers became "native informants," so to speak? What about representations and ideological constructions – colonialist and nationalists? As postcolonial feminists, critics, and academics, "we must not duplicate the colonial narrative of a rescuing mission" (Grewal and Kaplan 9). Instead, we must share the "critique of hegemony and the burden of representation" (Grewal and Kaplan 9).

However, my contention is not that feminists cannot communicate and collaborate across racial or class boundaries and borders. As Leela Gandhi posits, "In the course of its quarrel with liberal feminism, postcolonialism – as we have been arguing – fails conclusively to resolve the conflicting claim of 'feminist emancipation' and 'cultural emancipation'" (93). If, as Gandhi claims, "postcolonial theory betrays its own uneasy complicity with nationalist discourses whenever it announces itself as the only legitimate mouthpiece of native women" (95), can "postcolonialism and feminism ... exceed the limits of their representative histories" (98)? Thus, once again we are in the middle of the binary logic of Western knowledge systems. We must find other ways of dissent, as Vinay Lal suggests, and refashion liberation and emancipation through competing universalisms and not fall prey to binary logic.

Therefore, when we read postcolonial women's texts, we have to keep in mind that the representation of the identity of the postcolonial woman has to do with the operation of ideology and the gaps and absences the texts produce. The identity of the postcolonial woman is ever-shifting as she is being formed by the ideologies that surround her. Thus, for a politically engaged postcolonial feminist critique, one has to analyze not only what the text reveals but also what it conceals, or what it cannot say: "It is the significant *silences* of a text, in its gaps and absences that the presence of ideology can be most positively felt. It is these silences which the critic must make 'speak'" (Macherey 132). Because the way ideology operates is itself full of contradictions, the text tries to offer a symbolic or enforced resolution. In reading postcolonial women's texts, the feminist critic makes the silences of the text reveal culturally oppositional construction for redefinition of female roles. Although the elite Western-educated women gained substantially in terms of modernization and emancipation through Western education in the material realm, it is important to note that the models of liberation conceptualized by them are limited due to their consciousness and status, which are produced within a given class ideology and within various transnational locales. Their models of liberation, if emulated, will only lead to further *despair* and *despondency* (Ngugi) for the underprivileged and oppressed, especially if Western education and its fruits are dangled as a carrot seemingly leading to happiness and liberation for the oppressed masses in the Global South.

In conclusion, then, let me reiterate that some of the women writers whose work I discuss in this book are particularly aware of the oppressive ideals of womanhood imposed on them during nationalism. They question the idealization of woman as Earth Mother/Motherland or as the pure and self-sacrificing wife. They condemn practices such as arranged marriage, female circumcision, and polygamy. Some of the writers try to associate the notions of patriarchal oppression with cultural colonization and neocolonialism. For many writers, however, raising consciousness becomes complicated with national identities; do they speak and risk being accused of being "native informant," or do they not speak and risk being accused of being ignorant and oppressed "native" women? There are many postcolonial women writers who want to bring about change within the hegemonic structures in a selective way. To reiterate, these writers envision a cultural script and an alternate space, where "competing universalism" and the "ecology of plurality" (Lal, *Empire* 158) exist. Writers such as Dangarembga and Aparna Sen bring into sharp focus the postcolonial condition of their representational subjects; they show how cultural constructions of gender identities are interrelated with cultural colonization in their countries. For example, Dangarembga writes about cultural colonization as a form of "mental disease," a "nervous condition," or as I see it, cultural madness, for both the male and the female subjects. I discuss various forms of madness, cultural and social, where female identity is seen as deviant due to its conflicted nature, defined and constructed as it is in terms of an Other in the postcolonial and transnational spaces. Postcolonial female writers highlight "nervous" female characters, who find themselves the victims of cultural and economic colonization in a globalized world. However, they do not simply replicate masculinist and bourgeois modernist agendas of individualism as Bharati Mukherjee has been accused of doing. Certain African female writers, too, have been complicit with modernist agendas. For example, Ogunyemi argues that female oppression and "the cycle of poverty might be broken, if [the young girl] goes to school long enough to obtain the wherewithal to sustain a fulfilling motherhood"; otherwise she will be "exploited and overworked" (9). My question is: If social, economic and structural changes do not occur, what good is an education for the oppressed?

Ultimately, I show that while some writers conceptualize women's equality in terms of educational and professional opportunity, sexual liberation, and individualism, others, although also limited by their own class ideology, realize that the paradigm of liberation that focuses only on individual freedom without looking at the larger socioeconomic and political conditions in a postcolonial and global world is rather limiting. This book addresses how many women writers reinscribe themselves to disrupt the dominant narratives through painful and maddening inscriptions, and the narrative space that opens up for reinscription can be incredibly empowering for some; the nervous and alienated subject learns to negotiate its subjecthood and identity within the many shifting positions, such as race, class, gender, and caste, and learns to reconcile the many subjectivities within a given hegemony for collective social change. These madwomen either learn to collapse discursive boundaries and binaries in attempts to create equal alternative spaces (which, even if possible, are in the long run in danger of being co-opted by the dominant power structures and institutions), or negotiate within given hegemonies for empowering subjecthood devoid of modernist agendas. They accomplish the task by refusing to be victims of globalization, while keeping in mind the limited opportunities afforded to other, oppressed women *and* men, who, due to increased penetration of the capitalist world economy, continue to suffer deprivation and are indeed the most disenfranchised of all.

2

Dominant Epistemologies and Alternative Readings: Gender and Globalization

The paradigm of femininity constructed by discourses of colonialism and nationalism still predominates, to varying degrees, in postcolonial South Asia, the Caribbean, and in many parts of Africa. In this chapter, I outline important moments of European colonial history and literature and examine the representation and construction of the colonized. I examine gender indentity construction in national discourse in the late nineteenth and early twentieth centuries and analyze the continuing debates regarding nationalism and gender. How do women in postcolonial spaces resist gender identity construction in the era of globalization?

The result of nationalism was confusing for many women, as it was riddled with ambiguity and conflict. On the one hand, it promised women greater freedom, while on the other hand, their material conditions remained unaltered; we see such ambiguities and conflicts reflected in postcolonial women writers and their representational subjects. With the introduction of European languages and Western education into colonized spaces, an emergent middle class in colonized countries came to speak and write in the colonizers' language. Many women in colonized countries who questioned gender identity construction belonged to this class.

Thus, focusing on colonial and national constructions of female identity will lead to a discussion of why some Western-educated women writers continue to see resistance in purely Western, albeit altered terms, while others learn to negotiate for empowering gender identities in hybrid spaces without employing easy binaries of East/West or Modernity/Tradition. However, the majority of the so-called feminist texts read in the West are of the former variety. This, then, is the starting point of my investigations into why certain literature is still privileged in the West and Westernized social and economic spaces, and how it recasts and reproduces the ideological concerns of the dominant class/caste in postcolonial, neo-colonial, and transnational spaces.

To begin with, let us examine colonial rhetoric. Colonized nations have been repeatedly represented by colonialist discourse as feminine, requiring "paternal governance" (McLuskie and Innes 4). British imperialism in India, for example, defined itself as a civilizing mission, particularly in relation to the condition of women. Constructing the Indian woman as the passive victim of brutal patriarchal oppression helped British colonialism justify its intervention in the cultural and economic sphere of the indigenous peoples. In "Can the Subaltern Speak?" Gayatri Chakraborty Spivak refers to the British abolition of the practice of *suttee* in India as "White men saving brown women from brown men"; as Spivak explains, in the discourse of colonialism, the colonizers constructed their argument on the bodies of the oppressed Indian womanhood, and especially *suttee*, as justification for penetration into India, which indeed had nothing to do with the actual oppressed Indian woman (120–30). Such penetrations were justified as the obligation and moral duties of the enlightened colonizers, who used the rhetoric of civilization, such as Kipling's famous "White Man's Burden," for the continued oppression and exploitation of the colonized cultures, resources, and peoples.

During early interventions into India by the West, textual representations of Indian men as inferior and oppressive of Indian women abound. Let me give just one brief example from a myriad of such writings from that time: James Mill writes as early as 1817 that he considers Indian culture primitive, rude, immoral, and fundamentally lacking in the qualities that "preside over the progress of civilized society" (309). Of particular concern, for my purposes, is the representation of women in his writing. According to Mill, one has to see the status of women to realize how civilized a society is. He claims that in civilized society, women are exalted, while among "rude" people, women are degraded. He portrays Indian women to be in

> a state of dependence more strict and humiliating than that which is ordained for the weaker sex.... Nothing can exceed the habitual contempt which Hindus entertain for their women.... They are held in extreme degradation, excluded from the sacred books, deprived of education and of a share in the paternal property.... That remarkable barbarity, the wife held unworthy to eat with her husband, is prevalent in Hindustan. (312)

Mill further maintains that the practice of gender segregation came about because of the whole spirit of Hindu society, where women must be constantly guarded at all times for fear of their innate tendency toward infidelity and sexual excesses. At the same time, the poor passive and suffering Indian woman must be saved from the degenerate Hindu man. Such conflicted views and the perceived degeneracy of Hindu society and lowly position of Hindu women justified continued colonial intervention into Indian culture and society, while at the same time feminizing the Indian males as being unfit for self-rule.[1]

Despite colonial assertions of wanting to liberate oppressed Indian womanhood, colonial involvement was never meant to be liberating for the colonized women. In fact, in many parts of the world, colonial intervention lowered women's social standing and position. For example, Joanne Liddle and Rama Joshi argue that British intervention disrupted the maintenance of a matrilineal form of family organization of the Nayars of Malabar in Kerala (28). The British imposed legal restrictions in the nineteenth century by reorganizing the Nayars' family structure to a more manageable, and clearly patriarchal, form. Therefore, they maintain, colonial intervention, while proclaiming to liberate oppressed Indian women, resulted not only in the reinforcement of existing patriarchal practices in some cultures, but also in the introduction of specific forms of gender inequalities transported from Victorian England to many matrilineal societies (29). Here, clearly, British intervention altered and lowered Indian women's social condition.

Additionally, colonial ideology represented and constructed the Indian woman as the darker, inferior "other" of the Victorian gentlewoman

(Burton 295). In the colonial ideology of civilization, writes Antoinette Burton, the Victorian woman held an important symbolic space where she played an important part in the project of empire as a missionary or a teacher. Basing her concern for the "oppressed" Indian womanhood on common ideas of gender and motherhood, the British woman was allowed to penetrate into the forbidden spaces of the *zenana* (domestic spaces), ostensibly on a civilizing mission (Burton 295). Still, White women, throughout their entire attempt to liberate Indian women, "remained unambiguous about their own racial superiority and moral purity, a conviction that allowed them to speak for the Indian woman and silence her in the project of her liberation" (Burton 295). Take, for example, Katherine Mayo, who, in the discourse of colonialism, and through her text, shows the ideological framework that was used to construct the Indian woman. Mayo's book, *Mother India*, published in 1927 when Indian nationalists were intensifying their efforts against the British, was extremely popular and influential. This work is just one example of the colonial project using the representation and construction of the silent, suffering mass of Indian womanhood as a justification for colonial penetration and continued exploitation.

Mayo uses Orientalist (see Edward Said) language in providing empirical reality based on what she calls scientific data. She assures her Western audience that her book does not concern itself with politics or religion or the arts. Rather, her book concerns itself with the matter of "public health and its contributing factor, [and] the object of systematic and scientific inquiry" (12). She then goes on to document "empirical" proof of every aspect of Indian life, examining the personal habits of all people and looking for an essential Indian character, "not only of today but of long-past history" (16). She has a simple approach in understanding India's cultural, social, political, and economic history: one must understand the sexual practices of the natives. Mayo then concludes that India's problems and its inability to govern itself stem from Indian's sexual practices and their excesses:

> The whole practices of the Hindu's woes, material and spiritual – poverty, sickness, ignorance, political minority, melancholy, ineffectiveness, not forgetting that subconscious conviction of inferiority ... rests upon a rock-bottom physical

base. This base is, simply, his manner of getting into the world and his sex-life thenceforth. (22)

The most important and fascinating aspect of *Mother India*, in view of my project, is the construction of Indian women and the apparent attempt at engaging with Indian women's oppression. The author writes in great detail about oppressive practices, such as the *purdah*, child marriage, frequent pregnancies, primitive care during confinement, widowhood, and *sati*, which, she claims, drain the Indians of physical and mental strength, leaving them incapable of taking care of the important needs of their society. On the one hand, Mayo portrays the Indian woman as a passive victim of patriarchal oppression: she is weak, innocent, and helpless as a child. On the other hand, she portrays the Indian woman as the product of degrading, perverse traditions, cultural and sexual, unexposed to liberal education. As a result, Mayo suggests, the Indian woman fails in the discipline and sublimation of her sexuality. Occupied with matters of sexuality, the Indian woman teaches her child "from earliest grasp of word and act, to dwell upon sex relations" (23). She is the medium through which perverse sexual practices are transmitted, sapping the race of its physical and moral strength. As can be seen, contradictions and ambiguity abound in colonialism's cultural constructions of Indian womanhood. Such representations not only produced unlimited sympathy for the victimized womanhood of India and thereby justified colonialist intervention in the natives' domestic and cultural sphere, but they also provided a discursive space for the colonialists to fulfill their roles as social reformers (Mitra, "Colonialism" 46). The outcomes of such conflicted representations served the colonizers well.

Partha Chatterjee, in "Colonialism, Nationalism, and Colonialized Women: The Contest in India," argues that "by assuming a position of sympathy for the unfree and oppressed womanhood of India, the colonial mind was able to transform this figure of the Indian woman into a sign of the inherently oppressive and unfree nature of the entire cultural tradition of a country" (662). Thus, for the colonizers, the Indian woman's sexuality became extremely threatening, while, paradoxically, her passive suffering demanded reformist intervention. She became at once sexually alluring *and* threatening.

Frantz Fanon, writing in the context of French colonialism in Algeria (which resonates eerily in the twenty-first century in the context of Afghanistan and Iraq), maintains that the ambiguous figure of the colonized, native woman points to a complex psychology of colonialism. While the European finds the veiled Algerian woman sexually alluring, Fanon states that there is also

> the crystallization of an aggressiveness, the strain of a kind of violence before the Algerian woman. Unveiling this woman is revealing her beauty; it is baring her secret, breaking her resistance, making her available for adventure. Hiding the face is also disguising a secret; it is also creating a world of mystery, of the hidden. In a confused way, the European experiences his relation with the Algerian woman in a highly complex level.... [The Algerian woman] who sees without being seen frustrates the colonizer. There is no reciprocity. She does not yield herself, does not give herself, does not offer herself. (Fanon, *Wretched* 54)

This resistance, however, must crumble in the face of colonial intervention for the colonial enterprise to succeed. The colonizers need to "unveil" the native woman so that she will support Western penetration into the native society. Her unveiling, whether voluntary or involuntary, whether by coercion or Western education, will allow the ideology of liberal humanism to triumph. The unveiled woman will be easily co-opted, and as in other African nations, and as the educational debates suggest, women will then impart Western cultural practices to their children. Fanon points out that

> every rejected veil disclosed to the eyes of the colonialists horizons until then forbidden, and revealed to them, piece by piece, the flesh of Algeria laid bare. The occupier's aggressiveness, and hence his hopes, multiplied ten-fold each time a new face was uncovered. Every new Algerian woman unveiled announced to the occupier an Algerian society whose systems of defense were in the process of dislocation, open and breached. Every veil that fell, every body that became liberated

from the traditional embrace of the haïk, every face that offered itself to the bold and impatient glance of the occupier, was a negative expression of the fact that Algeria was beginning to deny herself and was accepting the rape of the colonizer. Algerian society with every abandoned veil seemed to express its willingness to attend the master's school and to decide to change its habits under the occupier's direction and patronage. (43)

Civilizing the native woman by removing the veil, thereby "saving" her, became the primary aspect of the colonial strategy of destructuring and destabilizing the colonized culture, resulting ultimately in economic and cultural control of the colonized. Fanon contends that due to that relentless project, "reactionary forms of behavior on the part of the colonized" were inevitable (46).

Therefore, nationalism in colonized countries constructed its oppositional rhetoric around the figure of the woman, in one way or the other. To counter the construction of the colonized women as the backward, passive victims of brutal patriarchal traditions by the British colonizers, women were "allowed" to be educated in schools outside the home by the emergent elite. According to Kumari Jayawardena, "Mass education was a concept of the bourgeois world, brought into these countries by the colonizing powers" (6). The bourgeois man, himself the product of Western education or missionary influence, needed a "new woman," and he demanded an "enlightened" woman, a "woman who was 'presentable' in colonial society yet whose role was primarily at home" (12). Many of the social reformers among the "indigenous bourgeoisie were men who saw the social evils of their societies as threats to the stability of bourgeois family life, and who, therefore, campaigned for reforms in order to *strengthen* the basic structure of society rather than reform them" (original emphasis, 9). The discussion about women and education is resonant of Victorian England and the "woman question." Many women in colonial India, no longer veiled or secluded, were allowed to be educated. Jayawardena's argument regarding women's education, and its analogous strengthening of the marriage institution, claims that

> education for women in Asiatic countries thus had a dual function. It brought bourgeois women out of their homes and into various professions, into social work, and into the political sphere claiming the right of suffrage. It transformed them in the image of the "emancipated" women of the Western society. On the other hand, as nationalist reformers took over, education became a conservative influence; it began to hark back to traditional ideals, to emphasize the role of women as wives and mothers. (19)

Thus, and as Fanon contends regarding such reactionary politics, women were constructed to be *both* modern *and* traditional. The social reform movement in India was linked to the issue of "preserving and strengthening basic family structures and creating good wives and mothers" (Jayawardena 87). Female education became an important question at this time since reformists thought that education was necessary to eliminate social evils, but the concept of education, as we have seen, was limited to producing better wives and mothers.

As Elleke Boehmer points out in regard to Africa, the concept "of the gendered configuration of the postcolonial nation, and specifically, of the nation embodied *as* woman *by* male leaders, artists and writers" is prevalent in texts "across time, and across nations, including anticolonial nations, if with inevitable cultural modifications, of women as the *bearers* of national culture" ("Stories of Women" 4). How did this "apparent constant" (Boehmer 4) of woman as nation come about in the first place? In *Motherlands: Black Women's Writing from Africa, the Caribbean and South Asia*, Susheila Nasta contends that women were represented in nationalist texts as

> The "mulatto figure" (often portrayed as an exotic, luscious fruit), or the powerful matriarch in Caribbean literature, "Mother of Gold" the fertile earth mother in African literature; female goddesses entrapped by tradition and religion in "Mother India." (xiv)

Nasta suggests that although these women were "represented as powerful symbolic forces, repositories of culture and creativity, they were essentially silent and silenced by the structures around them" (xiv). The social and public spaces were, at this time, gendered, and many women, even those "refined" through Western education, were mainly confined in the domestic spaces.

Take, for example, Rabindranath Tagore's *The Home and the World*, written in the aftermath of the Swadeshi (literally meaning "homemade" or "indigenous") movement in India, where the author utilizes the dichotomy of the home and the world, or the spiritual and the material, in his criticism of complicity and resistance in (post)colonial text; the author points to the ideological turmoil at the centre of nationalist endeavours to resolve the women question.[2] Ania Loomba writes that "National fantasies, be they colonial, anti-colonial or postcolonial, also play upon the connections between women, land or nations ... the nation state and its guiding principles are often imagined *as* a woman" (180). The family becomes the extension of the nation, and as a result, the family becomes "the antithesis of a nation or 'private' realm as opposed to the public space of the nation" (181). The turmoil became more apparent during nationalism when women participated in the nationalist movements that affected and produced changes in the domestic sphere.

Tagore's text shows how gender is inscribed at the centre of nationalist thought and action and how the disciplining of women and their sexuality for nationalistic purposes affected them. Indrani Mitra, in her essay "'I Will Make Bimala One with My Country': Gender and Nationalism in Tagore's *The Home and the* World," discusses the failure of the nationalist project founded on "false essentialism," which resulted in failure to strike the appropriate balance between home and the world, the public and the private, the material and the spiritual (244). Mitra argues that the nationalist project regarding the "new woman" is "founded upon an ideology that constructs 'home' as the symbolic space of nationalist politics and non-violent activism as its only true form" (244). Mitra contextualizes the text by placing it within the *Swadeshi* era in Bengal, 1903–1908.

In *The Home and the World*, we see a reconstruction of the female character, Bimala, by her husband, Nikhil, a rich landlord. Nikhil represents the native elite as the gatekeepers of traditional practices yet, at the same time, placed in the position of modernizers and reformers during colonialism. We see Bimala, who, with her husband's support and encouragement, leaves the seclusion of the *zenana* to enter the public sphere; she is being reformed by her husband and enlightened under his liberal tutelage and patriarchal authority. In this public space, she meets Sandip, her husband's friend, a fiery nationalist. Bimala's reconstruction must signify the idealized union between male and female, West and East, and to fulfill this purpose she is being educated under a well-bred English governess. Now she can venture into the "world" without jeopardizing the "home." At such a moment, ideally, tradition and modernity would come together harmoniously. However, the outcome of such an experiment proves disastrous for Nikhil because Bimala falls in love with Sandip, and her sexual attraction for another man signals disorder and the destruction of the "home" (Mitra, "'I Will Make Bimala'" 248).

As Mitra argues, the anxiety and conflict brought on by modernity is manifested in the paradoxical restructuring of the domestic sphere during nationalist movements. On the one hand, women had to be educated so that they would become more suitable for their Western-educated husbands, while, on the other, patriarchal control of female sexuality became an added concern due to modernity (Mitra, "'I Will Make Bimala'" 248–49). As in Africa, modern and educated women came to be viewed as sexually liberated and, therefore, possibly lascivious (see, for example, Mariama Bâ's *So Long a Letter*). These women's sexuality was to be controlled and contained for the culture to remain pure and untainted by Western notions of liberation.

The group that came to redefine the Indian woman, based on traditional elements drawn from inherited caste ideologies, modified and refined through contact with Western education, was the newly emergent middle class. Accordingly, women needed to be refashioned; however, their essential feminine qualities should not be changed (Mitra, "'I Will Make Bimala'" 250). In the educational debates of the time, education for the upper-caste and upper-class women emphasized the cultivation of Victorian ideals of femininity and stressed the "cultivation of genteel norms and domestic virtue" (Sumanta Banerjee 128). The dichotomies inherent in nationalist discourses – of the home and world, private and public – transformed to that of the mind and body and finally came to rest on the male and female psyche. Regarding nationalist discourse, Sumanta Banerjee notes the following:

> A woman's nature is generally emotional while a man's is rational. Only that therefore can be termed authentic female education which primarily aims at improving the heart of a woman, and only secondarily at improving her mind.... The main aim of real female education is to train, improve and nourish the gentle and noble qualities of her heart.... Under such a system [of education], attempts should be made through ... religious education, moral education, reading of poems which inspire noble feelings, and training in music which rouses pure thoughts, so that women can become tenderhearted, affectionate, compassionate and genuinely devout to be able to be virtuous and religious minded. (162–63)

Once the distinction between male and female was established in essentialist terms to construct social roles, femininity could be adjusted in accordance to the nationalist needs as it evolved into the twentieth century.

Chatterjee explains that while men adjusted themselves in the material or public realm, which was reflected in their dress, food habits, religious observances, and social interaction, women had to compensate by being pure in the domestic and spiritual realm. Although Westernized manners, such as reading a novel or wearing a blouse and petticoat with the sari, were accepted as a sign of decency and privilege, drinking or smoking in the manner of men was unacceptable. Women were given the responsibility of carrying out religious duties and taking care of family life and family ties: "The new patriarchy advocated by nationalism conferred upon women the honour of a new social responsibility; and by associating the task of 'female emancipation' with the historical goal of sovereign nationhood, bound them to new, yet entirely legitimate, subordination" (Chatterjee, "Nationalist" 248). Chatterjee contends that this coercive authority was expressed most generally in "an inverted ideological form of the relation of power between the sexes: the adulation of woman as goddess or as mother" (248). He emphasizes that the image of woman as goddess or mother serves to erase her sexuality, and consequently, makes her less dangerous.

Satyajit Ray's film *Devi: The Goddess* (1960),[3] set in 1860 Bengal, focuses on the national reconstruction of the female as goddess or mother and its consequences on women. The plot of the story revolves around a young woman, Daya, her modern, Western-educated husband, Uma, and her traditional father-in-law. Uma leaves Daya, and his Brahmin home, to study English at the University of Calcutta. Uma speaks in favour of the Brahmo Samaj movement,[4] which preaches the importance of learning the English language and ways and gives up Indian "cult" religions for Christian-influenced monotheism. He believes one should replace traditional medicine with modern medicine and support for the younger generation against the total power traditionally accorded the Hindu father. Uma's father worships the goddess Kali, the mother goddess, who is both a destroyer and a creator.

One night, the father has a dream in which Daya's eyes become the eyes of Kali, and on waking, he starts to worship his daughter-in-law and bows down before her as the incarnation of Kali. Daya's older brother-in-law and the holy men in the village follow suit and start worshipping Daya. A beggar brings his sick child to her, and he miraculously recovers in her presence. When the husband, recalled by the sister-in-law, returns and begs his wife to run away from this madness, she refuses to leave, wondering if, indeed, she really is a goddess. As people gather from far and near to worship the living goddess, her young nephew falls ill, and the family expects her to perform a miracle. When she fails, the family is at once grief-stricken and angry at his death. When Uma returns home, he finds his wife, presumed mad, running out into the flower-filled fields. At the end of the movie, her image dissolves into the image of the smiling stone face of the goddess Kali.

Thus, the film opens with the image of Kali and ends with it. Daya is mother to her nephew, to her father-in-law, and even to her parrot, which calls her "Ma." On her wedding night, her husband tells her, "You are a china doll. You are a goddess." She is at once represented as a creator and destroyer, and is placed directly within the conflicted space set up by the different generations and different cultures – between modernity and tradition.

The film calls attention to the two forces of nationalist thinking on the woman question – the modern notions of sexual equality and reform voiced by the young, Western-educated husband, and the destructive elements of tradition in the deification of woman as mother, which takes nightmarish forms in the father's fantasies.[5] I examine the aftermath of such ambiguous and conflicted reconstructions in postcolonial women's texts. While the above examples are limited in that they represent only a tiny population of the vast Indian subcontinent, the idea, in very generalized terms, is to show how modernity transformed the domestic spaces and how it impacted certain women's roles within it. While the domestic spaces can transform modernity, as seen by Gandhi's use of non-violence and passive resistance, which he claims he learnt from women, my main concern here is to point out the hegemonic position of the "new" woman in nationalist thinking and reconstruction in the late nineteenth and early twentieth centuries. Nationalism created a discursive space for the selective modernization of colonized woman as long as she remained pure and traditional (Mitra, "'I Will Make Bimala'" 251).

Tanika Sarkar argues that when the essential values of society came to be located on the "chaste and virtuous" woman, the actual doors of the *zenana* could be unlocked; as long as woman remained essentially feminine – essentially virtuous – she could be refashioned to suit the need of a changing society (2011–55). Thus, the upper- and middle-class patriarchal control of female sexuality changed from what was seen as the coercive system of the *zenana* to the more contractual form of companionate marriage as represented in Tagore's *The Home and the World*, which ultimately still supports patriarchal structures.

Even in Jawaharlal Nehru's *The Discovery of India*, the author realizes the difficult position of the "new woman" in the emergent nation. Discussing his wife Kamala, Nehru writes, "She became a symbol of Indian women, or of woman herself" (33). Nehru supports Kamala's political role and her participation in anti-colonial movements. "She wanted to play her own part in the national struggle and not be merely a hanger on and a shadow of her husband" (30). He discusses Kamala's desire to deconstruct the binaries:

> Like Chitra in Tagore's play, she seemed to say to me: "I am Chitra. No goddess to be worshipped, nor yet the object of common pity to be brushed aside like a moth with indifference. If you deign to keep me by your side in the path of danger and daring, if you allow me to share the great duties of your life, then you will know my true self." (30).

In spite of Nehru's assertion, he is aware that his ideas are not compatible with the emergent nation's idea of gender and equality. He writes,

"Kamala and I were unlike; we did not complement each other" (33). To him Kamala "was not the type of modern girl, with the modern girl's habits and lack of poise; yet she took easily enough to modern ways. But essentially she was an Indian girl and, more importantly, a Kashmiri girl, sensitive and proud, childlike and grown-up, foolish and wise" (29). Thus the distance created from the material sphere where human relationships could be cultivated fails for him, and it prevents him from knowing her "true self" (33). This failure leads him to suggest that "The idea [couple] is terribly difficult to grasp or to hold ... marriage is an odd affair, and it had not ceased to be even after years of experience ... [and] often ignored in our fierce arguments about politics and economics" (34). He wonders if the East and the West, wisdom and science, have to be sacrificed "one for the other," at the "stage of the world's history when the only alternative to such a union is likely to be the destruction and undoing of both" (34). Can the material be brought into the domestic spaces, and the spiritual taken to the public spaces without chaos? Or are they to be kept separated for various vested interests and reasons?

On the one hand, as we have seen, nationalism reinforced the patriarchal repression of women by ideologically separating the home and the world. On the other hand, nationalist ideology created a discursive space for the discriminating modernization of the domestic sphere and the reformation of women's place in it. Upper-class women were no longer barred from public spaces, as they had to go out to be educated, leaving the *zenana* quarters behind. The new woman's "spiritual qualities," such as "self-sacrifice, benevolence, devotion, religiosity, etc.," did not impede her movement into the public sphere; "on the contrary, [they] facilitated it, making it possible for her to go out into the world under conditions that would not threaten her femininity. (Chatterjee, "Nationalist" 249).

Thus, the result for nationalism turned out to be confusing and ambivalent for the new woman. On the one hand, the notion of liberating her became just empty rhetoric, as reformation did not change the material or social position of the Indian woman; on the other hand, it allowed the middle-class woman an entry into the public sphere, and we will find Indian women writers, who belong to this class, exploring space previously prohibited to them. However, we see post-independent India's cultural representations still reflecting the effects of women's reconstructions with its ambiguity and conflict in postcolonial women writers.

Social histories of the nineteenth and twentieth centuries discuss the social conditions of women in India during the colonial period, as well as during nationalist movements. Sociologists look at these two important circumstances – colonialism and nationalism – as determinants that have affected women's roles and conditions in contemporary India. They write about the reformation of oppressive patriarchal practices instituted by enlightened, Western-educated intellectuals. Women are guaranteed equal rights in the Indian constitution.

Feminists have been questioning those so-called progressive legal changes by looking at the actual condition of the majority of Indian women. There is continued underrepresentation of women in the political and economic sphere which prevents them from participating in the decision-making processes of the country. Thus, in recent decades, feminists and activists have started to reorganize and concentrate on the studies of the status of Indian women's oppression. As indicated, the group that earlier came to redefine the status of Indian women were the upper-caste and upper-class members of the Western-educated elite. The national culture that they defined for themselves drew from their traditional ideologies, which were transformed due to their Western thinking and education.

Therefore, traditional cultural practices modified by modern Western thinking became the location of the national project on the woman question. Chatterjee discusses how the figure of the Indian woman came to be located at the very centre of a national culture defined by the indigenous cultural elites in "The Nationalist Resolution of the Women's Question." According to him, nationalism reconciled the contrary pulls of tradition and modernity through the discursive division of the material and the spiritual. The East was subjugated due to the superiority of the material culture of the West, with its technological and economic institutions, and its modern statecraft. The native people, therefore, had to learn those "superior techniques of organizing material life and incorporating them within their own cultures" (237). They realized they were in need of modernizing reforms.

However, this did not mean that they were inferior in all domains, and to emphasize that, national culture located its self-identity in the spiritual domain, which is located with the domestic spaces of the home (Chatterjee, "Nationalist" 238). It was in this location that the "superior" self-identity of the East was made manifest, which was believed to be far superior to that of the West (238). Chatterjee argues that nationalism formulated an ideological framework to cultivate the material techniques of modern Western civilization while "retaining and strengthening the distinctive spiritual essence of the national culture" (238). Furthermore, in the discourse of nationalism, the binaries of material/spiritual, outer/inner, public/private, world/home constructed a space from which the colonized resisted colonial domination, and that space was the feminine one of the home.

> The world is the external, the domain of the material; the home represents our inner spiritual self, our true identity. The world is a treacherous terrain of the pursuit of material interests, where practical considerations reign supreme. It is also typically the domain of the male. The home in its essence must remain unaffected by the profane activities of the material world – and woman is its representation (Chatterjee, "Nationalist" 239)

Woman, although altered by the contact with Western ideas, can remain virtually pure in the domestic spaces due to her spiritual qualities. Thus nationalist discourse constructed another ideological framework to define social roles by gender.

According to Chatterjee's argument, then, the material/spiritual, world/home dichotomy corresponds to masculine/feminine virtues. Adjustments have to be made in these spaces, and men will bear the major responsibilities in the "external world of material activity, and men would bear the brunt of this task" (Chatterjee, "Nationalist" 243). As the family, too, was part of the social fabric, it could not be protected entirely from the outer world, though some changes and adjustments in the organization of the home would have to be made. Chatterjee notes, however, that

> the crucial requirement was to retain the inner spirituality of indigenous social life. The home was the principal site for expressing the spiritual qualities of the national culture, and women must take the main responsibility of protecting and nurturing this quality. No matter what the changes in the external conditions of life for women, they must not, in other words, become *essentially* westernized. It followed, as a simple

criterion for judging the desirability of reform, that the essential distinction between the social roles of men and women in terms of material and spiritual virtues must at all times be maintained. There would have to be a marked *difference* in the degree and manner of westernization of women, as distinct from men, in the modern world of nation. (original emphasis, Chatterjee, "Nationalist" 243)

While men's essential qualities could be altered with the needs of the time, women's essential qualities, such as her spiritualism, must not change in spite of her contamination with Western ideals. Thus, nationalism came to locate itself on the physical body of the Indian woman. As can also be seen from Tanika Sarkar's study of the nationalist writings of the nineteenth century, woman's body was the sign for the last inviolate space, the figure for national independence:

The woman's body was the ultimate site of virtue, of stability, the last refuge of freedom.... Through a steady process of regression, this independent self-hood had been folded back from the public domain to the interior space of the household, and then further pushed back into the hidden depth of an inviolate, chaste, pure female body. (2014)

As in Africa, where the "binary opposition of Mother Africa as the past or nation restored versus prostitute as the nation present degraded forcibly" (Petty 22) suggests, nationalism's anxiety and its resolution played out on the woman's body – as pure or defiled. Chatterjee claims that the "material/spiritual dichotomy, to which the terms 'world' and 'home' correspond, had acquired ... a very special significance in the nationalist mind" (239). He elaborates:

The world was where the European power had challenged the non European peoples and, by virtue of its superior material culture, had subjugated them. But it had failed to colonize the inner, essential identity of the East which lay in its distinctive, superior, spiritual culture. That is where the East was undominated, sovereign, master of its own fate. (Chatterjee, "Nationalist" 239)

And it was on the chaste and pure unconquered woman's body that nationalism posited its identity. Thus, equating national independence with the purity of Indian women resulted in an obsessive concern with "the sign of the final surrender, the fatal invasion of that sacred space" (Sarkar 2014). This anxiety is manifested in the nationalist debate about the woman question, especially in the debates around the question of women's education and became of central importance with the emergence of Gandhi in Indian nationalism, which coincided with the integration of women in large numbers into the liberation movement in the twentieth century.

The reason for Gandhi's serious involvement at this time is located in the historical experience of the moment: the beginning of mass political action against imperialism, involving both men and women in large numbers. Gandhi's writings at this time reveal an increasing concern with those social institutions and practices such as *purdah* that restricted women's participation in the national awakening (Sujata Patel 379). Patel argues that in the early stages of the movement (1917–1922), Gandhi clearly subscribed to the ideology of separate spheres, although he also invested the private space of the home with a new political life in the project of *satyagraha* (civil disobedience, non-cooperation), whose success was closely related to the issues of domestic economy. Gandhi used the spinning wheel as the symbol of *satyagraha*, which is connected to women's traditional role. Thus Gandhi could, at this time, conceptualize for women a meaningful role in the nationalist politics, without disturbing the sanctity of the domestic sphere and women's roles in it. Soon the idealized domestic sphere and the ideal domestic woman emerged as the prominent symbol of national regeneration. Gandhi believed in the essentialism of the two sexes and explained the social manifestations of the biological complementarity of the separate sphere which supposedly reflected an "egalitarian" partnership:

> Men and women are of equal rank, but they are not identical. They are a peerless pair, being supplementary to each other.... Man is supreme in the outward activities of a married pair and, therefore, it is in the fitness of things that he should have

a greater knowledge thereof. On the other hand, home life is entirely in the sphere of woman, and therefore, in domestic affairs, in the upbringing and education of children, women ought to have more knowledge. (Gandhi 207–8)

Soon the idealized domestic sphere and the ideal domestic woman emerged as the prominent symbol of national regeneration.

Patel explains the relevance of Gandhian nationalism for the domestic sphere and the figure of the moral woman in it. For example, the success of *swadeshi* (development of indigenous economy), a necessary prerequisite for *swaraj* (self-rule), critically hinged on the revival, on a symbolic plane, of the home as the site of economic production. The most suggestive symbols of *satyagraha* – the spinning wheel and, later, salt – were obviously connected to a home-based economy and thus, to the sphere of female activity. Patel claims that even though it is assumed that Gandhi "mobilized a large mass of Indian women," his construct of women too is "drawn from a space inhabited by an urbanized, middle-class, upper-caste Hindu male's perception of what a woman should be" (378). The unique achievement of Gandhian ideology, Patel states, "lies in its ability to reinstate woman as a creative and conscious agent in political activism," without displacing her from her "natural sphere" (379). Gandhi " [not only saw] women as the repository of all that is morally and spiritually good within the 'home,' he gave woman-in-the-home a specific space in his political ideology, thereby legitimizing this space" (Patel 379). As can be seen, the ideological base for nationalism under Gandhi was "discursively inscribed through the writings of bourgeois culture" (Patel 379). Because Gandhi politicized and legitimized the domestic space, women could join the nationalist struggles with their "superior moral and spiritual" strength. Again, as in Africa (see Chapter 1), women who fought in anticolonial movements had to wage another war against the males of the nation for economic equality. Many middle-class and educated women writers who examine their unaltered material positions write about such matters; the conflict inherent in such conditions is reflected in cultural representations produced by them. Caught as they are between various discursive and ideological constructs, the modern postcolonial women negotiate their identity in conflicting and indefinite territories. We can see such ambiguities reflected in cultural productions, representations, and receptions of texts by women writers, such as Bharati Mukherjee, Aparna Sen, Farida Karodia, Mariama Bâ, and Myriam Warner-Vierya, for example, who are Western-educated and Westernized women. We see the protagonists of these authors resisting cultural constructions of identity, such as wife, mother, and so forth; sometimes such resistance takes extreme and violent forms, and we see the protagonist going "mad."

How do we interpret representations of madness by female writers inhabiting these conflicted spaces? How do we read and analyze them? In *The Wretched of the Earth,* Fanon provides useful analyses for an interpretation of madness in postcolonial texts and the effects of colonization on both the colonizer and the colonized. The use of language and ideology in the tactics of colonization and decolonization in Algeria is particularly useful in its application to other postcolonial countries. Fanon states in the very beginning of the book that "decolonization is a violent phenomenon" (35). He calls colonization "violence in its natural state, and it will yield only when confronted with greater violence" (61). This violence occurs, explains Fanon, because of cultural alienation, which is brought about not only by economics but also by psychological, as well as cultural, conditions. Women in postcolonial societies became alienated due to colonialism and nationalism. On the one hand, they were encouraged to become "new women" through nationalistic discourse, and, on the other, they were urged to become more traditional and self-sacrificing. How do women, in a postcolonial world, address such ambiguities? Can they address them without falling prey to the pitfalls of language?

At first, like the earlier women writers Sandra Gilbert and Susan Gubar write about, women in postcolonial societies too "either are inclined to immobilize themselves with suffocating tight-laces in the glass coffins of patriarchy, or they are tempted to destroy themselves by doing fiery and suicidal tarantellas out of the looking glass;" then, later, they "explode" out of the "glass coffin of the male-authored text" and the "old silent dance of death" which then becomes "a dance of triumph, a dance into speech, a dance of authority" (44). Or do they? And if they do, how do we, as postcolonial/transnational feminist critics, read them? For to read these texts without the antecedent historical and cultural references is to fall into the very traps set by modernity and globalization and see them simply as writing about oppressive home cultures, or as creating mad female subjects resisting brutal indigenous patriarchies.

Fanon states that decolonization "brings a natural rhythm into existence, introduced by new men [and women], and with it a new language and a new humanity" (36). Maybe postcolonial women writers are using this "new language" to address women's continued oppression and to look for resistance strategies. However, what happens when women write in postcolonial spaces, which Mary Louise Pratt defines as "social spaces where cultures meet, clash, and grapple with each other, often in contexts of highly asymmetrical relations of power, such as colonialism, slavery, or their aftermaths as they are lived out in many parts of the world" (530)? She states that "autoethnography, transculturation, critiques, collaboration, bilingualism, mediation, parody, denunciation, imaginary, dialogue, vernacular expression" occur in the contact zone. However, when postcolonial female writers write in this zone, "miscomprehension, incomprehension … absolute heterogeneity of meanings" are some of the perils we will have to confront (530). Many of the postcolonial female texts are misread, miscomprehended or even misinterpreted, sometimes unknowingly, sometimes blatantly. Thus, women's writing in a postcolonial world has to be read in a new way. What happens when women write or read in a "new way"?

Fanon's notion of "occult instability," where postcolonial people dwell when they are trying to give shape to a national culture, is useful here. Fanon states that we "must join the people in that fluctuating movement which they are just giving shape to … which will be the signal for everything to be called into question … it is to the zone of occult instability where the people dwell that we must come" (*The Wretched* 227). Women, too, try to redefine their identities and reconstruct their social conditions within such spaces. We too, as readers, must call everything into question, and we too must come to this "occult zone of instability" for a new understanding to occur. This space is also Foucault's "limit of madness," the space where the "line between reason and unreason" is not "accessible" to readers; a new language – "a very original and crude language, much more primordial than that of science" – becomes available to the interpreters of madness, such as myself, a conflicted subject, and may yet represent "those stammering, imperfect words without fixed syntax" in which an "exchange between madness and unreason sometimes occurs" (Foucault, qtd. in Miller 106).

In order to read postcolonial women's texts, then, particularly women writing madness and nervous conditions, let us return for a moment to

The Madwoman in the Attic. There, Gilbert and Gubar state that women a few generations ago who were "presumptuous" enough to attempt "the pen" had to deal with "enormous anxiety," as they were seen only as beings to be acted upon by men "both as literary and sensual objects" (8). Many women writing madness, too, are "searching ... into the mirror of the male-inscribed literary text," and readers who try to uncover the feminist poetics in these texts do see "an enraged prisoner" beyond the "mask" (15). Their efforts to write the "I" for self determination through the pen are denied them. They either become the "angel-woman" or the "monster-woman," and the outcome of their earlier attempt at writing is "ambivalent" (34). To be constructed by patriarchal discourse, which is contrary in itself, in many ways, is to be "trained to ill health," be it mental, psychic, or physical (55), as the subject constructed by patriarchal discourse has to navigate territories that are oftentimes conflictual. Thus, "surrounded as she is by images of disease, traditions of disease, and invitation to disease, and dis-ease, it is no wonder that the woman writer has held many mirrors of discomforts to her own nature" (57). While Gilbert and Gubar discuss Western patriarchal constructions of gender identity, these ideas, when transposed on to the colonized cultures, wreak havoc on the postcolonial female psyche.

And while Gilbert and Gubar base their analyses of feminist texts on Western literary traditions, the codes of postcolonial feminist writing, too, are subsumed by Western patriarchal conventions, constructed as they are by colonialism. To paraphrase Gilbert and Gubar and ask along with them, when postcolonial female writers write for self-definition, do they imitate the discourse and conventions of colonialism or nationalism, or do they "talk back" to them in their "own vocabulary, [their] own timbre, insisting on [their] own viewpoints" (46)?

What literary choices do postcolonial women make, then? What of postcolonial feminist poetics in English literature? Many postcolonial female writers, writing madness, too, are trapped within a masculinist discursive paradigm. As Trinh T. Minh-ha posits,

> All deviations from the dominant stream of thought, that is to say, the belief in a permanent essence of wo/man and in an invariant but fragile identity, whose "loss" is considered to be a "specifically human danger," can easily fit into the categories

of the "mentally ill" or the "mentally underdeveloped." It is probably difficult to a "normal," probing mind to recognize that to seek is to lose, for seeking presupposes a separation between seeker and the sought, the continuing me and the changes it undergoes. What if the popularized story of the identity crisis proves to be only a story and nothing else? Can identity, indeed, be viewed other than as a by-product of a "manhandling" of life, one that, in fact, refers no more to a consistent "pattern of sameness" than to an inconsequential process of otherness? How am I to lose, maintain, or gain an (fe/male) identity when it is impossible to me to take up a position outside this identity from which I presumably reach in and feel it? (*Women* 90)

If, as Minh-ha suggests, trying to claim a unique identity outside of the "master's logic" can land one in a "hospital, a 'rehabilitation' center, a concentration camp, or a res-er-va-tion," (95), how can women reclaim a unique female identity inside the dominant discursive system? Must they dismantle the system, as Minh-ha suggests? Yet, again, as Minh-ha claims, "gender, in its own way, baffles definition" (116), and if "each society has its own politics of truth ... [then] being truthful is being in the in-between of all regimes of truth ... outside specific time, outside specific space (121), then what language do postcolonial female writers use? Which discursive system do they inhabit?

In *Writing Madness: Borderlines of the Body in African Literature*, Flora Veit-Wild states that "writing madness ... [relates] to the paradigm of writing the body ... 'as the borderlines of the body'" (3). She argues:

Borderlines of the body mark the boundaries between the mental and physical world, reality and unreality (imagination), self and other, the individual and the community; they also imply being on the verge/on the edge, with a hint at the possibilities/danger of trespassing the lines, of the transgression or violation of certain boundaries, limits, dividing lines, or regulations. (3).

Three phenomena occur when postcolonial feminists strive toward creating an individual subjectivity through writing madness. First, they go through the earlier phase of using the masculinist poetics for self-representation (see the earlier discussion on Cazenave); then, they go through the oppositional phase, when they "other" themselves; finally, after passing through these various phases, they come to the in-between space, what Homi Bhabha calls the "Third Space" for rearticulation. This space is the space of conflict, or contrary and maddening reception and understanding, and only in the hybrid social spaces are their poetics read as empowering, albeit sometimes through misreadings – as their poetics are sometimes viewed through universal feminist perspectives and other times through a critical postcolonial feminist lens.

I will locate my chosen texts in this postcolonial "Third Space" from which postcolonial feminists, themselves the bearers of hybrid identity (as they are formed by the oppositional rhetoric and discourse of colonialism and nationalism) translate and negotiate meanings and identities, particularly within the global context of resurgent debates about nationalism during the past few decades. However, we must keep in mind the position of women writers who are able to write in English and publish primarily in the West.

Are these writers Indian, African, Caribbean, or are they simply Western? Tim Brennan, in his essay "Cosmopolitans and Celebrities," claims that what often produces the illusion of the obsolescence of nationalism is the "cosmopolitan embrace" which catapulted into fame writers such as Bharati Mukherjee, Salman Rushdie, Derek Walcott, and Carlos Fuentes:

> Propelled and defined by the media and market, cosmopolitanism today involves not so much an elite at home, as it does spokespersons for a kind of perennial immigration, valorized by a rhetoric of wandering, and rife with allusions to the all-seeing eye of the nomadic sensibility.... Operating within a world literature whose traditional national boundaries are (for them) meaningless, writers like Fuentes and Rushdie at the same time possess "calling cards" in the international book markets because of their authentic native attachment to a specific Third World locale. (2)

Brennan's remarks highlight the debates of the postcolonial diaspora in which literary figures from "Third World" countries are accused of commodifying their national identities for international consumption. I will look at the cultural productions coming out of the postcolonial spaces where identities are negotiated and reconceptualized. Who are these hybrid writers who can still use their cultural capital and yet refuse to be identified with the nation of origin? Bharati Mukherjee, for example, refuses to be termed an Indian writer and prefers to be categorized as an American writer. She appears wrapped in an American flag *sari* as she makes the proclamation of being American.[6] Can such spaces be used for individual empowerment without the complication of nationalism?

For Bhabha, the space of the "displaced," the "hybrid," is an empowered space which can produce counter-narratives of nations that challenge and displace fixed geopolitical boundaries. In "DissemiNation," Bhabha writes, "The boundaries that secure the cohesive limits of the western nation may imperceptibly turn into a contentious internal liminality that provides a place from which to speak both of, and as, the minority, the exilic, the marginal and the emergent" (300). This hybrid space is also the place to strategize resistance and generate an emergent sensibility that produces counter-discursive and reading practices.

In subsequent chapters, I focus on the politics of gender in these discourses of resistance in order to discuss postcolonial women writers negotiating their national and gender identities. I argue that this identity is rooted in gendered identity constructions. We have to keep in mind that in the process of the formulation of a national identity by the colonized, Western concepts of progressive individualism were assimilated selectively. Women's subjectivities and the indigenous patriarchal interpretations of "Indianness" or "Africanness" conflicted, and this conflict is reflected in women's writings that are shaped in resistance to such processes. However, women writers who address resistance to cultural constructions of identities or show "resistant representations" are misread as writing simply about oppressive patriarchal practices. According to Amina Mama,

> The collective African [and South Asian] experience – being conquered by the colonizing powers; being culturally and materially subjected to a nineteenth-century European racial hierarchy and its gender politics; being indoctrinated

into all-male European racial administrative systems, and the insidious paternalism of the new religious and educational systems; and facing the continued flow of material and human resources from Africa [and South Asia] – has persistently affected all aspects of social, cultural, political, and economic life in postcolonial African [and South Asian] states. ("Sheroes and Villains" 47)

Thus, it is necessary to examine gender violence, imperial roots, as well as neocolonial power structures that continue to construct ambivalent and conflicted subjects. Today, in the post-9/11 world, and in an era of widespread globalization with "signs of galloping U.S. imperialism" (Loomba et al., *Postcolonial Studies and Beyond* 1), ideas of national belonging become complex. Thus, the United States and the rest of the West are seen as liberating for women and minorities, while the Global South continues to be posited as oppressive and limiting.

Nation as tradition or "Nation *is* tradition" (Menon 207) is again rampant. The idea of America in the discourse of neo-liberalism functions as a place where "possible struggles for rights through consumerist practices and imaginaries … came to be used both inside and outside the territorial boundaries of the United States" (Grewal, *Feminisms* 2). Additionally, "American was important to so many across the world because its power enabled the American nation-state to disseminate the promise of democratic citizenship and belongings through consumer practices as well as disciplinarily technologies" (2).

When "Nation *is* tradition" is again rampant, there are many challenges facing women of the world. "The challenge for feminist practice," suggests Menon, "as a radical critique of capitalism and dominant cultures is to disaggregate the strands of these assertions (nation is tradition) and to carve out a different space of resistance" (207). This space, too, is conflicted as, on the one hand, "globalization in the *economic* sphere 'has offered an expanded and varied life for the rich and made the poor poorer,' [and] in the *cultural* realm, it has 'opened up a new channel of hope for the historically suppressed masses'" (Kancha Ilaiah, qtd. in Menon 218–19). While Illiah points to the lower castes here, women too fall into the category of the oppressed, and the cultural spaces that Ilaiah points to are the "world's egalitarian knowledge systems … characterized [by] the access to

English" (Menon 218-19). Here too the ambiguities, conflicts, and ironies are widespread, as globalization will not alter the material conditions of the oppressed but will provide access to English and the *egalitarian* knowledge systems through which some can represent their oppressions for neo-liberal consumption, a conviction that allowed them to speak for the Indian woman and silence her in the project of her liberation.

While Paul Zeleza states that "Globalization, as a process and project of neo-liberalism reinforces and recasts the ... internal and external, institutional and intellectual, paradigmatic and pedagogical, political and practical" challenges faced by African universities and intellectual communities, as well as the "gender implications" in these changes, he still feels that the "engendering" of globalization can be "Africanized" (80). Instead of seeing African intellectuals in the Western world as a brain drain, he suggests that many African scholars view it as "brain gain" (80) if we use the exchange in a fruitful and collaborative manner, and do not fall prey to the "seductions of the Northern academies to become native ventriloquists, complicit 'others' who validate narratives that seek to marginalize Africa" (80). And more importantly, "Critical to the engendering of globalization is the articulation of clear feminist critiques and constructions of globalization" (81). How does literature on "gender and globalization," with its "androcentric assumptions," expose "neo-liberal agendas [which] mobilize gender, region, sexuality, class, and race to reinscribe differences and hierarchies" (82)? Race and gender differences and class hierarchies are represented in unproblematic ways in dominant literary spaces. How do women write against "gendered, racialized, and regionalized processes of global capitalist expansion" (82)? Zeleza suggests that for a successful feminist criticism, scholars who examine "the impact of globalization on African politics, economies, and societies, including the higher education sector and intellectual production," must "strip the theories of globalization of their Eurocentric and androcentric biases, to show that while indeed powerful, the processes associated with globalization are subject to contestation, the contestation of alternative visions and values, ideas and imaginations of a global order that is truly equitable and humane for both women and men in the worlds we now call the global North and global South" (83). If not contestation, then, we need to infuse postcolonial views into the language of globalization, as this book hopes to do.

However, if we examine Vinay Lal's contention about systems of knowledge, we might have to ask Zeleza the question, how? How do we go about this contestation that he discusses? According to Lal in *Empire of Knowledge*,

> Nothing is as much global as the knowledge systems that perform the interpretive, political, cultural, and managerial work which characterizes modernity in the era of globalization, and consequently it becomes imperative to provide a cartography of the global framework of knowledge, politics, and culture, as well as of those paths which open up alternative frameworks to a more pluralistic future. (4)

In other words, instead of using old frameworks of inquiry, we must be open to new and alternative ways of writing and reading, which, sadly, are always contested in the "liberal" West and its Ivory Towers.

One might ask how one is to reach these alternative frameworks. Lal provides a solution. He states that "The true function of the intellectual is to be resistant to the dominant epistemologies and political practices, and to investigate precisely that element of knowledge which gives it the quality of being taken for granted. To do otherwise is to abdicate the responsibilities of the intellectual" (4). As a postcolonial transnational feminist critique, this book investigates the reception of my chosen texts to question the "quality of being taken for granted" within the dominant epistemological frameworks to provide alternative readings.

However, there is a danger to providing such alternatives. When I examine these texts that provide neo-liberal ideas of globalization and critique them for their limitations, I might be viewed as being backward and a traditionalist. As Lal suggests, to question the "logic of development was to place oneself among primitives and traditionalists, and to be viewed as an obdurate native who refused to be reformed" (9). What becomes of critics who, like me, continue to resist and to rewrite the agendas of modernity and globalization? There is a fear.

They are punished. They become "victims of development … lying in unmarked graves" (9). States Lal, "The victim of development has no name, and was asked to march to the tune of development, laying aside his or her lands, honor, traditions, and culture in the name of the nation. The victim of development is not even a victim; he or she is a statistic" (9). It is the "insanity of development" and the unnamed statistic that I will try to give a name to in this book, although I must perforce use the same language of development and enlightenment, progress and democracy, freedom and liberalization, criticism and resistance that is bequeathed to me as a postcolonial scholar.

However, without the alternative readings, postcolonial writers are in danger of simply being raw material for the enrichment of the Western academy and the West, leading to further disenfranchisement of many in the Global South and indeed, in the Global North. As Wallerstein explains, each segment and section of society is impacted by the "world system theory," particularly the Global South due to its being involved in "the world-economy system as a peripheral, raw material producing area" (*The Capitalist World Economy* 7). He explains further,

> It is only with the emergence of the modern world-economy in sixteenth-century Europe that we saw the full development and economic predominance of market trade. This was the system called capitalism. Capitalism and a world-economy (that is, a single division of labor but multiple polities and cultures) are obverse sides of the same coin. One does not cause the other. We are merely defining the same indivisible phenomenon by different characteristics. (*The Capitalist World Economy* 6)

Therefore, each society is impacted by the capitalist world economy – in the economic as well as cultural spheres. All postcolonial societies have been raw material producing sites for a long time as part of the capitalist system. Thus, in my analysis, I suggest that postcolonial writers are indeed still being used as raw material in the cultural sphere. For as Wallerstein posits, "Power lies in the control of the economic institutions," and more importantly for my purposes, "Power lies in the control of cultural institutions" (*Unthinking Social Science* 36). Yet women writers who write to resist may or may not be aware of their co-optation and exploitation; nevertheless, they continue to write resistance literature in the hope of alleviating gender oppression. However, what happens when they write about gender oppression using the idiom of modernity in national and international spaces is the thrust of my analysis.

Additionally, I locate my texts in the conflicted space where the "nervous" subjects – alienated, dislocated, mad – formed by the oppositional discourses of colonialism and nationalism, of West and East, of home and the world, of masculine and feminine, of globalization and neocolonialism, resist cultural inscriptions for nebulous reinscriptions and empowerment. They attempt to rewrite history for an egalitarian future. "You can't escape history because it is everywhere," states Adrienne Rich, adding that "History is made of people like us, carriers of behavior and assumptions of a given time and place" (*Blood, Bread and Poetry* 144–51). The question is, can feminists rewrite history through resistance? As Wallerstein claims regarding resisting the forces of capitalism, "The antisystemic movements are themselves institutional products of the capitalist world-economy, formed in the crucible of its *contradictions*, permeated by its metaphysical presuppositions, constrained by the working of its other institutions" (emphasis added, *Unthinking* 37). Nationalism, according to Wallerstein, in "historical terms, is a very new concept," a "late product" of the modern world-system (*Unthinking* 134), and may not last through the twenty-first century. "This should make us hesitate at least in asserting the long-lasting quality of Indianness (or Africanness) as a social reality" (134).

As African, Caribbean, and South Asian women writers grapple with notions of Africanness and Indianness, of belonging to the nation, "the historical ground on which we stand is about as stable as that covering a fault line in the earth," states Wallerstein (134). If our "sociological (including cultural) analysis is to end up with a historical interpretation of the concrete" (134), what if in the global world-economy of today, we come to a "new order" (147) of things?

Now seems to be the beginning of the new order of things as powers shift. Yet we see more violence, incivility, and oppression – gender, race, class, caste, sexuality, religion – in the Global North as well as Global South today. How can postcolonial feminists write about cultural and psychological madness and conflicts brought upon by such conditions? Can women writers writing oppression for gender empowerment "assert the connection between the individual and community and in which community reflects cultural identity" (Fayad 106)? For identity to be empowering, the postcolonial notion of ambivalence must be used. "Ambivalence is able to avoid the problematics of either/or by rejecting boundaries set up between the dichotomies of modern/traditional and everything they entail" (Fayad 106). History as a category and foundation for the national narrative must be questioned. For an empowering postcolonial feminist historiography will build a "postcolonial female subject that embraces rather than excludes the *complexities* and *contradictions* of inescapable hybrid identities" (emphasis added, Fayad 106). In other words, trying to escape from one discursive system into another, where another set of oppressions exists, might not be empowering after all, but embracing ambiguities can actually lead to expansion – of the psyche and then of the social spaces leading to new understanding of subjectivities and representations.

3

The Indian Diaspora and Cultural Alienation in Bharati Mukherjee's Texts

PART ONE:
DISLOCATION AND PSYCHIC VIOLENCE IN *WIFE*

In many transnational female-authored texts, representations of Indian culture and womanhood are riddled with conflicts and ambiguities. I argue that these conflicts and ambiguities are due to the diasporic writers' conflicted psyches, formed as they are by the ethos of modernity, and also due to their location and class status. In writing about Indian female subject formation in the West, many authors draw upon an essentialized notion of Indianness in a stereotypical and reductive manner, adding to the idea of Indian culture as backward and in continued need of reformation. In my discussion of Bharati Mukherjee's *Wife*, I will demonstrate Mukherjee's Westernized consciousness and her awareness of Westernized and Western audiences, which provide her texts with interesting insights into her troubling representations.

The representations, in and of themselves, are stereotypical, which is troubling enough, but what is dangerous is that these representations add to the hegemonic notions of Indian womanhood and culture as backward and needing further modernization through penetrative globalization agendas. This idea of modernization is tied to the liberalization of the marketplace and to furthering the class divide, leading to further disenfranchisement of many women, which is becoming imminent in the Indian subcontinent.

Mukherjee, who once lived in a Westernized, upper-class neighbourhood of Calcutta, sees Indian society as tradition-bound, as can be seen in her earlier novel, *The Tiger's Daughter*. She has lived in the West since the early 1960s. In her texts, we see her rejection of the tradition-bound society of the East as she reaches out for the more empowering, individualistic society of the West. This reconstruction is not without struggle or loss, which she addresses in a number of novels, but in *Wife* we see the psychic struggle of an immigrant woman who is caught between two discursive systems – East and West – leading to trauma and violence.

However, the reality is that the immigrant's resistance to and compliance with the hegemonic discourses change with the context of oppression; this is why the immigrant comes to occupy many shifting subjectivities. Yet, such complexities are not represented in Mukherjee's texts.

The Tiger's Daughter, an earlier novel, deals with the return of the immigrant from the West to the traditional space of the old. Mukherjee's changing imagination is textualized in ways that indicate her consciousness is being redefined in and by the West. She describes her upper-class, convent-educated friends as a dying class, living lives of decadence and material comforts, signifying spiritual death. Although they appear to live liberated lifestyles of Westernized Indians, Mukherjee draws attention to the fact that they still believe in the traditional arranged marriage where parents "initiate serious talk" with foreign-educated and brilliant "boys" from the same caste and class. The protagonist, Tara, after seven years in liberal Western institutions such as Vassar and the University of Wisconsin, Madison, seems to fall prey to the "passive" and "fatalistic" attitudes of the Indian community. This novel contains many of the author's own misgivings about India and the Indian community and their inability or unwillingness to adapt to the changing times – a world she had left behind when she relocated to the West.

Mukherjee, educated at the prestigious Loreto House Convent School by Irish nuns, suggests that in early childhood, the two world views – of her home and school life – clashed. She writes about her sense of alienation from her home culture in *Days and Nights in Calcutta*, stating that her "imagination created two distinct systems of cartography [where] multiheaded serpents who were also cosmic oceans and anthropomorphic gods did not stand a chance of survival" against the mapping of the "New Testament" (917). Additionally, as a child, Mukherjee had spent some time in England, and when her family returned to India, she was further alienated from her middle-class, joint-family existence. With her father's growing success as a chemist and industrialist, the family moved away from the joint-family household into an exclusive, Westernized neighbourhood, where a *durban* always guarded the compound gates, regulating and checking unwanted visitors. The isolation and separation of the upper classes from the everyday Indian culture had begun. This isolation and alienation was further complicated when Mukherjee married the Canadian writer Clark Blaise, whom she met at the Iowa Writers' Workshop in the United States, and went to live in Canada, where she was "simultaneously invisible" as a writer "and overexposed" as a racial minority (Mukherjee, "An Invisible Woman" 36) until she came to live in the United States as a naturalized citizen.

Mukherjee discusses the problem of identity politics for the English-speaking postcolonial writer in *Days and Nights*:

> I am a late-blooming colonial who writes in a borrowed tongue (English), lives permanently in an alien country (Canada), and publishes in and is read, when read at all, in another alien country, the United States. My Indianness is fragile; it has to be professed and fought for even though I look so unmistakably Indian. Language transforms our way of apprehending the world; I fear that my decades-long use of English as a first language has cut me off from my *desh* (country). (170)

By the end of her year in India, when Mukherjee finally prepares to leave, she realizes she does not need to "discard [her] Western education in order to retrieve the dim shape of [her] Indian one"; in the future, she would return to India but would see it as "just another Asian country," and she would be "just another knowledgeable but desolate tourist," believing that if she stayed on, "the country [would] fail [her] more than [she] had by settling abroad" (284). Her touristy world view about Indianness is textualized in many interesting albeit problematic manners in most of her texts.

In *The Tiger's Daughter*, Tara, who is visiting India, cannot wait to go back to the United States and to her white American husband, David. And in *Days and Nights*, Mukherjee, even though she acknowledges a sense of loss at not ever having a *desh*, celebrates the possibilities of the writer's ability to "demolish and reinvent" a homeland: "It was hard to give up my faintly Chekhovian image of India. But if that was about to disappear, could I not invent a more exciting – perhaps a more psychologically accurate – a more precisely metaphoric India: many more Indias" (285)? While Mukherjee may be writing to redefine herself in new terms, her unfortunate representations of India as chaotic, passive, helpless, backward, violent, and fatalistic add to the valorization of the West as rational and progressive. Such representations suggest that the author still continues to think and write in a manner which is Orientalist, adding to damaging stereotypes of the Global South.

Aijaz Ahmad's criticism regarding the position of such Anglophone Indian writers as the spokespersons of Indian culture clearly underlines this issue:

> The few writers who happen to write in English are valorized beyond measure. Witness, for example the characterization of Salman Rushdie's *Midnight's Children* in the *New York Times* as "a continent finding its voice" – as if one has no voice if one does not speak in English.... The retribution visited upon the head of an Asian, an African, an Arab writing in English is that he/she is immediately elevated to the lonely splendour of a "representative" – of a race, a continent, a civilization, even the "third world." (5)

Such tokenism can be dangerous, particularly in a world polarized by world views where the East/West, primitive/civilized notions are still privileged, as can be seen by the West's rhetoric in the War on Terror and the attacks on Iraq, as well as the threat to bomb any other "rogue" nations that do not comply with the hegemonic notions of liberation and freedom.

First of all, we have to keep in mind why English was introduced as the official language in India: to subjugate the natives and to create a class of Indians who would help in the administration of the British Raj (Macaulay). The conflicted consciousness of the colonized that was constructed by imperialism due to the binary nature of colonial language continues to manifest itself in the writings of many postcolonial writers, particularly in this era of globalization.

Mukherjee's texts locate themselves within this conflicted cultural space in the category of postcolonial literature where nations construct gendered national identities. She writes about India and uses "Indianness," showing the author's affinity with the Indian nation and pointing to a colonized past, while forming a postcolonial present in the United States. As Anindyo Roy writes:

> To assign a specific tradition to the literature written by and about the new Indian diaspora is also to acknowledge that this tradition is marked by the presence of a "postcolonial" discourse. The terms "diaspora" and "postcolonial" belong to a specific historical condition that is released by India's emergence as a "free" nation and by her entry into a new transnational geopolitical sphere. (127)

Roy's terms "postcolonial" and "diaspora" point to the temporal and spatial components of Mukherjee's *Wife*, where she writes about Dimple Dasgupta, a young Bengali wife who immigrates to the United States – an opposition to Tara in *The Tiger's Daughter*, who returns to the nation of origin. Although *Wife* was published before *Days and Nights*, it can be situated around the time that Mukherjee starts to completely affiliate herself with the West. *Days and Nights* was published in 1977; Mukherjee landed in India for the year on a "Sunday morning, May 13, 1973" (10) with her husband and children. While *The Tiger's Daughter* maps Mukherjee's slow disassociation and withdrawal from the old world, *Wife* represents the possibilities of the new world for the immigrant. The reason Dimple fails to take the *advantages* offered by the new world is discussed in the following paragraphs.

While her experiences as an "invisible minority" in Canada were traumatic for Mukherjee, Feroza Jussawalla points out that Mukherjee celebrates the "exuberance" that an immigrant feels at the melting pot theory of assimilation in the United States (591). That such assimilation is problematic in a nation that celebrates multiculturalism and difference rather than belonging is ignored by Mukherjee. Additionally, in an interview with Ameena Meer, Mukherjee affirms, "I totally consider myself an American writer.... Now my roots are here and my emotions are here in North America" ("Immigrant Writing" 28). Mukherjee's celebration of the United States and her continuing use of "Indianness" as backward and "traditional" in texts after texts, which are published and consumed predominantly in the West, continue to be a matter of a critical postcolonial debate (Feroza Jussawala; Anindyo Roy; Indrani Mitra; Indrapal Grewal; Gurleen Grewal, among others).

Mukherjee's statements regarding assimilation in the melting pot draw a strident comment from Jussawalla, who finds in postcolonial writers like Mukherjee "a new hegemonic discourse of those who see themselves as assimilated and assimilable. The irony is that in separating themselves from other South Asian immigrants and in hoping to be accepted among the mainstream of the majority, these writers only extend and perpetuate a new colonial mentality" (590). Although Jussawalla's criticism of Mukherjee is justified, Mukherjee herself, after her naturalization as a United States citizen in 1988, locates herself in the mainstream American tradition but in a special space. While claiming to speak for the "new American from non-traditional immigrant countries," she states:

> They all shed past lives and languages, and have traveled half the world in every direction to come here and begin again. They're bursting with stories, too many to begin telling. They've lived through centuries of history in a single lifetime – village-born, colonized, traditionally raised, educated. What they have assimilated in 30 years has taken the West 10 times that number of years to create. ("Immigrant Writing" 28)

Mukherjee sees the new world full of potential where negotiations for gendered and national identities occur in an alien, albeit liberating, world. Although she has written extensively about immigrant experiences of people from all over the world in her later works, the works that focus on Indian immigrants seem more popular. Additionally, while most immigrants to the West are predominantly from urban areas and are Western-educated, in *Wife* we see a village girl who comes to the United States. Here, the village is shown as the pit of traditionalism from which the protagonist is eager to escape. Yet, even in the urban areas, the representations of Indians are imbued with the same binaries of modernity and tradition.

And although Mukherjee claims that *The Tiger's Daughter* is not autobiographical, there are moments in the text that reflect the author's own experience. For example, she states, "There were just so many aspects of India that I disliked by then. So a lot of my stories since are really about transformation – psychological – especially among women" (Connell 15). She critiques the limited space available for negotiation of gender roles for women in postcolonial India. Women's national identity, therefore, becomes difficult and, for some like Mukherjee, distant.

Why do texts such as Mukherjee's resonate with so many women, particularly Western and Westernized Indian women? Indrani Mitra, writing in connection with postcolonial women writers, examines the disillusionment felt by postcolonial Indian women within the women's movement in postcolonial India; she argues that while the constitution guarantees equal rights "designed especially [for] egalitarian sexual relations and women's access to education and professional opportunities," social reforms without "fundamental structural changes in bourgeois society" lead to continued oppression and equality remains just a myth for many Indian women ("Colonialism" 179). For the educated, upper-class woman, to whom the promise of liberation was most immediate, the experience of modern India is one of conflict and alienation. Mukherjee speaks to this stratum of society, as well as to other Orientalists, who continue to see India as traditional and backward. They do not appear to complicate the oppression of women by situating it within the historical and cultural contexts of a classed and gendered society.

Mukherjee interrogates the question of subjectivity and agency from the perspective of a middle-class postcolonial, female subject. In her earlier novels, set in the early and mid-1970s, the realities of women's material existence have changed only slightly. For middle-class Indian women, the idea of companionate marriage had expanded to include educated Indian women, although the prospect of liberation proved disillusioning for them. Postcolonial writers such as Mukherjee question the confined spaces in which educated and upper- and middle-class women play their demarcated roles.

In her later novels, written after she immigrated to the West, she explores the possibilities for liberation through transformation for oppressed, rural, and lower- middle-class women in the New World. For example, in *Jasmine* (1989), Mukherjee maps the immigrant experience of a protagonist who finds the West exciting and full of possibilities; Jyoti, a woman from rural Punjab, after a series of traumatic experiences as an Indian woman, finally transforms herself by finding an "authentic" American identity in America as Jasmine. When faced with postcolonial criticism due to such reductive constructions of gendered identity, Mukherjee defends her position:

> The kind of women I write about, and I'm not generalizing about women in the South Asian community here, but the kinds of women who attract me, who intrigue me, are those who are adaptable ... and that adaptability is working to the women's advantage when we come over here as immigrants. The males function very well as engineers or doctors or whatever, and they earn good money, but they have locked their hearts against mainstream culture.... For an Indian woman to learn to drive, put on pants, cash checks, is a big leap. They are exhilarated by that change. They are no longer having to do what mother-in-law tyrannically forced them to. (Connell 32)

Though her argument is somewhat reductive, Mukherjee here points to the fact that national identity is obviously a privilege which economically independent males can lay claim to, but for Indian women, who must negotiate their identities outside of the traditional Indian family, it becomes difficult, yet paradoxically exhilarating. However, such exhilarations come after a great loss and compromise. From Tara to Dimple to Jasmine, we see a slow transformation of the female characters who must negotiate their identities in the new world, and although this transformation is not without violence, in which one self seems to annihilate another in the in-between contradictory spaces, where the new is not yet constructed, Mukherjee simply celebrates what she calls the "exuberance" of the immigrant experience.

Sneja Gunew discusses the constructions of identities and the violence that seems inherent in the construction of the Self. In the discussion on violence and multiculturalism, Gunew asks an important question: "[I]f you are constructed in one particular kind of language, what violence does it do to your subjectivity if one then has to move into another language and suppress whatever selves or subjectivities were constructed by the first" (419)? In the act of becoming, when the old subjectivity – in the act of repression – and the new subjectivity – in the act of emergence – collide, psychological violence is inevitable. Mukherjee uses these ideas of violence which takes textual forms in many different, albeit slightly generalized and problematic, ways in her texts. We see the use of violence and its textualization in *The Tiger's Daughter* when Tara is sexually assaulted by the old politician; in *Wife*, we see it when Dimple aborts her fetus and when she stabs her husband; and in *Jasmine*, we see it when Jasmine reconstructs herself as Kali in order to avenge her rape by slicing her tongue and then killing her rapist.

We also see epistemological violence in *Jasmine* when Jasmine reinvents herself. Jasmine, an illegal immigrant, a young widow, transforms herself from Jyoti to Jasmine to Jassy to Jase and finally to Jane in the United States, moving rapidly from one locale to another: starting from rural India (Hasnapur), proceeding to a city in Punjab (Jallandhar), arriving in Florida, moving to Queens, then to Manhattan, and ultimately settling for some time in Iowa. Jasmine does not transform herself gradually; she reinvents herself by killing her old selves: "There are no harmless, compassionate ways to make oneself. We murder who we were so we can rebirth ourselves in the images of dreams" (*Jasmine* 25).

However, Jasmine's desire to come to the United States stems from the desire to commit *sati* on the campus where her now deceased husband, a victim of Sikh terrorism, was to attend engineering school in Florida. She buys a fake visa to the United States (with the support of her brothers, one might add); when she arrives in Florida after a nightmarish journey, she is attacked by a white man who rapes her. After she stabs her rapist in the guise of Kali, she sets her clothes and her husband's clothes (which she was supposed to burn along with herself at the campus) on fire in a dumpster. At this point, she emerges, phoenix-like, from the symbolic burning and is free to find a new identity for herself in the new world. While Mukherjee investigates the possibilities offered by the New World for reconstructions of identity, her simple binary representations continue to be problematic.

For example, after her husband's death, Jasmine, now living in the modern Punjabi city, arbitrarily decides to commit *sati*. Mukherjee's representation of India and Indian customs reinforces the idea of India as backward and tradition bound. In her discussion of *Jasmine*, Gurleen Grewal castigates Mukherjee for her serious omission in situating the Western audience and trivializing the practice of *sati*. Grewal states that such "gross misconceptions" suggest that women might travel halfway around the globe to commit *sati*:

> Reading *Jasmine*, one might think sati was being practiced as a matter of routine and choice by contemporary Hindu widows.... Mukherjee's protagonist is neither coerced by relatives avaricious for her husband's money, nor so bereft of options that death is her only alternative. Extricated from relations of power and property, the practice of sati, as an arena of both oppression and of women's resistance to oppression, is rendered meaningless in *Jasmine*. ("Born Again" 188)

Grewal's criticism is valid, as Jasmine's brothers fund her trip to the United States of America, and later, as Jasmine sees the possibilities of the West, she decides to become a *liberated* American woman. Thus, in her representation of the assimilationist protagonist, who rejects tradition-bound culture, nation, and her gendered identity, Mukherjee reinforces imperialist constructs of Indian women as oppressed and brutalized (see Chapter 2). Mukherjee is clearly limited in her conceptualization of liberation due to her class status and her Westernized consciousness.

As Chandra Talpade Mohanty suggests, such a representation of "third world women as a group or category ... automatically defined as religious (read 'not progressive'), family oriented (read 'traditional'), legal minors (read 'they-are-still-not-conscious-of-their-rights'), illiterate (read 'ignorant'), domestic (read 'backward'), and sometimes revolutionary (read 'their-country-is-in-a-state-of-war; they must fight!')" (*Third World Women* 72) reinforces the notion of "western women as secular, liberated, and having control of their own lives" (Grewal "Born Again" 187). While Mukherjee must surely be aware of the problematics of representation, the textualization of the oppressed Indian woman continues to proliferate in her texts.

Though "Mukherjee is ... careful to suggest that America is no Eden: it is a brave new world that includes the violence of rape, murder, and suicide" (Grewal 187), she shows Jasmine can become "American" by simply rejecting the old and claiming the new. When Jasmine burns her clothes in the trash bin, Mukherjee seems to suggest that Jasmine can symbolically trash the old traditions and, hence, her traditional identity.

Jasmine's widowhood shows her as a completely disempowered figure in contemporary Indian society. In a society where widows are seen as inauspicious, Jasmine's desire to commit *sati*, although in an alien land, changes the meaning of *sati* in the postcolonial context. A Hindu/Indian religious rite which had not only been discussed and written about in colonial India, but also has a prominent place in contemporary discourses involving national identity, *sati* problematizes the construction of a postcolonial feminist identity in *Jasmine*. Why does Mukherjee write about *sati* in this context?

Mukherjee's use of the practice of *sati* brings to mind its colonial context and historicizes postcolonial female subjectivity in terms of British imperialism. Nationalism and the "woman question" came into discourse at a period in Indian history when the ritual of *sati* became a signifier for discursively dismissing Indian national identity formation. Therefore, Mukherjee's representation of Jasmine and her desire to commit *sati* helps reinforce the construct of the monolithic image of the "third world woman" as a "religious, family oriented, legal minor, illiterate, domestic" even while it helps to constitute certain postcolonial female writers such as Mukherjee as "secular, liberated, and having control of [their lives]" (Mohanty 73).

Mukherjee blurs the differences of class between the Jyoti of the village and Jane in Iowa; Jyoti is a peasant girl from a village, and Jane appears to be a Westernized and Western-educated woman like Mukherjee. The implication for "illiterate," non-Western immigrants in the United States is that one can acquire class privileges if one so desires. Grewal claims that the life of a peasant girl, Jyoti, is "expendable": "[her] death by a symbolic burning in the trash can, and subsequent transformation into Jane is a colonial legacy; Mukherjee, however, does not acknowledge the psychic violence in the legacy she claims" (Grewal 193).

I argue that Mukherjee does acknowledge the psychic violence, but not in *Jasmine*, where she appears to be celebrating Jasmine's successful "assimilation," but in *Wife*, although, here, too, trauma is posited in troubling ways. It appears that she realizes the psychic violence one can undergo when one resists the hegemony of the Old World in order to comply with the hegemony of the New. It is important for my argument to locate *Wife* before *Jasmine* and after *The Tiger's Daughter* and *Days and Nights*. In *Jasmine*, we see Jasmine becoming a successful "American," and in *The Tiger's Daughter* and *Days and Nights*, Tara and Mukherjee, who feel increasingly alienated in India, relinquish their "Indianness." In *Wife*, we see Dimple Dasgupta, who, although resisting her "Indianness" actively, is unable to use what Mukherjee posits as the space of transformation and liberation in the United States. She is unsuccessful in forging an "American" identity for herself because her Indian identity, which was forged in the aftermath of British colonialism, has been strongly influenced by Western binary logic. It is this conflict that problematizes Dimple's identity construction in the New World. The reductive and stereotypical accounts of young women in India waiting to be married are relevant here.

Dimple, who is waiting to have her marriage arranged with a "suitable boy," nevertheless daydreams about love. Where is the space for notions of romantic love in India where the system of arranged marriages prevail? While her parents are searching for the perfect match in the newspaper (matrimonial section) advertisement, where males seek "a beautiful, fair, tall, educated young girl of good conduct, within their caste," Dimple dreams of freedom: "Marriage would bring her freedom, cocktail parties on carpeted lawns, fund-raising dinners for noble charities. Marriage would bring her love" (*Wife* 5). Dimple, however, is flat-chested. Her mother, in the meantime, seeing her daughter's pain, "prescribe[s] pre-bath mustard oil massages, ground almond and honey packs, Ping-Pong [table tennis], homeopathic pills and prayer to Lord Shiva, the Divine Husband" (5). We can see Westernization rearing its head in the promise of romantic love after marriage, and cocktail parties on lawns, while traditional discourse manifests itself in the arranged marriage system and the prayer to Lord Shiva. Mukherjee highlights the idea of privileging women as wives and mothers, and we can see that nationalist ideology, whereby woman is exalted as the caretaker of the inner sphere of the home, still prevails in many so-called postcolonial texts.

Jasmine's father, Mr. Dasgupta, who is an electrical engineer of modest income, cannot afford a substantial dowry for his daughter's wedding. Yet besides all the wedding arrangements, including a lavish meal ("eighty-five kilos of fish"), he is able to give the girl "the usual gold ornaments (which normally is a full set, including a heavy necklace, bracelets, ring and earrings made of twenty-four-carat gold), saris (which are normally rich embroidered silks), watch, fountain pen and some furniture" (15). In fact, Amit, the groom, takes some cash in lieu of furniture, for he is planning to settle in the West, and the cash will come in handy. While it is accurate to state that the dowry system is extremely unfair, and dowry deaths – where brides are murdered, typically through burning, for being unable or unwilling to bring more money from their homes, and their murders generally reported as accidents or suicides – have escalated in post-independent India, such representations, rendered as they are simply in gendered terms, fail to analyze the rise in dowry deaths in the context of the scramble for middle-class status by many poor Indians in modern, post-independent India.

When she finds that married life is not what she had dreamed about – cocktail parties, fund-raising dinners and love – we see a bored and depressed Dimple. To combat her boredom, while waiting for her husband to come home, Dimple takes to reading English magazines to improve her reading skills. One day she finds the following letter from a female reader who supports the idea of arranged marriages and is opposed to divorce: "Are you forgetting the unforgettable Sita of legends? Can she recall how she walked through fire to please Ram, her kingly husband? Did Sita humiliate him by refusing to stroll through fire in front of his subjects and friends? Let us carry the torch (excusable pun) of Sita's docility!" (*Wife* 28). Mukherjee's consciousness of her Westernized audience is manifested in such representational writings, where she has to explain the ideology of "sacrificial" women; most Indians do not talk or write about Sita[1] explicitly; the message is implicit and is practised, not preached. Such representation verifies critics' accusations of Mukherjee's ongoing constructions of "Third World" subjects for "First World" consumption, for it is a known fact that Mukherjee's novels are predominantly consumed in the West (Indrapal Grewal, *Transnational* 65–79). For example, in *The Tiger's Daughter*, Tara is forever referring to her absent American husband, David Cartwright, and it is through his eyes (or the eyes of Clark Blaise's camera in *Days and Nights*) that we see India, just as we see a middle-class, married woman's life through a Westernized filter.

Mukherjee shows us that Dimple has in her the makings of an independent, liberated woman, or is it really the making of a "mad" woman? We see the conflict – which is produced in the postcolonial woman's psyche – when Dimple becomes pregnant soon after her marriage. She resents it, unlike most married women, resisting the patriarchal construct of motherhood, an indication that Dimple is not passive. "She gave vicious squeezes to her stomach as if to force a vile thing out of hiding" (*Wife* 31). The only reality at that point is her vomit, not the "reality" of motherhood. She forces herself to vomit by inserting her fingers down her throat. "[The vomit] was hers" (31). Claiming her vomit as her own and making it an empowering experience, and finding pleasure and excitement in the smell of vomit that clings to her body, she feels empowered in being able to control her own body. For her "vomiting was real … but pregnancy was not" (32). Thinking "bitterly that no one had consulted her before depositing it in her body" (33), she feels helpless, and the feeling enrages her. One day she jumps rope "until her legs grew numb, her stomach burned; then she poured water from the heavy bucket over her head, shoulders, over the tight curve of her stomach. She had poured until the last of the blood [as she miscarries] washed off her legs; then she had collapsed" (43). While Jasmine rids herself of old cultural tradition by the symbolic burning of her clothes, Dimple aborts her baby and is then ready for the liberatory possibilities of the New World (to which she is immigrating soon). While her Western audience might see her act of abortion as liberation and empowering, for the Indian audience, this act should be incomprehensible. How would a traditionally raised Indian woman read such an act – as an act of "madness"? Is it not madness not to become a mother and be valorized in the traditional family? Women acquire privilege and power through becoming the bearers of children, and by extension, the nation. Within the domestic spaces inhabited by most middle-class Indian women, such an action as Dimple's would be odd, if not incomprehensible. It might be read as a necessity due to health or monetary reasons, not as liberatory or empowering.

The tension between the traditional and the modern, between the East and the West, manifests itself when Dimple moves to America with Amit a few months after her marriage. After he gets a job as a boiler maintenance engineer, Dimple is represented as being kept isolated in an apartment all day as she does not have transportation, nor does she know how to drive. Also, she is unsure about her English-speaking skills.

Dimple meets and is fascinated by an Americanized Indian woman, Ina Mullick. However, Dimple is not allowed to make friends with Ina because Amit considers her too "Americanized"; she might give Dimple some "bad ideas." The "bad idea" is that Ina goes to night school, though Amit insists that Ina is just opening herself up for being mugged in the subway. An Indian woman has no right to put herself in such unsafe situations, especially "with so many Indians around, a television, and a child, a woman shouldn't get time to get crazy ideas" (69). Mukherjee shows Amit's anxiety about the West and its "liberating" influences, which manifests itself in such representations.

The constructions of gender identity in most minority communities in the United States are complicated with racial oppression. In order to fight their marginalization in the dominant discourse, the middle-class, Western-educated Indians seek to validate their identity through the private sphere. While the public sphere, where success is coded in material gains, is open to educated Indians, the private and cultural spaces of America are shut off to most Indians. Thus, Indians, mostly men, can be progressive and Westernized in the public spaces, but the domestic and private space must remain Indian, therefore traditional.

In spite of all the warnings about "crazy ideas," Dimple makes friends with Ina, whose friendship with Milt, a young white American man, she envies. Even though Ina is married, she has a comfortable friendship with another man. Dimple aspires to be like Ina, who is spontaneous and funny, but must keep her friendship with Ina and Milt a secret. Feeling alienated and lonely, she spends more time watching soap operas and other programs on television and starts confusing her reality with that of the characters on television. The two hegemonies – Western and Patriarchal – are reconstructing Dimple's psyche through different ideological discursive systems at this point.

Judith Butler's explanation of "prior hegemony," which presupposes a latter hegemony, is useful in my discussion of resistance to hegemonic discourses. "Prior hegemony" in my discussion refers to the "Western" or "Colonial" discourse, while the latter hegemony refers to the patriarchal or nationalist discourse (*Bodies That Matter* 133). It is useful to remember that in the liminal spaces of oppositional discourses, according to Butler, prior hegemony often wields more power over the latter, which remains, to a large extent, a minority discourse. However, when the two discourses collide, there is a possibility that the latter hegemony can also reproduce the ideologies of the prior hegemony. In *Bodies That Matter*, Butler states, "Importantly, however, that prior hegemony also works through and as its 'resistance' so that the relation between the marginalized community and the dominative is not, strictly speaking, oppositional. The citing of the dominant norms does not, in this instance, displace the norm" (133). Dimple tries to "cite" the dominant norms by looking for Marsha's (the woman whose apartment they are subletting) Western clothing and trying it on. She starts daydreaming about liberty and freedom. But as a caretaker of tradition and culture, and caught between two world views, Dimple starts dreading even her dreams, which she cannot share with anyone. She becomes "a small stiff lump, hair arranged like black bat wings against the sky blue pillow" (128). Caught in such a dismal situation, Dimple feels that catching a fatal disease, like leukemia, is preferable and more "glamorous." Her reality turns to dreaming, and her journey to "madness" begins. Was she a prime candidate for "madness" right from the beginning, when she resisted the cultural text by getting rid of the baby? Or does it start one afternoon when she has sex with the tall and good-looking Milt, a "genuine American," who considers her beautiful, and who finds the dimple on her cheeks charming?

She thinks that having casual sex with Milt will turn her into an American; instead, she feels disappointed and guilty:

> She has mismanaged [sex with Milt] all; she'd seen enough TV and read enough novels to know this was the time to lie in bed, to hum little songs, to pinch, pull, slap; it was not the time to reach for dark glasses and sensible undergarments and make discreet inquiries about the young man's job. She was so much worse off than ever, more lonely, more cut off from Amit, from the Indians, left only with borrowed disguises. She felt like a shadow without feelings. Whatever she did, no matter how coolly she planned it, would be wrong. (*Wife* 200)

For Mukherjee's women protagonists, identity construction entails finding out about their sexuality, which might lead them to liberation and happiness. If she can have casual sex, she must be turning "American." Yet Dimple starts to contemplate suicide as a way out: "One [way] was to stand under a warm shower and slice open a jugular.... She could see pretty jet sprays of pinkish blood.... She would like to make one extravagant gesture in her life" (154). Mukherjee claims that Dimple's contemplation of suicide is very Indian, very traditional: "Dimple, if she had remained in Calcutta, would have gone into depression, and she would have found a very convenient way out for unhappy Bengali wives – suicide" (Connell 20). Mukherjee's rewriting of "sanctioned suicide" (Spivak, "Can the Subaltern Speak?" 120–30) in India, where women do not commit suicide because they cannot "find" themselves, but because of severe physical, economic, and psychological oppression from greedy in-laws due to their inability to give dowry, shows her subject position as Westernized. Alienation and displacement can lead one to see oppressions differently: in India, economic difficulties are paramount; in America, where prosperity reigns, it is the "human condition" that calls for suicide! If one cannot find oneself, one can annihilate oneself!

But Dimple, whose resistance to the hegemonies of both India and the United States is not successful, decides to end her oppression by destroying the obstacle to her successful assimilation: "That night, trapped between the cold wall and Amit's heavy body, in post nightmare lucidity, she sought revenge ... [Yet] her own intensity shocked her – she had not considered herself susceptible to violence – so she tried to explain it away as unnatural sexual desire. 'Love is dread,' she whispered loudly to the sleeper" (*Wife* 117). As she considers killing Amit by "applying light, rhythmical pressure" on Amit's neck, she begins "to feel that violence was right, even decent.... Her own body seemed curiously alien to her, filled with hate, malice, and insane desire to hurt, yet weightless, almost airborne" (117).

Why is it that when she is thinks of death and pain, she feels airborne and light? Why does she feel violence is right, even decent? Why is death and dying, or is it killing, so full of promise? Here Dimple's feelings of violence against her husband symbolize her resistance against patriarchal ideology, where the man can adapt in the material world, while keeping the space of the home "inviolate." Violence then moves from one space to another. From contemplating killing herself, Dimple now wonders about killing her husband. Her frustration at being unable to transform her identity to that of liberated Americans in the new world is trivialized over and over again in the text. When they go out visiting other Indian friends, Dimple finds her husband's presence oppressive, for he does not allow her to taste any alcoholic drinks. If he were not there, she might have "permitted herself a sip or two" of beer, "but Amit will always be there beside her ... acting as her conscience and common sense. It was sad, she thought, how marriage cuts off glittering alternatives" (127). Here, of course, Amit represents the old order, the traditional Indian world of customs and tradition, so finally, one day, she "sneaked up on him and chose a spot ... then she brought her right hand up and with the knife stabbed the magical circle once, twice, seven times, each time a little harder" (213), and she kills her husband. Or does she?

Dimple remembers that on TV women get away with murder. But that question, whether she finally killed her husband or not, is somehow not important, for in the act of killing her husband, she is symbolically destroying the self that cannot be reconstructed. She erases one of the maddening inscriptions: the inscription of traditional Indian, and hopes to reinscribe herself as American, and therefore, liberated. The conflict between the two ideologies is necessary, according to Mukherjee, in order to remake the self in terms of the new immigrant aesthetics. When she was asked, "Do you see immigration as an experience of reincarnation?" Mukherjee answered, "Absolutely! I have been murdered and reborn at least three times" (Connell 18). Dimple kills her fractured self many times before she reconstructs herself through murder. Does that action mean that Dimple is privileging her selfhood and becoming complicit with Western notions of a liberated woman? Mukherjee sees Dimple's action as resistance and condones it as progress. "In the United States, she suddenly learns to ask herself 'self'-oriented questions. Am I happy? Am I unhappy? And that, to me, is progress. So, instead of committing suicide, turning society-mandated violence inward, she, in a misguided act, kills the enemy.... It's meant to be a positive act. Self-assertive" (Connell 21–23). The novel, while attempting to examine the conflicted space in which an Indian woman reconstructs her identity where the older paradigms are no longer functional and new ones are yet to actuate, is ultimately limiting as a model for liberation, because Mukherjee reductively suggests one can simply reject the past for autonomy and liberation. Additionally, she does not allow for multiplicities of identities in a multicultural space that is supposed to be the United States of America.

The female protagonists of Mukherjee's fiction, like many immigrant women in the United States, claims Mukherjee, are "between roles.... There isn't a role model for the 'Jasmines' or the 'Dimples.' They have to invent their roles, survive and revise as best they can" (Connell 23). Mukherjee's texts do bring to the fore the problematic space that an immigrant community inhabits where notions of traditional femininity are still imposed in an effort to minimize the colonizing influence of the dominant community, where racism rears its ugly head perpetually. In this conflicted space, the postcolonial female's negotiation for her identity in a transnational diasporic space is riddled with conflict, a conflict represented in a "maddening" space by often alienated subjects themselves. Therefore, we must keep in mind the transnational diasporic subjects' psychic constructions when we read these so-called feminist texts. We must not duplicate a colonialist rendering of subject formation in our readings, which frames gender oppression in the Indian community in monolithic terms, but must situate these texts squarely in the cultural space where their production and consumption take place.

PART TWO:
DESIRABLE DAUGHTERS AND THE IMMIGRANT IMAGINATION

In my discussion of Bharati Mukherjee's *Desirable Daughters*, published almost two decades after her earlier texts discussed in Part One, I will share some interesting insights about Mukherjee's own ideas of exile and alienation coming full circle as she attempts to reconcile the psychic contradictions and conflicts of the postcolonial female subject and cultural identity formation in the diaspora. However, her text is still haunted with the construction of the modern subject in reductive ways. In this section, I will illustrate Mukherjee's continued stereotyping and misrepresentation of both the American as well as the Indian experiences of postcolonial female subjects.

Tara Chatterjee, the protagonist of *Desirable Daughters* currently living in America, divorces Biswapriya Chatterjee – "who was, and probably still is, wealthy beyond counting or caring" (23) – and was educated, like Mukherjee herself, at Loreto House, a prestigious convent school run by Irish nuns.

Mukherjee writes about her sense of alienation from her Bengali culture as early as 1977 in *Days and Nights in Calcutta*. As discussed in Part One, with her father's growing success as a chemist and industrialist, the family moved away from the joint-family household into an exclusive, Westernized neighbourhood, where a *durban* always guarded the compound gates, regulating and checking unwanted visitors. Such too is the fate of Tara and her two sisters, Padma and Parvati, who are not allowed out on the street, symbolically separating the public and the private. The narrator explains, "Our car was equipped with window shades. We had a driver and the driver had a guard" (*Desirable Daughters* 29). For true liberation to occur, these female protagonists of Mukherjee's must leave the "oppressive" Indian homes and cultures behind.

In many of her novels, Mukherjee explores the possibilities for liberation through transformation – especially for oppressed, middle-class Indian women – in the New World. From Tara Banerjee (*The Tiger's Daughter*) to Dimple (*Wife*) to Jasmine (*Jasmine*) to Tara Chatterjee (*Desirable Daughters*), we see a slow transformation of the female characters who negotiate their identities in the New World, and although this transformation is not without violence or loss in which one self seems to annihilate another, it is still seen as liberatory.

However, Mukherjee apparently realizes at this time in her life, after raising two sons in the West, that it is not easy to murder one's self off as easily as she had thought. The past seems to haunt the author, as seen in the representation of Tara in *Desirable Daughters*. The narrative begins with the mythic marriage ceremony of Tara Lata Gangooly, a child bride, whose intended dies of a snakebite even though the proper worship and rituals for the snake goddess have been made; the intended's greedy family demand the dowry money anyway, because they claim that the boy died due to a curse and that the bride was a "home-destroying, misfortune-showing daughter" (10). The father, Jai Krishan Gangooly, who is a Hindu and who believes that an unmarried daughter will not attain Nirvana and might be reborn as a woman, saves her from that fate by marrying her to a tree. She is now a married woman just like her two older sisters. She goes on to live for seventy years and gradually changes the world by becoming a freedom fighter; she is eventually killed by the British.

Tara Chatterjee considers herself the mirror image of the ancestral Tara. The narrator then proceeds with the story of the "three great-granddaughters of Jai Krishan Gangooly" (7), Padma, Parvati, and Tara. Tara is recently divorced from Bishwapriya Chatterjee, a billionaire software tycoon, and is living with her white America lover, Andy, who is an ex-hippie, and who, I argue, exoticizes Buddhism. She is raising her fifteen-year-old gay son. Tara is still friends with Bish, and the causes of the divorce seem to be fairly simple; Bish is a typical Hindu man, a householder who performs his dharma well – the dharma of the householder involves paying off the debts to one's ancestors which are discharged by marrying and having children; a debt to the gods that is discharged by the household rituals and sacrifices; and a debt to the teacher that is discharged by appropriately teaching one's wife or children. This, however, is not enough for the Westernized Tara. She needs someone who is less serious and dutiful; she needs "Andy, good old 'boys-just-want-to-have-fun' Andras Karolyi," her "balding, red-bearded, former biker, former bad-boy, Hungarian Buddhist contractor/yoga instructor ... [her] carpenter" (25), who got her with a "backrub," and who, even though a practising Buddhist, has "never taken a deep interest in [Tara's] Indian life" (46–47). She explains,

> "Love" is a slippery word when both partners bring their own definition. Love, to Bish, is the residue of providing for parents and family, contributing to good causes and community charities, earning professional respect, and being recognized for hard work and honesty. Love is indistinguishable from status and honors. I can't imagine my carpenter, Andy, bringing anything more complicated to it than, say, "fun." Love is having fun with someone, more fun with that person than with anyone else, over a long haul. (27)

Here, too, Mukherjee falls into reductive and easy binaries regarding love vs. arranged marriage, duty vs. dharma, liberated fun sexuality vs. sexual oppression and couches them in the inherited rhetoric of emancipation constructed by the elite in India during the nationalist era.

The narrator compares the lifestyles of her two sisters, who seem to be living ordinary lives as opposed to Tara's American life. Of her two sisters, Parvati lives in India in a very traditional household even though she had a love marriage; she had fallen in love with an Indian student while studying in America. The eldest sister, Padma, who lives in New Jersey, is married to a Harish Mehta, an "American," according to the narrator, as like Padma, "he'd blotted out all that was inconvenient or didn't fit" (183). Padma, according to the narrator, "had been the 'new girl' [in India] and our father had destroyed the opportunity" (179), the opportunity to be liberated and Westernized.

However, Tara discovers that Padma might have had a secret love affair in India with Ronald Dey, a Christian Bengali; she is suddenly confronted with the reality of her "nephew," Chris Day, when he appears from India, ostensibly looking for his mother, Padma. She visualizes her sister's affair in India as liberating, for she exclaims, "Passion like Didi's is foreign in our family; recklessness unknown. She is our *true American*, our improviser ..." (emphasis added, 31). She continues, "Something marked Didi as different" (31), and, of course, the difference is "genetic," just as Jasmine's transformation in *Jasmine* is represented as genetic. Because she had always been marked as different, and therefore American, Padma now lives the Diva lifestyle in New Jersey as a "fag hag" and is famous in the Indian enclave as a television star. However, she commodifies Indianness and is more Indian than the Indians in India. Tara states, "In San Francisco, I barely knew any Indians" (181). Both the sisters use the idea of Indianness for different purposes, one to "sell" it and one to reject it.

Mukherjee's *The Tiger's Daughter* contains many of the author's own misgivings about India and the Indian community and its inability or unwillingness to adapt to the changing times – a world she had left behind when she relocated to the West. The narrator of *Desirable Daughters*, too, makes similar claims:

> "Love" in my childhood and adolescence (although we didn't have an "adolescence" and we were never "teenagers") was indistinguishable from duty and obedience. Our bodies changed, but our behavior never did. Rebellion sounded like a lot of fun, but in Calcutta there was nothing to rebel against. Where would it get you? My life was a long childhood until I was thrown into marriage.... Love was a spectrum upon which [many different men] lay within a narrow, caste-bound zone of contention. In the third-largest population in the world, even a narrow range is not a constricted choice. (29)

However, this community can apparently remake itself in the West. She states that she belongs to an elite minority group and accepts that she is blessed. In her earlier novel, *The Tiger's Daughter*, Mukherjee shows the same community as being tradition bound, fixed and oppressive. So how is *Desirable Daughters* different from her earlier texts? How is she redefining the passive and fixed India? She seems to be gesturing toward the essentialized core of Indianness that one is inextricably tied to.

What about the Indian communities of the New World that she had demonized as living in ethnic ghettos in *Jasmine* and *Wife*? In *Desirable Daughters*, we see the author making an attempt to resurrect the image, particularly of the Bengali community, as well as the feminized Indian manhood of her earlier texts.

Let's examine her most recent novel a little more closely. The protagonist of *Desirable Daughters*, too, is named Tara, and we see many more specific autobiographical elements in her latest novel. Tara's ancestors are from the upper-class Brahmin community, the "Bhadra lok" and she is a descendant of a "Bhadra mahila," an educated and genteel Bengali woman; this community was one of the first communities in India to be "civilized" (*Desirable Daughters* 7). Also, interestingly enough, it is only in this novel that Mukherjee suddenly seems to become aware of the debate and discussion that has been raging in academia regarding the position of the Bhadra lok and especially the Bhadra mahilla during colonial rule in India. Partha Chatterjee, among others, has written extensively in "The Nation and Its Women" about the "women's question," which became a "central issue in the most controversial debates over social reforms in early and mid-nineteenth century Bengal – the period of its co-called renaissance" (*The Nation and Its Fragments* 116–34). While the author tackles the very complex question regarding the "new woman" and her identity construction through oppositional discourses of tradition vs. modernity/nationalism, I want to point to his assertion that "in setting up new patriarchy as a hegemonic construct, nationalist discourse not only demarcated its cultural essence as distinct from that of the West but also from that of the mass of the people [i.e., Indian Muslims, Muslim women, and the majority of the masses]" (134). In a similar vein, the narrator of *Desirable Daughters* explains,

> The Hindu Bengalis were the first Indians to master the English language and to learn their master's ways, the first to flatter him by emulation, and the first to earn his distrust by unbidden demonstrations of wit and industry. Because they were a minority in their desh, their homeland, depended on mastering or manipulating British power and Muslim psychology, the Hindus of east Bengal felt themselves superior even to the Hindus of the capital city of Calcutta. (6)

One such man is the great-grandfather of the current Tara, Jai Krishna Gangooly, a pleader in a Decca High Court, who is cast as "the apostle of enlightenment and upholder of law against outmoded customs, or the adjudicator of outrages undefined and unimaginable under British law," and is also someone who is in conflict with the "majesty of law" as he is searching "for an uncorrupted, un-British, un-Muslim, fully Hindu consciousness" (9). Strange that the narrator admits Gangooly's search for a "fully Hindu consciousness," for in the following paragraphs remaining in this chapter, I shall show that even though Mukherjee appears to want to repair some of the damaging (mis)representations of the Indian minorities resplendent in her earlier texts (for example, the Sikh "terrorist" in *Jasmine*), and to showing a fuller picture of the New Jersey Indians as compared to *Jasmine* and *Wife*, she continues to (mis)represent and generalize the Indian diaspora and its struggle for empowerment by falling into her earlier notions of "Indianness" as either passive or excessive, and "Americanness" as liberating.

In comparison to *Jasmine*, where a member of the Sikh community is represented as a terrorist, in *Desirable Daughter*, the Sikh man, Sgt. Jasbir Singh Sidhu, B.A., M.A., Ph.D., Doctor Jack, who, unlike Sukhi, the terrorist and murderer of Jasmine's husband in *Jasmine*, is himself a victim of Sikh fundamentalists. His father, who was a policeman in India, was marked as a traitor by them and killed. He has lived in Vancouver since he was two and is now a SFPD member. When she goes to the police station to report on her misgivings about Chris Dey, she asks to see a culturally sensitive officer; to begin with, she is assigned a Bangladeshi officer, Farookh Ahmed, but she doesn't think a "Muslim would understand"; so, due to her request, she is assigned "a tall Sikh with a trimmed beard and a thoroughly American manner and accent. But for the powder-blue turban, he looked more like a college student than an officer of the SFPD" (139).

While trying to do justice to the complexity of the Sikh situation post-1984, she falls into the stereotyping of Muslims. First, she does not see Farookh Ahmed because of his Muslim background; second, the imposter, Abbas Sattar Hai, who is pretending to be her nephew, Chris Dey, viciously murders her real nephew; third, he is shown as a member of the Muslim community and, in fact, as belonging to the notorious underworld Muslim Dawood Gang operating out of Bombay. Hai ends up blowing up Tara's house with explosives, while she is being romantically reconciled with her divorced husband in a sexual fantasy worthy of our soap operas after Andy walks out on her due to the SFPD's investigation of the Dey's case. (The audience is to assume that Andy has a criminal past, you know, as he is a "violent" Hungarian!)

While the crime situation in Bombay's underworld is no doubt complex and dangerous, the assumption that crimes committed in America are by recent immigrants, and moreover, by those "violent Muslims," lands Mukherjee's narrative from the frying pan into the fire. The increasing disenfranchisement of Asian American youths in America, and specifically in California, and the proliferation of Asian American gangs, is here trivialized and the magnitude negated. For how can there be Asian American gangs in California when the Asian students perform their dharma so well (44)? And does not everyone live a wonderfully "ethnically ambiguous life," "drinking coffee" and "walking their dogs" and being on first-name basis with the service people – Ib, Selim, Moh, Safid, Ali – who are apparently all employed and equally hardworking like the Palestinians (25)? And don't forget the laundromats and restaurants owned by the Japanese!

Yet, Mukherjee also seems to make a genuine effort to reclaim the "decadent" and "traditional" Bengalis' lifestyle of *The Tiger's Daughter* by portraying her parents' retreat to Rishikesh, to explain Hinduism and the four stages of Hindu life – brahmacarya, gârhastya, vânaprasty, sannyâsa, namely, student, householder, forest-dweller, and ascetic in *Desirable Daughters*. Tara explains about her extremely Westernized father at this stage of his life by stating, "My father has made connections on a cosmic level, the rest of it didn't really matter" (304). In her earlier novels, the protagonists long for sexual liberation and freedom; indeed, Tara Chatterjee of *Desirable Daughters*, too, desires and celebrates the sexual exuberance of the Americans, yet at the same time, for the first time, Mukherjee seems to valorize the Indian arranged marriage system, in her own conflicted way! She contrasts the two men in her life – one Indian, the other Hungarian:

> The two long-term lovers in my life are such opposites there are no points of comparison. [She then goes on to compare them, anyway!] Whatever one is, the other isn't. Andy isn't rushed, he isn't methodical, but sometimes his presence is his

absence. Sometimes I feel I should call him back. I never had to do that with Bish. Thousand of years of arranged marriages had somehow habituated us even before laying eyes on each other; there would be nothing in our sexuality that was, finally, exotic. (77)

And earlier, she states that Andy was not interested in her Indian past, just like Bud Ripplemeyer of *Jasmine*; as if to say it is not the exoticness that brings exuberance to their lovemaking, it must be something else. Yet it is only in Bish that she finds complete acceptance.

Mukherjee attempts to make amends for her earlier stereotype about unfeeling Indian husbands and rescuing white lovers, but the textuality of her attempts appears contradictory. The narrator of *Desirable Daughters* continues, "Bish is generous and protective [even as a divorced man]; he has more than enough to provide. Indian men, whatever their faults, are programmed to provide for their wives and children. If I had wanted only to be provided for, stupendously provided for inside the gated community, endlessly on display at dinners and openings, I would have stayed in Altherton" (27). But, of course, she chooses liberation, represented by love and sexual freedom.

Stereotypes of immigrants in San Francisco, too, abound – no one can make out anyone's ethnicity; the narrator explains, "I am one with the neighborhood, a young woman like so many others on the street: ethnically ambiguous, hanging out in the coffee shop, walking the dogs, strolling with boyfriends, none of us with apparent source of income" (25). With the exception, of course, of the hardworking "crack-of-dawn rising, late night closing Palestinians, whose shifting rosters of uncles and cousins seems uniformly gifted in providing our needs and anticipating our desires" (25). The new immigrants wear ill-fitting clothes, "laughable clothes" (35), and illegal aliens, who are "food handlers or sales assistants," have "watchful postures," but then later she laments she cannot tell Indians apart because she's lost her "Indian radar" (118)!

In her earlier novels, Mukherjee simply rejects the past for autonomy and liberation by reaching out to the West and Western ideals. However, in *Desirable Daughters*, she seems to return full circle to *her* India of the old Bengal with its superstitions and caste-bound traditions. Tara states:

> I realized the futility of questioning fate, or blind random chance, or character. If Didi [Padma] had married, would she have stayed in Calcutta? I could not imagine it. Would she have made a loving mother? If she had acted, would she have risen to diva status? Something else, equally calamitous would have happened on the same date, at the same minute. Perhaps an earthquake, a plane crash, an automobile accident. Who are we to question God? (303)

Indians, as you know, are fatalistic!

The female protagonists of Mukherjee's earlier fiction, like many immigrant women in the United States, claims Mukherjee, are "between roles" and must "reinvent themselves" (Cornell 23). Mukherjee's texts have, to a limited extent, brought to the fore the problematic space that an immigrant community inhabits. But her texts are only useful if we, as critics and readers, complicate the issues of the politics of representations in the West as well as the author's postcolonial condition and cosmopolitanism. As we know, in the Indian immigrant community, where notions of traditional femininity are still imposed in efforts to minimize the colonizing influence and racism of the dominant community, the postcolonial female's negotiation for her identity in a postcolonial space *is*, no doubt, riddled with conflict.

In *Desirable Daughters*, the sexually liberated and fully empowered Tara, even though artificially widowed (her hair is singed off due to the blast and she is wearing a wig; the illusions point to the traditional Bengali widows and their disempowerment) tries to reconcile the conflict and contradiction of the diasporic Indian women's subject formation by returning to the beginning; instead of the earlier versions of killing one self for the empowerment of the other, she seems to nudge the subject toward the hybrid "Third Space" of Homi Bhaba for reconciliation; however, even though the attempt is recognized, the text ends up with too many contradictions, stereotypes, and broad generalizations. This shows that even though Mukherjee appears to be aware of the postcolonial criticism of her texts, she still continues to inhabit a very problematic space and her conflicted consciousness still haunts her tales.

As she is one of the most-read Indian authors (examine any Asian American Anthology and you are sure to see one of her stories), her representations of Indians and Indianness, and particularly Indian women, contribute to ongoing paternalism of the Global South by the Global West; too, such discursive formations have also furthered the West's effort at market liberalization of India, adding to further oppression of the working class and continued marginalization of Indian men and women due to the hierarchical nature of the global economic system.[2]

4

Postcoloniality and Indian Female Sexuality in Aparna Sen's Film *Parama*

Aparna Sen's *Parama* – released in 1985 – aroused much interest in the Indian viewing public and was widely discussed in terms of its feminist thrust. This attention was due primarily to the fact that both the director, Aparna Sen, and the actress of the film, Rakhee Gulzar, popularly known as Rakhee, are stars in their own rights; also, both Sen and Rakhee are divorced women; Sen's remarriage at that time to a much younger man, Mukul Sharma, who plays photographer Rahul in the film, added to the media interest. In this chapter, I will examine the filmic narrative to pose questions related to a postcolonial feminist reading by examining the social position of the director and by critiquing the reception of this film in India.

Like the other chapters, this one also asks: How do we read texts that represent generalized views of oppressed and powerless Indian women, while at the same time representing Indian patriarchy as monolithically oppressive and backward? Is Sen perpetuating the colonial ideology of the oppressed Third World woman who needs to be rescued, or is she too trapped in various patriarchal and feminists discourses necessarily depicting oppression only through narratives of modernity and tradition in a postcolonial world? Or, and here is my main point, is the director a transgressive artist showing empowerment and rearticulation of identity through the power of imagination and fantasy by showing madness as resistance?

Parama proved controversial, as it was very unusual to depict a sexual relationship between a married woman and a younger man at the time of the film's release. What is ironic is that the sexually explicit scenes in the film contributed, to a large extent, to the film's commercial success in India. While Sen's intention was to make a feminist film, the great response from a large crowd of sexually repressed male spectators – the censor board in India strictly controls sexually implicit portrayals or nudity, giving such films an "A" (Adult) certification – made it all the more popular (Arora 295).

Parama is the story of a married, middle-class woman who lives in an extended family structure of Bengal. Parama's life is drastically altered when New Yorker Rahul, a photographer for *Life*, comes to Bengal for a photo shoot of an Indian "housewife" and chooses Parama as his subject. Rahul, a diasporic Indian, eventually persuades Parama to explore her own dreams and ambitions. He encourages her to play the *sitar*, which she used to play before her marriage and which she has since neglected. Under his influence, Parama starts exploring her sexuality, which leads her into an extramarital affair with him. Rahul promises he will take her to America, where they will roam the country, giving sitar recitals while he accompanies her on the *tabla*. Her husband is mostly away on business trips, making it convenient for the two to spend time together exploring Calcutta, until Rahul is reassigned to another place. He leaves India, never to return, but the intimate photographs of Parama do appear in *Life* magazine and are seen by her family members. This incident precipitates a psychic and familial crisis for Parama, who is ostracized by family and community and suffers an emotional breakdown. She tries, unsuccessfully, to commit suicide, and ends up in the hospital with a fractured skull. She recovers physically after her surgery, but goes through a "mental breakdown" and becomes uninterested in anyone or anything, though her husband and her family are anxious for her to return home. In the hospital, however, she talks only to her divorced feminist friend Sheela (portrayed in the film by the director herself). She finally agrees to return home, but only on the condition that she be allowed to work outside of the home.

In this film, Sen deals with the psychic trauma that is part of a married, middle-class woman's life when the meaning of her life is restructured according to Westernized notions of individuality and sexual liberation. Can the character Parama, who suffers a nervous breakdown, reconstruct a new identity within the "Third Space" (Bhabha) that opens up as the two discursive systems of tradition and modernity clash in postcolonial India? How do we read a text about madness and gender without complicating the politics of location and reception, both of the film and the director?

There were various reactions to *Parama* when it was released in India. While the criticism varies, critics have been harsh to Sen when they maintain that the feminist bent of the film is flawed due to its easy and seemingly enforced resolution, while others comment on Sen's Westernized sensibilities.

Film critic Poonam Arora contends that in *Parama*, Sen provides a critique of Western ethnography, revealing the problems in the photographer's misreading of Parama in "Western bourgeois terms" (293–304). Arora critiques the photographer's "liberal tutelage" of Parama, which "encourages her self-expression and individuality" (300), because he disregards Hindu familial structures:

> Individualism is a nonconcept in Hindu philosophy as well as Indian society. In Hinduism, one's subjectivity is defined by one's *Bhumika*, what translates as one's familial and social role. Thus Parama is addressed as daughter-in-law, sister-in-law, wife of a maternal uncle, wife of a paternal uncle, mother, or wife. The photographer is the only one who refuses to recognize her various other roles and insists on calling her by her first name; an act that not only disregards the sanctity of familial relations, but also tears the fine fabric of that society. (301)

In other words, Rahul's intervention into Parama's life resembles colonial intervention into the cultural sphere of the colonized.

Radha Subramanyam disagrees with Arora, arguing that the film's approach resembles the photographer's in the way it "conceptualizes subjects, subjectivity and resistance" (147–48). She argues that

> the film itself privileges a postenlightenment narrative of independence and empowerment for its feminist and individual claims. Far from being a critique of western ethnographic constructions of the subject, or showing the inadequacies of western liberal tutelage, the film draws deeply, for its feminist argument, on western liberal notions of the subject. (149)

Subramanyam critiques the narrative structure that pays more attention to the oppressive family relationships than to any critique of ethnography. Whereas Arora sees Rahul, the photographer, as a "brown sahib" (historically, a native who was educated and trained to be the mediator between the colonial ruler and the native population), "a pseudo-westerner" whose "loyalties were and still are with the colonial ruler" (299), Subramanyam argues that the gaze of the photographer and that of Sen, the director of the film, are "congruent."

However, I argue that although the position of the Westernized photographer is problematic, and he does act as an ethnographer in photographing Parama for *Life*, Sen does not simply position Rahul as a "brown sahib"; Rahul is a diasporic postcolonial subject, an immigrant from India, whose family settled in the United States when he was quite young. He himself is a subject formed by the discursive systems of Indian patriarchal discourse interwoven with Western individualism. To name Rahul's intervention in Parama's life as similar to colonial intervention of the British Raj constructs him as a mercenary exploiter. Granted, Rahul appears Westernized and intervenes in Parama's familial and sexual life in a manner that would rarely ever be done by an Indian from India; his ideas of sexuality and individualism are Western and he sees Parama as limited in her abilities to savour life and sexuality fully. His ideas of Indianness are the ideas that inhabit a diasporic community's imagination in transnational spaces. These ideas are taken to the far reaches of the world through immigrant narratives as well as through the Indian cinema. If he acts as an ethnographer (internalizing the myths of traditional and sexually repressed Indian women), myths deployed by the indigenous patriarchy during and after colonialism and nationalism remain current. Additionally, and more significantly, many diasporic Indian men are unable to resist mainstream forces like media stereotypes and racism, and have been racialized, feminized, and discriminated against in America.

If, as a diasporic subject, Rahul constructs his masculinity in opposition to the traditional Indian woman, we can see the hegemonic cultural and social forces working behind such constructions.

Arora also claims individualism is a nonconcept in Hindu philosophy, as well as in Indian society. Is she discussing contemporary Hindu society? Notions of individuality had already been introduced and selectively absorbed by the Indian populace when Western education was implemented in nineteenth-century India. This class of Indians, from the late eighteenth to the early nineteenth century, consisted mainly of an English-educated, middle-class elite employed in government jobs or were part of the landowning elite. Middle-class Indian women had already made their entry into the public sphere during this time, producing texts written in English, conforming to the notion of femininity influenced by the English missionaries, administrators, and educators, tempered by indigenous patriarchy; nuclear families also came to be formed at this time.[1] Therefore, to claim that Rahul is introducing a concept unheard of in Indian society seems a bit farfetched.

While it is tempting to read *Parama* as a colonial narrative, and see Rahul as a colonizer or an agent of colonialism who must "unveil" the mysteries of the native woman, thereby supporting "Western penetration into the native society" (Fanon, *A Dying Colonialism* 43), it is more useful for my purposes to look at it as a text that complicates the notions of companionate marriage, as opposed to the coercive system of the *zenana* and arranged marriages and of patriarchal control of female sexuality, in Westernized and elite female-authored texts.

While love and courtship were central themes in the developing, nineteenth-century English novel, relationships between men and women as individuals were not prevalent in India at that time. Meenakshi Mukherjee discusses the ways the concept of love was in "dissonance with the subjectivity" of the ideal woman constructed by nationalism: "In the contemporary Indian setting, however, romantic love could only be illicit, involving either a widow or a courtesan – since only these two categories of women were without legal 'proprietors' and thus seemed to embody a certain amount of unharnessed sexual energy" (*Realism and Domestic Fiction* 41). Therefore, love became necessarily associated with the fallen woman. Such an attitude was inherited by Indians, and it shows in Indian literary texts. As such, for the Indian woman, whose social identity is defined within such contradictions, the notions of love, romance, and courtship are problematic. Most middle-class Indians' imitation of the ideal of companionate marriage, which was never clearly articulated in terms of romantic love, created ambivalence in the middle-class Indian woman's imagination. Although the system of companionate marriage, which was introduced during colonialism, with its notion of romantic love and mutual affection, still supports patriarchal structures, it was desirable to the educated Indian woman as it seems consensual; yet it enables the continuation of traditional roles for women as wives and mothers. Thus the ambivalence and confusion inherent in the rhetoric of nationalism follows postcolonial Indian women, as can be seen in the film.

In her marriage, Parama appears content in her many roles as mother, daughter-in-law, sister-in-law, aunt-in-law; the household revolves around her in terms of activities and around her-mother-in-law in terms of respect and honour. Parama has control of the house – spending money, paying the servants, shopping – and she has the key to the house, which is symbolic of the power of the lady of the house. She has access to the family car and a chauffeur and can visit her many modern friends, who are activists, artisans, or academics, as they move in and out of the domestic sphere into the public domain.

When Parama hears about her friends' many activities outside the home, she is surprised that they have time to do anything outside the home, for she stays so busy she does not even have time to play the *sitar* anymore. While talking to her friends, she appears nostalgic at not being able to play the *sitar*, giving a small self-deprecating laugh, but does not act in the least bit deprived, only surprised. However, it is only later, when she comes into contact with Rahul, and especially when she relinquishes some of her familial duties, that we begin to see the hegemony of the West, with its notion of individuality, begin to make a stronger mark on Parama. Before her contact with Rahul, Westernization affected her but only to the extent that she was allowed to be educated – like the selectively modernized colonized woman – to the extent of becoming a fitting wife and mother for her urbane and Westernized husband. The postcolonial Indian man, who becomes Westernized in the material realm, finds his identity only in the spiritual, hence traditional realm. While in the public sphere identity is ordered through material wealth and Westernization, in the private sphere, the family is organized in terms of family values (Chatterjee, "Nationalist" 243).

Subramanyam accuses Sen's narrative of privileging a post-Enlightenment ideology of individualism for its feminist thrust (147). She refers to examples, such as the sexually explicit scenes and shots where Parama responds to the family's needs, claiming the film depends precisely on the notion of the subject for its criticism of patriarchal Indian society. Yes, the first few frames of Parama are through a photographer's lens, and when that lens is removed, she performs her religious and familial duties, constantly moving and smiling, and being praised by her mother-in-law. She is superbly confident and in complete control of the domestic sphere. However, Subramanyam sees Parama as completely disempowered. She writes that in each of the shots, "A woman is constantly, repeatedly, asked to perform a series of roles. Demands are being made on her continually without regard for her needs and desires" (150). Here Subramanyam herself constructs desire in purely Western terms and sees Parama's many roles as limiting and unfulfilling.

Here desire is constructed according to communal and individual categories. Middle-class Indian women "need" and "desire" to be a mother, wife, sister-in-law, daughter-in-law, etc., in such a household as Parama's. Many women enjoy the empowerment that comes with such roles, no matter how coercive or oppressive they are considered. It is only through such gender roles that women acquire position and prestige, translating into power. Without such roles, access to power and agency are often denied them. As Parama moves in and out of the different roles, we see a supremely confident and contented middle-class Indian woman. She performs her gender role well while partaking of its many privileges.

While there are many role models, such as wife, mother, daughter, etc., within the Indian context, the role of lover – primarily seen by the middle-classes through its representations in Indian cinema, strictly controlled by the Indian censor board – is wrapped in mystery and silence. In Indian popular cinema, the love scene or the "bedroom" scenes are still performed in enigmatic ways, often with the screen fading into black, or alternatively, focusing on kissing birds and shaking bushes. Kissing scenes remain at the experimental level in Indian cinema and are still quite rare. Therefore, sexuality, in terms of sexual liberation and sexual identity, does not exist in the social discourse of the majority of Indians, and the topic of sexuality itself is still taboo within Indian family structures.

Though social and gender identities are clearly formed in Indian society, sexual identity in terms of the bourgeois notion of sexualized love is still problematic and riddled with conflict. Such familial and sexual conflicts are represented in Bollywood cinema in superficial ways, while the Indian parallel, or art cinema, showcases them in complex and interesting ways. Domestic melodrama, as David N. Rodowick argues, "demands sexual identity to be determined by social identity" (240). In this way, Rodowick adds, "the family both legitimizes and conceals sexuality by restricting it to a social economy defined by marriage – men assume the place of their fathers in the network of authority, and women are mirrored in this network by their relationship to men as wives, mothers, daughters, etc." (240). In domestic melodrama, "the difficulty which individual characters find in their attempts to accept or conform to the set of symbolic positions around which the network of social relations adhere and where they can both 'be themselves' and 'at home'" leads to conflict (240). Here, sexual desire is seen as dangerous "to successful socialization and thus require the division of sexuality from sociality" (241). The manipulation of feminized bodies by patriarchy results in the representation of "feminine sexuality as excessive to the social system that seeks to contain it" (241). The internalization of such identity conflict leads to repression, which returns in the form of violent psychological disorders, such as hysteria, alcoholism or psychotic behavior (241).

While Rodowick discusses Western domestic melodrama, in Indian melodrama or Bollywood (as Indian cinema is popularly known), a hybrid of the Western and Eastern filmic tradition, the Indian woman's repressed sexuality also returns in many uncanny motifs. In *Parama*, Parama's pursuit of an active sexual life leads to a psychic conflict. However, it is not her sexuality that becomes problematic, but the naming of that sexuality for the sake of a sexual identity that leads to crisis. Thus, I argue that Sen provides a contradictory space and an oppositional viewpoint where it is not the male but the female character that tries to construct a sexual identity. It was and still is uncommon for Indian films to show sexually explicit scenes, but because Sen tries to articulate a specific sexual role for the bourgeois Indian woman, she provides a new and radical space for many such scenes in the film.

The spaces where a sexualized female subjectivity is produced are not clearly marked or predefined. Rahul asks the male family members' permission to shoot Parama for his project, showing him as a hybrid diasporic and postcolonial subject who is familiar with both Western and Eastern cultures. And it is Parama's husband who gives him permission to photograph her, in spite of Parama's discomfort. The husband does not show any anxiety about a much younger, liberal, and Westernized male being in close proximity with his wife. Conceptualization of a sexual identity that is not part of the domestic paradigm is not even a possibility here.

Consequently, Rahul and Parama spend many leisurely days together, roaming around Calcutta, while her husband is away on business trips. Rahul does not tell Parama what to think about or what to read or learn. Because Parama already participates in an existent postcolonial consciousness, though parts of this hegemony have taken a back seat due to her domestic roles, Rahul's questions of "What do you do all day? What do you think about?" lead her into a space previously shut off. They visit Parama's childhood home; here, she reminisces about her girlhood, hinting of early sexual desires, now long repressed, as she talks about the plant of Krishna, the lord of love (Arora 300). She tells Rahul that, try as she might, she does not remember the name of the plant, signifying the repression of sexual desires in many young girls in the Indian culture (Arora 300). For many young women, who may appear well read and knowledgeable about sexuality in an abstract way, any personal knowledge or understanding of sexuality is neither possible nor permitted.

Thus, in the representation of the "bedroom" scenes between Parama and her husband, we see them talking about his business or her desire for a new home while they are having sexual intercourse; in the middle-class, joint-family system of India, intimate conversation is often difficult, if not impossible, due to the close proximity of rooms. Whatever conversation occurs, it is before or after the act, or during it as seen in *Parama*, and mostly about mundane matters; this, however, is viewed by many Westernized audience as undesirable because it is very different from notions of romance as perceived in Hollywood cinema. For many Indian women, there is a particular intimacy in being able to communicate in such a manner. Even in most Bollywood films, as I indicated earlier, love scenes are never explicit, even between socially sanctioned couples.

The affair with Rahul constructs Parama as a sexual being. But although Parama is finally a sexualized person, she is unable to name herself. In the middle-class home that she comes from, there is no space for sexual identification; thus, Parama's sexual identity (not her sexuality) remains unnamed.

However, after Rahul leaves, promising to come back for her, he sends Parama the *Life* magazine at her home address and her nude photographs are inadvertently seen by her family members, exposing her affair with Rahul. This exposure leads to a crisis. Still, even at this point, Parama cannot articulate her sexual identity, even though she does not feel guilty or blame herself. Increasingly, she is alienated and isolated when the members of her family, including her son and teenaged daughter, shun her and all her previous roles defining her subjecthood are denied her. When her mother-in-law falls sick, Parama, whose previous care of her had brought forth lavish praise, is denied access to her room. In desperation, she asks her husband's forgiveness. Even at this point, Parama tries to define herself in terms of her old roles. She is punished when she can no longer play them, and we see her slowly going "mad" because she has neither language nor power to articulate her new identity. Because of her transgression, without language, she descends first into a void, and then into the "silence of madness."[2]

A subject who is being formed by opposing discourses of colonialism/nationalism, West/East or modernity/tradition undergoes conflict when the discourses collide; subject formation depends on how this conflict is resolved. If the hegemony of colonialism/Westernization is strong, then the conflict will lead to a crisis; if the traditional hegemony still has control over the consciousness of the subject, then the conflict is deferred until a later time. The transgressive new hybrid goes through a trying, albeit expansive, period in the rearticulating of subjectivity.

In the clash against the hegemonies of patriarchies, the Western hegemony, which is equally strong, if not stronger than the Indian patriarchy, renders Parama helpless, therefore, "mad." That is because the crisis has occurred too soon after her discovery of her new sexual identity; given time, she would have restructured her sexual and gender identity and would have been able to articulate her desires, even within the domestic sphere, in a powerful way (as she does later). James Miller discusses Michel Foucault's ideas of beginning anew in *The Passion of Michel Foucault*: "Discontinuity – the fact that within the space of a few years a culture sometimes ceases to think as it had been thinking up till then and begins to think other things in a new way – probably begins with an erosion *from outside* ... the moment they (society) mark a limit, they create a space for possible transgression" (qtd. in Miller 115). While Foucault is discussing culture per se, I argue that Parama becomes a metonym for Indian culture here. Because her act is seen as transgression, and *is* transgressive, Parama collapses. "Society in this way is made to seem innocent: The guilt is shifted inside" (qtd. in Miller 114). She will be able to rewrite herself, but not at this time. Parama, presently, is "caught ... in [the] culture's web of 'discursive practices,'" but may in time come "to speak of different objects, to have contrary opinions, and to make contradictory choices" (qtd. in Miller 161), but not now. When she does, the experience with Rahul will imbue her "with a new understanding of [her] sexuality ... with a new feeling of power – and a new, and utterly unexpected, sense of freedom" (qtd. in Miller 284). For Parama, first, language has to be freed from all its associations. As Foucault claims, "Language therefore calls into question the world and ultimately itself in a dizzying spiral of possibilities and impossibilities, realities and unrealities ... in a mad and lyrical embrace of the void, oblivion and death – 'that formless, silent, unsignifying region where language can free itself'" (qtd. in Miller 133). But Parama still needs to go through another transgressive and transformative experience; when she is unable to find language or support at this time, she slits her wrists in the bathroom in an attempt to commit suicide.

At this point, the narrative structure and representational forms erupt. The narrative is no longer linear; red color fills the screen, and Parama in a white sari (the colour a widow wears in India) with her long, beautiful hair shorn off (she had fallen in the bathroom and had to undergo surgery) gazes aimlessly. In Bengal, widows' heads used to be shaved: Parama's image at this time is that of a disempowered woman in Hindu society. Long hair also signifies class and femininity. The narrative structures break down and the screen erupts with distorted images. Parama sits passively on the hospital bed. A distorted close-up of each family member appears, and while their lips move, no sound emerges. After a few moments of this, Parama, who is completely detached from her surroundings, turns her head away. The fragmented shots and distorted visions suggest dissociation and detachment. Her husband, who had previously removed their children from her care and who had taken the house money away from her, now appears contrite and apologetic. When Parama does not respond to them, they think she has gone "mad," for how is it possible for the previously responsive Parama not to react to their needs? They want her back home, safe in her familiar familial role. They try to persuade her, with the help of her analyst, to admit her guilt so that she may be "cured." They misread Parama's detachment as the vacuous stare of a lunatic. How is it that she, who had begged to be forgiven, doesn't seem to care anymore?

Parama uses this liminal space for reconceptualization and rearticulation. A "Third Space" (Bhabha) has opened up for the nervous subject. She represents the subject whose psyche is split by the two equally powerful discourses. At this point, Parama dwells in the in-between stage, where she tries to give shape to her emerging subjectivity without negating her previous self. She looks for words and language in the new imagination that is being constructed for and by her.

Arora contends that Parama recovers from this sickness by recreating another reality for herself, another myth. She equates her love for the photographer with divine love – the love of Radha for Krishna. In Indian mythology, even though Radha is married, her love of Krishna is sanctioned in Hindu society as divine love. Therefore, as Arora argues, Parama, who is being "subjected" by two competing discursive structures, resists by "constructing herself according to a third discursive system – that of myth" (301). While Arora's essay concerns itself with Parama's "escape" through a third discursive system – that of myth – I look at the moments in the text where Parama has a "nervous breakdown" and creates yet another space for rearticulation of her new role. Why is it that in the hospital Parama remembers her widowed aunt who had gone mad? Her aunt had been locked up in her (and Parama's) childhood home because she had an affair with a man after she became widowed. How is Parama's "madness" different from her aunt's? Why is Sen juxtaposing the two "madnesses" in the film?

In the previous scenes, when she sees visions of her "mad" aunt, Parama compares her own conduct with that of her aunt. But after her "nervous breakdown," Parama no longer equates her "madness" with that of her aunt; she seems to be reconstructing her images. Her aunt's images are now sharp and clear. Her sympathies are clearly with her oppressed and "mad" aunt, and her feelings about her are no longer ambiguous or ambivalent. All of a sudden, Parama becomes resolute and firm. Her way is clear. She will return home, but on her own terms. And in this reconstruction, one person's help becomes crucial, and that person is Sheela, her transgressive friend. Sheela had refused to relocate with her husband to another city, choosing instead to work with spastic children in Calcutta. Parama asks her to find a job for her; Sheela reminds her that when Parama got married, her education was interrupted and she never earned her bachelor's degree. However, when Parama persists with her request, Sheela tells her about a sales job in a government cottage industry

– Khadi Bhawan – where she will earn only six hundred rupees. Khadi Bhawan stocks merchandize handmade by indigenous local artists – men and women – from poorer backgrounds. And although the money is not much, especially compared to her husband's financial position, she decides to accept the job. The public space she chooses for herself is not that of corporate capital.

Her family members are upset that she wants to work outside her home; her husband, who has long forgiven Parama her indiscretion, is insulted that *his* wife, a wife of an important businessman like him, should deem it prestigious to work for six hundred rupees outside her home and offers to increase her household money. She replies that it will still be his money. While this can be read as Parama's first step toward economic independence, I suggest that Parama is not so excited about economic independence as about an alternate space that opens up. In other words, the material world, the public sphere – particularly if it is in the non-corporate capital world – has to open up to women for rearticulation of their subjectivities. However, she fights to deconstruct the binary of inner/outer by deciding to return home to her family – as a working mother and wife, a contradictory state in that although a wife and mother works inside the home, her work is still not considered work because it is unpaid labour. She defines herself as a working wife, a concept which, although not privileged, is becoming extremely desirable in the marriage market in postcolonial India, in spite of the fact that a many Indian women, lower- as well as middle-class, have been in the work force for a long time.

And it is just after her announcement about her job that Parama, who has been trying to remember the name of the plant of Krishna, finally recalls it – Krishna Pallavi. It is precisely at this time that her teenaged daughter, who appears as a little feminist in the first part of the film but who has been shunning her mother, comes to sit by her side in a gesture of understanding and acceptance. As she reaches out to hold her daughter's hand, we see luminosity in Parama's pale face as she looks out the window to the plant of Krishna. Two phenomena occur here simultaneously: Parama again reconnects with a female member of her family, reinforcing the notion of women's community and solidarity within Indian patriarchal structures, but more importantly, Parama's sexuality, which became repressed during the aftermath of the recovery of the affair, finally resurfaces and she can name it. Instead of being displaced or returning as "uncanny," it resurfaces in this new space, for here Parama can finally see herself as a sexualized self. Thus, it is in this space of liminality that Parama finally recovers from her "madness" by reconstructing herself, free of guilt, as a sexualized subject. In her case, the stereotype of the "independent woman" does not include giving up her domestic space and the community of women; it just means that she reconstructs the traditional paradigm of marriage, where the domestic and economic spaces appear to merge. While this ending is seen as problematic by many critics, where they disagree with Sen's depiction of Parama's "paltry" job as "as a giant step for Indian womanhood" (Subramanyam 114), I suggest that Sen's portrayal of a woman who is sexually aware yet can continue in the domestic spaces as a wife and mother is indeed bold. Sen paved the way for later, more radical feminist films in India in which female sexuality became the central theme.[3] "A void, a moment of silence, a question without answer ... a breach without reconciliation" are created through such transgressive works of art, and "the world is made aware of its guilt" (Foucault, qtd. in Miller 228); transformation occurs in such moments.

Whereas in certain immigrant and diasporic writings, constructions of identity are necessarily violent, leading to the destruction of one or the other self, thus pointing to a certain notion of independence (see Chapter 3, for example), in earlier Indian women's writings, identity reconceptualizations are not so binary. The nervous subject that is being formed by opposing hegemonies has to learn to negotiate identity in eruptive and unknown territories and must utilize spaces that open up for rearticulation; such spaces are necessarily ambivalent and produce conflict in the subject being formed, and how one resolves this conflict depends on the many shifting positions, such as the race, class, and caste of the writers as well as their representational subjects. Therefore, to read *Parama* as transnational, postcolonial critics, we must also keep in mind transnational multicultural feminist theories, practices, and concerns that take into consideration the politics of location of both the author as well as the audience and the "mutual embeddedness ... of race, class, national, sexual, and gender-bases struggles ... and the political intersectionality of all these axes of stratifications" (Shohat 1).[4] Otherwise, misreadings and misunderstandings will lead to continued and prolonged oppression and marginalization of the people of the Global South.

5

Educational Debates and the Postcolonial Female Imagination in Mariama Bâ's *So Long a Letter*

Mariama Bâ's *So Long a Letter* shows the changing consciousness of the educated African woman writer who examines and questions women's social positions in a (post)colonial society. *So Long a Letter* helps situate my discussion on African women writers within the educational system in French West Africa during the 1930s and 1940s in order to see how the Western educational system impacted the construction of gender identity in Senegalese society during colonialism, and how it still impacts them in a postcolonial/neocolonial world. In this way, we can see how the selective modernization of African women, just as in India, altered their imagination and how many began to view their own culture as limited. Many female writers, such as Bâ, who critique Senegalese cultural practices, tend to use easy binaries of the East as limiting and the West as liberating, yet their texts betray interesting ambiguities and contradictions.

As seen in many colonized spaces, nationalism redefined the colonized in opposition to colonial representations of the colonized as inferior. Since nationalism was seen predominantly as a male enterprise, woman's place in literature came to be redefined through male perspectives. It is only in the 1980s that African women's literary voices began to be heard and they began to inscribe themselves into a male literary tradition. In *Contemporary African Literature and the Politics of Gender*, Florence Stratton provides the historical context in which African women begin to write. Stratton suggests that the colonial "trope of Africa as Female" was unproblematically "reiterated" in nationalist texts (18).

In Stratton's discussion of male literary tradition, she posits that women were not only excluded from participating in it, they "are also systematically excluded from the political, the economic, the judicial, and even the discoursal life of the community" (25). Did the exclusion occur because women did not participate in nationalist movements? Certainly not, indicates Stratton: "Of course, women all over Africa did, in fact, participate in the struggle against colonialism, sometimes as leaders. In Nigeria, [for example], there were mass protests by Igbo women against British and their agents which began in 1925 and culminated in the Women's War of 1929-30" (35). Yet, despite women's participation in anticolonial struggles, Négritude's deployment of Mother Africa as a trope for women became limiting for them because it excluded women "implicitly, if not explicitly, from authorship and citizenship" (Stratton 40). Why has the vision posited by the Négritude movement, while uplifting the image of the "savage" African male, further oppressed African women?

"Senghorian Négritude," asserts Stratton, "resorts to the binary logic of the western philosophical tradition, opposing feeling or emotion, which it equates with African civilization, to reason, which it identifies with western culture" (41). Such an engagement with colonial discourse managed to continue what JanMohamed calls the Manichean allegory. The continued deployment of the trope in male literary tradition delineates "a situation that is conventionally patriarchal. The speaker is invariably male, a western-educated intellectual" (Stratton 41).

Stratton posits that "lurking within Négritude ... is another manichean allegory ... the allegory of male and female, domination and subordination, mind and body, subject and object, self and other" (41). The feminization of Africa and the female body posits the male gaze as normative. "He is the active-subject-citizen. She is the passive object-nation" (51). Women are not only excluded from the male literary tradition as subjects; their objectification leads to their exclusion from cultural spaces as well.

Additionally, valorizing women as Mother Africa, or as the nation penetrated and violated, and therefore impure, also adds to the historical continuum of males as narrators (Stratton 53). "The main function of the prostitute metaphor, the flip side of the Mother Africa trope, is to reproduce the attitudes and beliefs necessary for preserving the otherness of women and hence to perpetuate their marginalization in society" (Stratton 53). As women are inscribed and "conscripted" through male narrative, they have to "repudiate" this trope; such an act will be an attempt to undermine "the manichean allegory" of gender (Stratton 54). When Senghor, in 1959, claimed that African woman does not need to be liberated as she has been free for thousand of years, Mariama Bâ responded thus:

> The woman writer in Africa has a special task. She has to present the position of women in Africa in all its aspects. There is still so much injustice.... In the family, in the institutions, in society, in the street, in political organizations, discrimination reigns supreme.... As women, we must work for our own future, we must overthrow the status quo which harms us and we must no longer submit to it. Like men, we must use literature as a non-violent but effective weapon. *We no longer accept the nostalgic praise to the African Mother who, in his anxiety, man confuses with Mother Africa.* Within African Literature, room must be made for women ... , room we will fight for with all our might. (qtd. in Stratton 54–55, original emphasis)

Thus, women writers have to reclaim a space for themselves in national historiography through a feminist literary tradition. Stratton states that the continued deployment of romanticized and idealized images of women in androcentric texts "mask the subordination of women in the patriarchal socio-political systems of African states from which they do ... need to be liberated" (55). Let us examine how certain women visualize liberation.

If, as Stephanie Newell suggests, "women's writing is not outside the dominant male zone," and the aesthetics of women's writing, which are "beset by legacies of colonialism," manage to "interrogate the totality of the society and claim it as a contexts for the redefinition of women" (20), why do women writers continue to posit liberation through a Westernized discursive system which ignores the social conditions of the culture? Is it because of the politics of location of certain writers?

Mariama Bâ is one such writer who questions traditional cultural constructions of women and tries to locate an alternate identity for them in a patriarchal society within (post)colonial social spaces. While the context for this text is Senegal, an ongoing dialogue is created between it and other postcolonial writers and texts, providing a platform for a comparative poetics of postcolonial literature. As Charlotte H. Bruner in *African Women's Writing* rightly points out, "Now African women writers are no longer isolated voices crying from a 'wilderness.' They are aware of each other.... And their wilderness is no bleak desert nor isolated jungle" (vii). And although her metaphors are problematic, to say the least, her sentiments are in the right place. While this chapter will provide a historical context for social change and the construction of the conflicted modern woman in colonial Senegalese society, it will also help to highlight the colonial and postcolonial condition of other African women writers and their texts, and place them within the postcolonial debate that this study is located in.

Bâ, one of the first Senegalese women to receive a Western education, shows the period of change in social and cultural structures in her text and discusses the socioeconomic and historical conditions of the African woman within a colonial and postcolonial context. Although there were many social changes during nationalist movements that reconstituted women's roles in modern Africa, texts such as Bâ's re-examine the question of women's liberation in the context of national liberation and Westernization. Bâ elaborates on the formation of the "new" woman within the Muslim African culture; this new woman is the product of a Western education, and she questions her role in the domestic sphere, which remains primarily unchanged.

Bâ brings up the female condition and the conflicted imagination and psyche produced by traditional African and modern French notions of womanhood in terms of family structures, particularly when faced with the Western educational system imposed by colonial administrators in French West Africa. In *So Long a Letter*, the protagonist, Ramatoulaye, a fifty-year-old Senegalese woman, recently widowed, is the first-person narrator. She is writing "so long a letter" to her friend, Aissatou, whom she recalls going to school with and who now lives in the United States.

Ramatoulaye fondly remembers going to the teachers' training college in Sebikotane in PontyVille, where she met her future husband, Modou Fall. She recalls being "the first pioneers of the promotion of African women," while remembering the contradictory reactions of Senegalese men: "Men would call us scatterbrained. Others labeled us devils. But many wanted to possess us" (14–15). The anxiety that Western education produced within the colonized culture is apparent in such statements.

While narrating the many happy memories of the Normal School for Women in Rufisque – the French teacher whom she loved, the women who shared the same dreams of "emancipation" as herself – Ramatoulaye describes the "aims of the wonderful French headmistress": "To lift us out of the bog of tradition, superstition and custom, to make us appreciate a multitude of civilizations without renouncing our vision of the world, cultivate our personalities, strengthen our qualities, to make up for our inadequacies, to develop universal values in us" (15). She assures the audience that the French headmistress was not patronizing, for "she knew how to discover and appreciate our qualities" (16). She adds that "the path chosen for our training and our blossoming had not been at all fortuitous. It has accorded with the profound choices made by New Africa for the promotion of the black woman" (16). Thus, we see that in the new consciousness of New Africa as well as in the new African woman, Western education is to bring choices, liberation, and positive change. What that liberation is bringing is questionable as social structures remain unchanged, but for Ramatoulaye, the promise of modernity portends flights into a realm of fantasy and romance incongruent with lived experiences.

When Aissatou marries Mawdo Bâ for love, it turns out to be what Ramatoulaye calls a "controversial marriage" (17) because Aissatou is a goldsmith's daughter and Mawdo's mother is a "Dioufene, a *Guelewar* (Princess) from the Sine" (17) and their two families are seen as incompatible. The traditionalists, when they see the path Western-educated elite are taking, declare, "School turns our girls ['short skirts'] into devils who lure our men away from the right path" (17). Such attitudes are not uncommon toward modern young women and are reflected in the educational debates of the 1930s and 1940s in French West Africa. Bâ's novel illustrates the ideological crisis of tradition and modernity in the cultural construction of women in colonized countries.

Ramatoulaye reflects on the old professions, like that of Aissatou's father; he was a goldsmith and his sons would have followed in his footsteps. But now she realizes that Aissatou's younger brother's "steps were directed towards the white man's school. Hard is the climb up the steep hill of knowledge to the white man's school: kindergarten remains a luxury that only those who are financially sound can offer their young ones" (18). She discusses the pitfalls of education, for many do not get access to higher education, and "apprenticeship to traditional crafts seem[s] degrading to whoever has the slightest book learning" (18). But even though she realizes there are drawbacks to "book learning," she sees it as useful and unavoidable: "We all agree that much dismantling was needed to introduce modernity within our traditions. Torn between the past and the present, we deplore 'hard sweat' that would be inevitable. We counted the possible losses. But we knew that nothing would be as before. We were full of nostalgia but were resolutely progressive" (19)

The ones who were resolutely progressive were the urban, upper-class elite of the colonized nation. Ramatoulaye rejoices in her friend's good fortune in marrying Mawdo, who "raised you up to his own level, he the son of a princess and you a child from the forges" (19). She reflects on the lifestyles of the urban elite when she reminisces about the picnics organized by them in Sangalkam at Mawdo's farm, which he had inherited from his father: "Sangalkam remains the refuge of people from Dakar, those who want a break from the frenzy of the city. The younger set, in particular, has bought land there and built country residences; these green, open spaces are conducive to rest, meditation and letting off steam by children" (22). The educated elite see the progress of the nation in terms set up by the colonizers. If they are to progress in the material sphere, they have to adapt to modernity and the lifestyles of the Whites.

In the next section of the letter, Ramatoulaye elaborates on the system of education and teachers, who are responsible for the "minds" of the young people and must work as an "army" to eradicate "ignorance": "Teachers ... form a noble army accomplishing daily feats, never praised, never decorated. An army forever on the move, forever vigilant. An army without drums, without gleaming uniforms. This army, thwarting traps and snares, everywhere plants the flag of knowledge and morality" (23). She narrates the role played by her generation in the making of a New Africa: "It was the privilege of our generation to be the link between two periods in our history, one of domination, the other of independence" (25). Ramatoulaye calls these educated, urban elite the "messengers of a new design. With independence achieved, we witnessed the birth of a republic, the birth of an anthem and the implantation of a flag" (25).

What of women's place within this new republic, and in particular, what of the educated woman with ideas of individualism and choice? Women's participation in the modern notion of individualism produced ambivalence, which is reflected in the formation of the female subject in women's texts. In a society where one does not choose one's mate, Ramatoulaye takes great pride in being one of the first ones to do so. The concept of marriage was being refashioned to meet the needs of the changing, urban society. The patriarchal control of female sexuality was changing from the traditional system of polygamy to the more liberal companionate marriage, with the promise of romantic love and mutual esteem. Nationalism constructed a discursive space for the accommodation of traditional roles. However, even though educated women had a "choice" in whom they could marry, the system of marriage remained unchanged for many modern women in that it enabled the persistence of the traditional family roles.

Ramatoulaye, too, has a choice in whom she marries. She has earlier rejected Daouda Dieng, her mother's obvious preference, and chooses instead to marry Modou for love. Falling in love seems to indicate she will achieve equality and freedom. We see a textual manifestation of what equality means to Ramatoulaye when she falls in love with Modou: "Modou Fall, the very moment you bowed before me, asking me to dance, I knew you were the one I was waiting for. Tall and athletically built, of course.... But above all you knew how to be tender. You could fathom every thought, every desire" (13). The concept of Christian monogamous romantic love impacts many lives. As a person who is placed in a historical moment of Westernization, we can see Ramatoulaye celebrating choice and love in modern terms.

Emmanuel Obiechina claims that formal literary study, Christian monogamy, and modern media are primarily responsible in bringing the concept of Western romantic tradition to West Africa (32–41). "The insistence of Christianity on monogamy meant that, at some stage or other, a single man would have to confront a single woman with whom he would have to forge a most individualistic and private relationship – that of the fusion of two personalities (or souls) into a mystical unity" (40). The ritual of romantic love was garnered and "learned from English literature, from boy-meets-girl romantic magazines, from romantic fiction and most dramatically, from the cinema and television" (40). Love songs added another dimension to this ethos. "The result," adds Obiechina, "has been the emergence of romantic love as a vital factor in modern West Africa" (40). Notions of romantic love were disseminated throughout colonial Africa.

The system of marriage in a Muslim society is very different from the Western system, yet Ramatoulaye's actions in selecting a mate for herself seem progressive and liberated. However, romantic love, with its idealized concept of male-female affinity, ultimately supports patriarchal institutions. While romantic love inspires Ramatoulaye and Aissatou to rebel against traditions, their actions mainly reflect their subject position as Western-educated.

The letter continues with the story of how Ramatoulaye survives, emotionally as well as economically, after Modou betrays her by marrying Binetou, a school friend of Daba, their daughter. Her husband neglects to tell her of his second wife, waiting until the day of the marriage. Yet, even after this incidence, Ramatoulaye continues to see love in its idealized version:

> To love one another! If only each partner could move sincerely toward the other! If each could only melt into the other! If each would praise the other's successes and failures! If each would only praise the other's qualities instead of listing his faults! If each could only correct bad habits without harping on about them! If each could penetrate the other's most secret haunts to forestall failure and be a support while tending to the evils that are repressed! (89)

Ramatoulaye sees marriage and romantic love as the inevitable outcome of the "complementarity of man and woman" (88). Her reaction toward marriage reflects the perspective of a middle-class, Western-educated woman.

Yes, she sees the "evil" inherent in the system of polygamy, as she is supposed to as a liberated, Western-educated woman. She speaks out against polygamy. When she becomes a widow and Tamsir asks to marry her, she lashes out at him, accusing him of exploiting his many wives: "You, the revered lord, you take it easy, obeyed at the crook of a finger. I shall never be the one to complete your collection" (58). She states that she will never be an extra burden to him, nor will she wait her turn for him to visit her on the allotted night. Additionally, she rejects Daouda's marriage proposal because she is not in love with him, and also because he is already married. While reiterating the oppressive nature of polygamy, she rejects the view that polygamy can be helpful if all the co-wives coexist peacefully, helping each other in bringing up the children and sharing household chores, particularly for the rural and non-Westernized communities. She declares, "You think the problem of polygamy is a simple one. Those who are involved in it know the constraints, the lies, the injustices that weigh down their consciences in return for the ephemeral joy of change" (68). She emphasizes the need for a greater community among women to alleviate the pain they suffer due to polygamy: "Abandoned yesterday because of a woman, I cannot lightly bring myself between you and your family" (68). Bâ's frustrations with the exploitative nature of polygamy are also directed toward other women. She sees the erosion of the communal space for women's solidarity but is unable to locate that erosion in the aftermath of colonialism and Westernization, nor does she tie it in with class.

Ultimately, Ramatoulaye rejects both Tamsir and Daouda for sentimental reasons: "You forget that I have a heart, a mind, that I am not an object to be passed from hand to hand. You don't know what marriage means to me: it is an act of faith and of love, the total surrender of oneself to the person one has chosen and who has chosen you (I emphasized the word 'chosen')" (58).

Ramatoulaye emphasizes the word chosen in order to show her preference for love marriages. She also rejects Daouda's marriage proposal, even though she knows he has loved her for a long time and is a reliable person, and she does like him, because, ultimately, she is not in love with him (68).

Yet Ramatoulaye is conflicted and split, and in spite of valorizing love and marriage, for her individualism is not paramount, but communal identity is:

> I remain persuaded of the inevitable and necessary complementarity of man and woman. Love, imperfect as it may be in its content and expression, remains the natural link between these two beings.... The success of the family is born of a couple's harmony, as the harmony of multiple instruments creates a pleasant symphony. The nation is made up of all the families, rich or poor, united or separated, aware or unaware. The success of the nation therefore depends inevitably on the family. (88–89)

Bâ is unable to move beyond colonial and nationalist discourses and continues to see female identity in traditional and familial terms – as wives and mothers. Therefore, we see ambiguity in her notion of romantic individualism which clashes with traditional and communal identity formation in Bâ's text.

Putting such ideas about Westernized women in their social context, Obiechina contextualizes traditional practices such as polygamy:

> Romantic love, whether as an autonomous experience or as a stepping stone to marriage, was played down and subordinated to familial and community interests. Because of the close linking of the fate of individuals to that of the group to which they belonged ... romantic individualism was curbed by stringent taboos.... In a situation of underdevelopment and fragile political and social infrastructure, families and communities depended for stability largely on the balancing of group relationships and the linking of families and segments in marriage alliances. (34)

And while Ramatoulaye sees Aissatou's divorce as empowering, ultimately, however, Ramatoulaye chooses not to leave her husband, explaining that it is because of her children; she lives a life of "despair," "rancour," and "sadness" (12). Bâ's protagonist is a Western-educated, middle-class woman who finds that her sense of self and her individual identity are continually clashing with the expectations of a patriarchal society. The exploitation in the relationship of power – economic and sexual – between the two sexes is reworked through the image and language of love and individualism by a strong, although exploited, woman in Bâ's text.

Bâ's novel shows resistance where the alienated subject displaces its anxiety onto another space in the character of Aissatou. Ramatoulaye recalls how Aissatou, who had defied conventions and caste barriers to marry Mawdo, had also felt betrayed by her husband when he, too, had brought home a second wife, Nabou. However, Aissatou refuses to be defined by patriarchal society, and chooses to leave with her four sons. She writes a letter to Mawdo in which she states that she finds his actions of "procreating without love" hateful, even if he was just trying to please his ailing mother; she then leaves him.

She rebuilds her life, but in another space. She goes back to school, leaving for France to be an interpreter and eventually working at the

Senegalese embassy in Washington, D.C. Thus, Aissatou rejects the "Old World" with its tradition-bound cultures for the transformative potential and liberation for the individual in the "New World." Bâ's text ends up questioning the national identity of women like Aissatou who are culturally alienated and who reject indigenous African customs (130). Aissatou cannot be a role model for the new Senegalese women.

It is Ramatoulaye who struggles with conflicts produced by the discourses of modernity and tradition in "New Africa." While she gains some sort of an independent identity in the public sphere due to her status as a teacher, in the domestic sphere her status remains ambiguous. For her, the available paradigm of womanhood in a transitional society is limited. She rejects Tamsir and Daouda but waits for a special man who will fulfill her. While she is passionately against polygamy, she accepts it, albeit unwillingly, by staying with Modou after he marries Binatou. Thus, although it appears as though Ramatoulaye could choose as a Western-educated woman, in actuality her choices are very limited. Thus, the rhetoric of modernity and liberation produces ambiguous results for many women who do not simply reject all traditional or African cultural practices as backward, or are unable or unwilling to relocate to the "liberal" West.

And although Aissatou represents the "liberated" woman, the text seems to emphasize the similarities between her and Ramatoulaye rather than the differences. And while comparing young Nabou's oral education and her life as a nurse, Ramatoulaye realizes that all of them are really alike and share the same oppressions and problems: "Young Nabou, responsible and aware, like you, like me! Even though she is not my friend, we often shared the same problems" (48). The narrative allows for the acceptance of traditional patriarchal roles and women's oppression within the domestic spaces.

Liberating possibilities are only hinted at in the margins of the discursive systems; however, such possibilities too appear ambiguous. One such conflict comes out of Ramatoulaye's relationship with her children and particularly with her daughters. While she thinks a liberal education will help them create their own subjectivity, she does not equate that with sexual liberation. She is troubled and shocked when her liberated daughter allows herself to become pregnant, as though such a thing could not be a possibility in one so educated. In the final analysis, Bâ's text allows her to question traditions, but she is unable to move toward another space, or see an alternative vision. What becomes so complex and tricky is that the traditional roles were rewritten as modern, and thus liberating, but they actually became coercive and oppressive. Ramatoulaye must remain in the domestic sphere so that the overall structure of neocolonial patriarchal society may survive. Even though a new imagination seems possible, it cannot be incorporated into the identity of the African woman. She still has to be either a housewife or mother in the manner of Ramatoulaye, or leave the home space in the manner of Aissatou. Bâ's text does bring out the complexities of redefining gender roles for the middle-class patriarchy, but it remains ambiguous and full of contradictions. She sees the role of the new women in terms set up by colonialism and nationalism during educational debates in colonial Africa – as "educated" and transformed wives and mothers. In her text, patriarchal roles and values of the middle-class women are challenged but not reconstituted; women's redefined roles do not allow them to negotiate for "emancipation" within the acceptable spaces provided for them in society. Bâ's text does not offer a radical revision of the women question; while it allows her to question traditions in terms of modernity, it is unable to show us an alternate future, for she sees the future of the nation as dependent on the traditional family model.

6

The Diasporic Search for Cultural Belonging in Myriam Warner-Vieyra's *Juletane*

In *Juletane*, Myriam Warner-Vieyra represents the life of a young Guadeloupean woman who lives in France and who now "returns" to Africa. The novella thus presents a woman from the African diaspora who returns to her mythical African homeland but finds herself marginalized due to her "otherness" in her "home" country. Her fragmented sense of self and her duality as a colonial subject leads to alienation, yet Warner-Vieyra, through her "mad" female character, tries to resist and subvert colonial and national discursive strategies. She may not always be successful in subverting the dominant paradigm, but she attempts to bring into sharp focus the alienation suffered by a diasporic subject in the many shifting spaces it comes to inhabit. The East/West binary provides interesting and ambiguous insights into the postcolonial condition of both the author and her representational subjects. The author herself is a Guadeloupean woman who lived in France for many years and has lived in Senegal for over forty years.

Colonialism and its persistent destructive powers in the Caribbean form the backdrop of this narrative. Bill Ashcroft, Gareth Griffiths, and

Helen Tiffin discuss the aftermaths of colonialism in the Caribbean in *The Empire Writes Back: Theory and Practice in Post-Colonial Literatures*:

> In the Caribbean, the European imperial enterprise ensured that the worst features of colonialism throughout the globe would all be combined in the region: the virtual annihilation of the native population of Caribs and Arawaks; the plundering and internecine piracy amongst European powers; the deracination and atrocities of the slave trade and plantation slavery ... (145–46)

The aftermaths of colonialism in the Caribbean proved disastrous for many, particularly those displaced and dislocated, first from Africa, then in the Caribbean, and further in Europe, never belonging, their subjectivity forever fragmented.

In this chapter, I look at some of the aftermaths of colonialism – such as the notion of "displacement," "exile," and "return" – and their personal and political implications for women from the Caribbean. As Carole Boyce Davies writes regarding Caribbean women writers, "Migration creates the desire for home, which in turn produces the writing of home" (13). For many writers from the Caribbean, the return to "home" or "nation of origin" was seen as the end of the sense of alienation that they felt. "Nostalgia is a powerful element in much Caribbean women's fiction, and usually regarded as a dangerous element in it," states Mary Condé ("Introduction" 2). Thus, for many, the return to home itself is riddled with conflict as "colonial imaginary space is split, the language of the experience of oppression at a symbolic distance from the European drawing room," posits Charlotte Sturgess (203). She adds, "Presence itself has then to be constantly mediated through discontinuity, and the strategies, diversions and subversions which attest to its complicated allegiances in post-colonial time and space render the securing of the subject in language both crucial and problematical" (Sturgess 203). Thus, subjectivity is constructed through "migrancy and loss" (Sturgess 203) for many Caribbean women writers.

Warner-Vieyra tries to expose and undermine dominant strategies of power that are manifested in forms of racism and sexism when she represents Juletane, who "returns" to her "home," the result of which remains ambiguous, and therefore maddening. I argue that, being a diasporic subject and as a Westernized person herself, the author's ideas of what she considers sexist and oppressive are themselves problematic due to their ambiguities.

Warner-Vieyra's novella is in the form of a diary, written by the late Juletane, but is being read simultaneously by Hélène (a social worker in Africa) and the audience after Juletane's death. Juletane and Hélène never meet in the course of their lives, although they had come close to meeting, once. Dr. Monravi, a French psychiatrist, had referred Juletane to her because they were both from the Island, but they could not meet at that time. However, after Juletane's death, the doctor gives Hélène Juletane's few possessions, including a diary. She had set the diary aside, and at a significant stage in her life, while she is packing, she rediscovers it. She is in the act of reading the diary as the narrative unfolds.

Juletane, a West Indian orphan living in Paris, was born in the French Antilles. When she meets Mamadou, an African student, she falls in love with him, marries him and "returns" with him to Africa, presumably Senegal. Through a chance encounter with a compatriot on the ship, Juletane finds out that Mamadou has a first wife and a child, and cannot believe or accept she is in a polygamous marriage. However, when Mamadou promises to leave his first wife once he finds a job, Juletane tries to save her marriage by becoming pregnant. After a brief period of happiness, she has a miscarriage, and feeling dejected and unwanted, she retreats to an inner room, refusing contact with anyone, and eventually starts a journal. Then, when her husband marries a third time, Juletane's descent into madness begins.

At the beginning of the novella, Juletane is represented as thinking that returning to Africa, "the land of her forefathers" (15), will define her as an African, and even though she appears unaware that her ideas of Africa and African customs are patriarchal in terms, she is aware of Africa as a land of her forefathers. However, when Mamadou offers her the position of a junior wife within a polygamous Muslim family, she describes her role as an "intruder" in an alien land.

Warner-Vieyra provides a critique of polygamy through this text, as does Mariama Bâ in *So Long a Letter*, attacking the unfairness of the African Muslim patriarchal system. Like Bâ, she also examines the notion of romantic love. When she first meets Mamadou, Juletane realizes that she has been looking for a "prince charming" (63). She is ecstatic when she finds out that Mamadou returns her love. She says, "I loved him with all the ardour and intensity of a first and only love.... Mamadou became my whole world" (13). Soon she finds that her ideals of romantic love are far different from those of her husband. Because of the social customs of the country, Awa, the first wife, accepts Juletane and is even kind to her in her own way. Juletane, who is unable to decipher such traditional, non-Western practices, decides to return to Paris; the only problem is lack of funds. She surmises that the only way she would fit into this household is as a mother, and when she becomes pregnant, she shares a short period of great joy and happiness with her husband.

However, after a car accident, which causes her to miscarry and leaves her sterile, her "inferior" position in the family becomes clear to her. First, she loses the dream of a romantic life with Mamadou, and then she loses all hope of being accepted as a mother. Removing herself from the social sphere and isolating herself in a tiny room, Juletane, seeing herself as useless because of her sterility and lack of romantic love, shaves her head, dons mourning clothes, and contemplates suicide. Finally, unable to separate the real from the imagined, Juletane has a nervous breakdown. Thus, Juletane's search for her identity leads her from space to alienated space: from her Island home to France and then to Africa, leading her to "choose" a tiny room, which ultimately leads into a confined space in a mental asylum. Such negations of space and speech lead to the silencing of the subject; here, the narrative and discursive structures are destabilized, leading to the disruption of narrative flow, hence read as madness.

Let us re-examine the trajectory of Juletane's journey into madness. Her resistance to patriarchy with its practice of polygamy leads her to encourage her husband's family to see her "madness." In her "madness," Juletane retreats into the inner spaces of the home, for she is unable to construct an identity in its open spaces: "I remain locked in our room without eating or drinking" (24). She looks out from her room into the inner courtyard, where, under a barren mango tree – a symbol of Juletane's existence – she views the comfortable figure of Awa with her children. Eventually, as the dominant discourses of Africa start to take over Juletane's consciousness, we see her increasingly dwelling on her barrenness.

That "madness" becomes more pronounced when Mamadou marries again. The new wife, Ndeye, too, hates Juletane and makes no effort to hide her hatred. From one of the windows facing the courtyard, Juletane surveys the first wife and her children and listens to the third wife's gossiping with her friends, yet she refuses to learn the West African language and continues to write in French. She does not participate in the Muslim festivals nor does she take part in the baptism of Mamadou's and Awa's son. She remains separated from the community that defines the identity of each of the family members. Alienated due to her colour, which is lighter than that of women around her, Juletane remains an outsider, a "Toubabesse" (a White woman), according to Ndeye, Mamadou's third wife; here, she is not even considered a black woman.

Over the years, we see Juletane's refusal to be defined by the other members of her family in the domestic sphere. One day, when she leaves her space to go into the living room to play her favourite record, Beethoven's *Ninth Symphony*, she is slapped by Ndeye for daring to invade her space. Because Juletane had so far refused to be part of the household, Mamadou and Awa refuse when she needs and asks for their help. Juletane no longer imagines herself as mad, for she refuses to speak and has, in fact, gone for two years without speaking to her husband, nor can she communicate with the other members of her family. Due to her silence, she is no longer part of the discursive community, and her sense of self is further splintered and fragmented.

Later, when Awa's children are found dead through poisoning, Juletane writes: "Did I pour the contents of the medicine bottle into the children's drinking cup? Or did I leave the bottle where they could reach it? I don't remember anything" (74). Did she kill the children in a rage? Was she insane at that time? Juletane has been named the madwoman, "*la folle*" by Ndeye, which has effectively erased her real name from everyone's memory, leading her to question her "madness":

> Here they call me the "madwoman," not very original. What do they know about madness? What if mad people weren't mad? What if certain types of behavior which simple, ordinary people call madness, were just wisdom, a reflection of the clear-sighted hypersensitivity of a pure, upright soul plunged into a real or imaginary affective void? (2)

In this void, devoid of dominant discursive inscription, the soul, through psychic transformation, can rewrite itself and the body can transcend ideological constructions. However, reinscription, in one form or the other, does not happen for Juletane, for she has been named by others, and although she tries resisting such naming, she has no means of transcending the Westernized cultural script. The self-imposed isolation, although painful, is not traumatic to such an extent as to alter her subjecthood and deem her mad. Her anger, however, propels her, and so she pours boiling oil on the sleeping Ndeye's face, declaring, "that slap in the face was the last drop that made my cup of passivity overflow and transformed my patience into a raging torrent" (50). Her aggression and attempt at agency confines her to a mental institution, where she dreams of going to a graveyard and seeing her own grave with no name on it. Awa kills herself by drowning in a well, and later, Mamadou dies in a car accident. Regretting that her husband died before he could read her diary, she finally stops writing, and three days later, she dies in the hospital. She couldn't conceive of a reality outside of patriarchy, be it Eastern or Western.

Although Juletane's narrative ends here, another story starts as Juletane's journal is finally read by Hélène, a Guadeloupean woman who has also lived in France, the Caribbean, and then West Africa. After reading the tragic account of Juletane's encounter with polygamy and oppressive patriarchal customs and traditions, Hélène's life is transformed due to the readings: "Juletane's diary had broken the block of ice around her heart" (79). She had been feeling like a displaced person before in Africa; now, she no longer feels "alienated," for she has found a sense of community with Juletane, even after her death. She understands Juletane's alienation, and although Juletane had refused to construct an identity for herself by redefining the traditional role of wife or mother, Hélène realizes that one can break down the binary of domestic and public.

Postcolonial African feminism's ambivalence when it comes to individual versus community identity is reflected in this novel. On the one hand, romantic individualism is privileged over communal identity, while on the other hand, individualism is not valorized if it means communal and familial identity are being denied. The text suggests that after reading Juletane's diary, Hélène – who had believed in a creed of "me first," as she considers herself "her own woman" – may now marry because she has become more "feminine," instead of marrying simply because she desired to "become a mother" (1). She used to be quite clear in what she desired in marriage:

> She had recently decided to get married for the simple reason that she wanted a child of her own. She was fond of her husband-to-be. He was ten years her junior, a handsome athletic man, six feet tall, eighty kilos, gentle as a lamb. She was his superior financially and intellectually. Too independent by nature, she could not have tolerated a husband who would dominate, make decisions, take the lead. (1)

After she reads Juletane's diary, she decides to marry for other reasons as she realizes that she does not have to choose one or the other. She remembers her childhood home, the Island, and thinks of her happy childhood as well as the good relationship that she still maintains with her family. Every month, she sends money home, "with a short letter, always promising a long one next time" (242). Although she feels she has nothing in common with her people from the Island, she starts thinking of her family kindly. Further, although Hélène had been hurt in love when her first fiancé left her for a white woman, and although she was planning to marry just for convenience's sake, she starts to transform after reading the diary. Thus, even though her role may have undergone transformation and she can marry someone of her choice while remaining financially independent, the patriarchal family and its patterns are still very much in position, although somewhat altered. Hélène's symbolic emancipation shows us an alternate reality, an alternate mythology. Even though Westernization did not bring emancipation in terms of liberty and economic independence for many women, educated women could envision change in the domestic space. Hélène's marriage to a much younger man shows that she could revise the traditional paradigm of marriage by rewriting the familiar scripts of family for personal fulfillment and empowerment.

By allowing Juletane to die, and by inserting Hélène's presence in the text, Warner-Vierya helps to redefine Hélène's identity. Initially, Juletane searches for a national identity, whereas Hélène searches for an individual identity, but national identity is not separate from communal identity, so Juletane, who is defined primarily by Western ideology of individualism, suffers when she is being interpellated by another ideology. Earlier in the narrative, it is disclosed that she may have had a miscarriage due to her transgression of an African cultural practice during pregnancy. Juletane begins to knit baby clothes for her unborn child, which is considered inauspicious. Ultimately, her refusal or inability to be defined by the dominant paradigms of Africanness causes her to lose her sanity.

According to Michael Seidel, "an exile is someone who inhabits one place and remembers or projects the reality of another" (ix). Thus, this conflicted and hybrid psyche in exile that is Juletane even rejects her body – on which one ideology is inscribed and another one is trying to take over – in various ways. In the beginning, when Mamadou spends time away from her in the company of Awa, she bashes her head against the wall, ending up with a scarred forehead. She also rejects her body and her sexuality when she becomes anorexic and grows extremely skinny. Her act of cutting off her hair is also a rejection of her pre-scribed body image. She wants to rewrite herself anew. She steals an old notebook of one of Awa's children and begins the process of reinscription through journalling. Juletane "imagines" herself through writing, but as we have seen, her redefinition proves to be limiting.

Odile Cazenave suggests that Warner Vieyra uses the outsider's view to critique "societal standards" and to contest "traditional roles;" she posits that "with a combination of techniques and strategies, in particular, violence, humiliation, and marginalization ... women writers ... have subverted ... the masculine paradigm ... [through the] choice of the marginal character" which is the result of the "revolutionary spirit" of such writers (10). However, I argue that although Warner-Vieyra critiques traditional cultural practices such as polygamy in her text, by providing an enforced resolution she seems to reinforce patriarchal ideology. However, as a Western-educated woman, her critique is directed at Muslim polygamous practices, which she contrasts with the notion of Christian monogamous, romantic love. Although Juletane is represented as resisting oppressive patriarchal practices, it is the Muslim practice of polygamy that she is resisting. Even though she goes mad in an attempt to resist, Mamadou is still the intended audience of her diary. Once he dies, she no longer sees the need to write, for she has wanted him to know how much she suffered for his betrayal.

Therefore, while Warner-Vieyra helps to raise consciousness in terms of women's suffering in a postcolonial society, the notion of romantic love and monogamous marriage fails to critique the oppressive social and economic structures from which many oppressive social practices arise. What is of crucial importance, however, is that while Juletane could not rewrite herself within the spaces provided for by patriarchy, Hélène learns to use the very space for rearticulation and renegotiation of female identity. Therefore, Juletane's resistance, although limiting for her, becomes empowering for Hélène because she learns to read and revise this cultural myth for her own self-empowerment through reimagining women's community. She does not give up one space for another; instead, she uses the liminal spaces of patriarchal ideology that open up for redefinition and rearticulation for self-empowerment within the given space. In the long run, such acts can be viewed as more productive and empowering than trying to recreate another hegemony within a closed structure of society, which will in the short run lead to failure and a nervous condition for the conflicted subject, or else co-optation by the dominant ideological paradigms for their own purposes. A paradigm shift accomodates only altered realities; on the other hand, subversions can occur only through complete dismantling and reconstruction, or through turning the paradigm on its head. Dismantling and reconstruction of oppressive structures only occur through revolutions or rebellions. So far, feminists have been only successful in altering realities in limited ways, and Hélène is one such example. Finally, my act of reading *Juletane* is to posit another reading, and to suggest that, perhaps, certain feminist readings can be limiting if we fail to contextualize the narrative and the writer within the larger discursive systems in postcolonial and global world spaces.

7

Maddening Inscriptions and Contradictory Subjectivities in Tsitsi Dangarembga's *Nervous Conditions*

How do postcolonial female authors represent patriarchal control of women and the regulatory power of ideology which become transparent in moments of contention between discourses of tradition and modernity? How do they represent traditionalists and their use of the modern/tradition, world/home, public/private binaries to retain control of the family institution? Westernization of the woman's body is seen as a threat to national identity, based as it on the artificial binary of indigenous/Western, tradition/modern, good/evil dualities, as if to be truly an African woman is to remain "essentially" African, therefore "pure," and if not, then the female body is seen as diseased or contaminated.

I will discuss Tsitsi Dangarembga's novel *Nervous Conditions*[1] in order to demonstrate how such women who resist the artificial binaries of good/evil and traditional/modern create a space for other women to re-articulate identity in newly emergent and constructed spaces. Postcolonial women writers are trying to recast female subjectivity and agency by allowing women to name the structure of oppressions in order to resist certain patriarchal oppressions within postcolonial frameworks. They try to show alternate spaces within global capitalism where identities can be refashioned for selfhood and empowerment, where women work toward social change and expansion, and where multiple identities can be incorporated into old ones, not simply by disrupting or dismantling pre-existing social structures but by altering and expanding them. For in reality, this is the only possibility there is, to recast and recreate within liminal social and economic spaces, rather than trying to dismantle or destroy pre-existing structural spaces, for destroying (even if it is possible) without renewing (as can be seen by the ongoing destruction of Zimbabwe's economy) is ultimately limiting and possibly self-destructive and maddening.

Dangarembga's *Nervous Conditions*, set in colonial Zimbabwe, known then as Rhodesia, examines issues of race, class, and gender oppressions in the postcolonial context and shows how these oppressions are played out on the site of women's bodies. Dangarembga, born in colonial Rhodesia in 1959 and spending her early childhood in England where her parents acquired Masters' degrees, received her schooling in Britain. The story, situated in colonial Rhodesia on the eve of its independence, critiques the (post)colonial patriarchal constructs which are the outcomes of European colonialism.

Nervous Conditions is a title that comes out of Jean-Paul Sartre's introduction to Frantz Fanon's *The Wretched of the Earth*, which explains that "[t]he colonial condition is a nervous condition" (20), as the subject, formed by the discourses of colonialism and nationalism, is pulled in oppositional directions by these two ideologies and is in danger of becoming split. According to Flora Veit-Wild, "*Nervous Conditions* insinuates that the process of mental colonisation is a gendered process and that women in particular react with nervous, psychosomatic symptoms" (141).

Dangarembga examines the aftermath of imperialism where women's bodies were seen as impure or diseased within patriarchal ideology due to their Westernization. However, women writers rewrite women's bodies as sites of resistance to the disabling colonialist and nationalist discourses and institutions. Unlike *So Long a Letter, Nervous Conditions* points to a community of women fighting to decolonize themselves against both colonial and patriarchal institutional oppression.

Tambu, the narrator, tells us that the story "is about my escape and Lucia's; about my mother's and Maiguru's entrapment; and about Nyasha's rebellion – Nyasha, far-minded and isolated, my uncle's daughter, whose rebellion may not in the end have been successful" (1). Even though Nyasha may have suffered due to her inability to change her circumstances, her resistance proves to be enabling for women, such as Tambu, who learn to question and resist certain patriarchal and colonial oppressions in other, less painful ways.

Nervous Conditions, narrated in the first person by Tambu, unfolds the tale of her struggle in the impoverished homestead to her eventual "escape" from it through education and "expansion." The narrative voice of Tambu, a peasant from a rural setting, starts the story with "I am not sorry my brother died" (1), foreshadowing gender battles and connecting her move to the urban setting of her uncle's mission with the death of her brother. She is happy to have escaped the poverty and oppression of the rural homestead, where she was denied education until her brother's death, hoping to be transformed in the urban setting of the mission. She moves in with her uncle Babamukuru, aunt Maiguru, and cousins Nyasha and Chido, in their beautiful and well-furnished mission home to attend the missionary school. The novel examines the oppressive social systems transformed in the aftermath of the brutal encounter with colonialism.

In the beginning, Tambu sees her educated aunt as having escaped class and patriarchal oppressions through education:

> My mother said being black was a burden because it made you poor, but Babamukuru was not poor. My mother said being a woman was a burden because you had to bear children and look after them and the husband. But I did not think this was true. Maiguru was well looked after by Babamukuru, in a big house on the mission which I had not seen but which I have heard rumours concerning its vastness and elegance. Maiguru was driven about in a car, looked well-kept and fresh, clean all the time. She was altogether a different kind of woman from my mother. I decided it was better to be like Maiguru, who was not poor and had not been crushed by the weight of womanhood. (16)

Tambu believes that education has transformed Maiguru, giving her freedom and material comfort, and releasing her from gender responsibilities.

Tambu's brother, Nhamo, sent to be educated at the mission so that he, like Babamukuru, would eventually take care of the family, unfortunately dies of a mysterious sickness. It is only after his death that Tambu is allowed to be educated and rejoices in no longer having to work hard at the homestead cultivating crops. She thinks that "at Babamukuru's I would have the leisure, be encouraged to consider questions that had to do with survival of the spirit, the creation of consciousness, rather than mere sustenance of the body" (59).

At Babamukuru's, Tambu is slowly acculturated and interpellated into the capitalist world economy and its "liberated" spaces. To Tambu, who sees the poverty and dirt of her homestead as backward, "the absence of dirt (at the mission) was proof of the other-worldly nature of [her new] home" (71); too, the excessive amount of food provided at the mission attests to ideas of modernity and development as opposed to the backwardness of the impoverished homestead. She sees the plants at Babamukuru's house and describes them as the ones she had seen in her English textbook, in the yard of "Ben and Betty's uncle in town," and finds them "liberating, the first of many [liberating things] that followed from [her] transition to the mission" (64). She exults in the idea "of planting things for merrier reasons than the chore of keeping breath in the body" (64) and rejoices in the liberating possibilities of education, seeing her mother as one "so thoroughly beaten and without self-respect" (124) due to "being female and poor and uneducated and black" (89). At this point, Tambu is unable to separate economic deprevation from gender and racial identity constructions.

However, Dangarembga does not provide us with a single-dimensional picture of the "Third World" woman; she provides us with representations of women of different classes, generations, and socioeconomic standings. Yet, as Tambu aptly claims, "The way all the conflicts came back to the question of femaleness" demonstrates the complicity of elite native patriarchy with colonialism in wishing to keep women in domestic roles where private spaces are still undervalued and underprivileged.

The patriarchal order is supported by the colonial enterprise in the pre- and post-capitalist neocolonial economies. Babamukuru, Nhamo, and Chido are products of colonial capitalism and education and are, in fact, complicit with colonialism in upholding what is considered by colonialists as traditional patriarchal institutions. At whatever cost, they will help in keeping the colonial enterprise alive, particularly if it means food on the table; they inadvertently become agents of colonial and neocolonial power structures. For example, when Babamukuru returns from

England, he is greeted enthusiastically as the saviour of the family, while Maiguru, who is equally educated, is ignored. While Babamukuru's status rises when he returns with a Western education, women's roles (even those of educated women) are still defined by their relationships to the males, respected only as wives and mothers, which in and of itself is acceptable, but when only the earning members are respected, the status of women within the family becomes problematic.

According to Veit-Wild, "Tsitsi Dangarembga's novel cannot (yet) offer a political perspective of resistance" (144). However, I disagree. By providing us with a context of patriarchal practices under colonial and neocolonial contexts, Dangarembga helps us to recognize that the power structures in (post)colonial societies are a mixture of complicity and confrontation that produce a "nervous" condition in the split postcolonial subject. Tambu's cousin, Nyasha, who had lived in England and had an English education, suffers from this nervous condition, and being aware of the oppressive systems of Westernization at work, informs Tambu,

> It's not England any more and I ought to adjust. But when you've seen different things you want to be sure you're adjusting to the right thing. You can't go on all the time being whatever necessary. You've got to have some convictions.... But once you get used to it, well, it just seems natural and you just carry on. And that's the end for you. You're trapped. They control everything you do. (117)

There is no space left for resistance for the conflicted subject. Tambu narrates the incident that occurs when Nyasha was reading D.H. Lawrence's *Lady Chatterley's Lover*. Babamukuru removes the objectionable book depicting female sexuality from the room where Nyasha kept it and refuses to give it back to her. Upset at such a treatment from her father, who states that "a good child" does not behave in such a manner, she refuses to eat and eventually becomes anorexic (83). According to Veit-Wild, "Nyasha, who had never had to suffer from insufficient food, reacts with the refusal to eat, and thus keeps her body 'clean'" (143). Veit-Wild claims that as Nyasha "has been exposed much more than her cousin to the European world, and has in various ways imbibed high doses of 'Englishness,' she is the one who suffers most from the predicament of the in-between, of living in a state of liminality. She is, one might argue, a mimic woman" (Veit-Wild 143); however, unlike her father, who mimics "unquestionably," "Nyasha's body expresses what the suffering person can no longer express with words" (Veit-Wild 142). Her father prevents her from becoming aware of her sexuality, therefore possibly preventing her sexual awakening. Nyasha represents the nervous and contaminated female body that has been produced in the oppositional discourses of colonialism and native patriarchy. The violence of the colonizers transforms itself to the violence of the colonized. Nyasha's problematic relationship to both discourses and the violence on her body is manifested in her illness as she suffers from a mental breakdown taking the form of anorexia leading to delusions. Nyasha's mental breakdown is a rejection of both Westernization and indigenous patriarchal practices, and the breakdown involves Nyasha's rejection of food. She denies the body that is inscribed by oppressive discourses, the body where her sexuality is repressed (therefore, pure). The text highlights the intersection of colonialism and patriarchy, and we see Nyasha's condition as symptomatic of the split subject who is trying to resist both the constructs of native and female.

Nyasha rejects her food and withdraws into another space again when she is physically punished for coming back late from a co-ed dance with white boys, wearing mini skirts, and behaving, in her father's words, like a "whore" (114). She has to remain pure so that she can retain her value in the marriage market, since the only roles available to women – Western-educated or not – are traditional ones. Their very existence appears to depend upon having a male for economic and social reasons.

Under colonial and global capitalism, women are becoming more subordinated than before, often losing their old and meaningful roles in the new socioeconomic schemes within the production processes. Thus, women's oppression and exploitation can be situated within the process of decolonization. According to Frantz Fanon, "When a colonialist country … proclaims to the nationalist leaders, 'If you wish for independence, take it, and go back to the Middle Ages,' the newly independent people tend to acquiesce and to accept the challenge.… In plain words, the colonial powers say, 'Since you want Independence, take it and starve'" (97). In a starving nation, economic imbalance and horizontal hostilities between and even among the different genders and sexualities are not surprising.

Yet, modernity and education are supposed to address all concerns and wipe out all oppressions. When she first arrives from the impoverished homestead, Tambu believes Maiguru "lived in the best possible circumstances, in the best possible worlds" (142), and she can't understand why her aunt could possibly suffer as Nyasha claims. Education is supposed to bring liberty, freedom, and happiness. Toward that end, when Tambu is getting ready to go to the convent, wondering if education will "lighten" the burden of her family, Nyasha, with her usual insight, comments: "There'll always be brothers and mealies and mothers too tired to clean latrines. Whether you go to the convent or not" (200), indicating, quite correctly, that poverty and gender disparity will not disappear with education and Westernization.

Lucia, the only woman on the homestead who resists patriarchal control of her sexuality for reproductive reasons and who remains unmarried, declares that she doesn't know how to obey a man because she is not married (153). When she starts having a sexual relationship with Takesure, she does so out of choice because "her body has appetites of which she was not ashamed" (171). Babamukuru, who is a Western-educated man, respects her individuality and sexual control, applauding her for being "like a man herself" (171). It is not older women like Lucia who must be controlled; it is young women like Nyasha who have to be kept pure for the modern marriage market; if she can't marry well, she might lose her social and economic standing; therefore, it is with Nyasha that Babamukuru's patriarchal control takes extreme forms.

Babamukuru himself has given up Shona traditions in favour of more Westernized and Christian ways. When Takesure sees Lucia's control of her body and her sexuality, he declares that "she is vicious and unnatural. She is uncontrollable" (146), hoping to find ways to outsmart her. It is then that Jeremiah, Tambu's father and Babamukuru's brother, reminds Babamukuru that there are problems everywhere in the family: "Nyasha is impossible these days, and Maiguru too" (146). He then recounts misfortunes in the family, where violence by the male against women is considered the outcome of forgetting traditional ceremonies of "cleansing," for if they had done so, they "could have got rid of this evil" (146). Here of course they are touching on the subject of Female Genital Mutilation (FGM), a custom that is no longer practised in Babamukuru's house. While this taboo topic is brought up here by Dangarembga to show the brutality of the practice, women in rural areas and in the poorer sections of society await this ceremony to be initiated into womanhood, and thereby become part of the social fabric of the adults, partaking in the privileges. Thus, FGM becomes a marker of womanhood; what matters is how that practice is utilized by the patriarchal community to provide access to social spaces, and how women use it to empower themselves, even if that empowerment is painful and limited. Women have been using painfully brutal means (for example, breast implants, botox, high-heels, liposuction, motherhood, to name just a few) to acquire privileges and power within hegemonic social spaces. Upper-class and Western-educated people can change social practices with hardly any economic consequences, but for the poorer section of society, punishments from the gods for what they perceive as not observing traditional practices manifesting in a poor harvest or famine become pressing issues, for both men and women. Otherwise, how else will they deal with persistent hunger and poverty in an unequal world?

In this text, however, even though female sexuality is seen as evil by traditional males, Nyasha realizes that it is also due to colonial intervention and Westernization that they all suffer oppression. Whereas Veit-Wild argues that Nyasha doesn't have words to express the extent of her oppression (143) and therefore suffers from anorexia, I suggest that her awareness of the global dimension of capitalist ideology is not to be negated. Nyasha sees oppression in terms of a patriarchy transformed by colonial intervention, seeing men, too, as powerless to resist colonial and capitalist oppression: "Do you see what they've done? They've taken us away, Lucia. Takesure. All of us. They've deprived you of you, him of him, ourselves of each other" (201). She continues, "We're groveling … for a job … for money. Daddy grovels to them. We grovel to him.… I'm not a good girl. I'm evil … I won't grovel. I won't die" (200). Nyasha sees oppression for both men and women in its complex global power relationship. She acknowledges the "nervous condition" of the trapped colonized who becomes a "hybrid": "I am not one of them but I'm not one of you" (201). She is neither a good native nor a good girl; she is merely alienated and fragmented. Yet this fragmented subject is capable of visualizing hierarchical oppression in a globalized world.

Nyasha also realizes that mere education is not going to transform economic and cultural oppression for most women. For an educated woman, Maiguru's condition does not change much, and she does not have much control in raising her children. She does try to resist by leaving her home in anger for five days, but nothing really changes when she returns, and Nyasha understands that Maiguru is trying to resist something more powerful than just Babamukuru. She cries: "It's not really him, you know.

I mean not really the person. It's everything, its everywhere. So where do you break out to? You're just one person and its everywhere. So where do you break out to? ... I don't know" (174). Tambu also realizes through education she has become like Nyasha, but the realization does not seem to offer liberation. Also, Nyasha's resistance to systems of oppression does not seem to bring her release; in fact, Tambu thinks that "Nyasha and Chido and Nhamo [have] all succumbed" to the "Englishness" (203). It is this that is so dangerous and insidious.

However, it is through Nyasha's resistance as well as the resistances of the other women that Tambu learns that education is not what is going to finally liberate her. Nyasha writes in her letter to Tambu, "You are very essential to me in bridging some of the gaps in my life" (196); Tambu also realizes that the bridge that connects her to other women and their resistance will lead to her empowerment. When Nyasha has a nervous breakdown and lies drugged in the hospital, Tambu realizes her interconnectedness with Nyasha. She writes, "Nyasha's progress is still in the balance, and so, as a result, [is] mine" (202). Through the community of women, and through their interconnections, Tambu can create an empowering subjecthood. She no longer valorizes Western education, Westernization, and individualism as the epitome of liberation and happiness. At the end of her narration, as she is headed to the Sacred Heart School, she makes this profound statement: "Although I was not aware of it then, no longer could I accept Sacred Heart and what it represents as a sunrise on my horizon. Quietly, unobtrusively and extremely fitfully, something in my mind began to assert itself, to question things and refuse to be brainwashed, bringing me to this time when I can set down this story" (204).

Even before this realization, Tambu had resisted; she had done so through an "illness" when she had refused to go to her parents' Christian wedding at the insistence of Babamukuru, rejecting the idea that they were living in sin. She also was resisting and refusing to play the good native and good daughter, and the site of conflict for control is also her body, as she has an out-of-body experience. Thus, Nyasha's mental breakdown and Tambu's "illness" or madness are representations of the violence inflicted upon (post)colonial women, while at the same time, they suggest possibilities for change. Consequently, Tambu's progression to a changing consciousness, although "a long and painful one," was a process that led to her "expansion" (204). Therefore, this text complicates notions of patriarchal domination by situating them within the matrix of colonialism and neocolonialism within a globalized world where gender, class, and racial oppression intersect within an impoverished nation, such as Zimbabwe.

8

Globalism and Transnationalism: Cultural Politics in the Texts of Mira Nair, Gurinder Chadha, Agnes Sam, and Farida Karodia

This chapter examines the poetics of resistance to gendered identity formations in the texts of women writers of the South Asian diaspora and their interconnections to the Indian and South African nation-states. In their re-envisioning of Indianness and Indian womanhood, certain writers are themselves limited due to their location and class politics. I will examine Mira Nair's film *Mississippi Masala*, Gurinder Chadha's film *Bhaji on the Beach*, Agnes Sam's collection of short stories *Jesus is Indian* and Farida Karodia's short story "Crossmatch," in order to revise their ideas of gender empowerment produced in resistance to certain constructions. In order to examine the Indian diaspora, we must first find out how Indians came to be scattered throughout the world. Additionally, how do they hold on to their cultural identity in the face of harsh conditions many of them faced? Does it matter that identity constructions in the diasporic spaces of the Global North are vastly different from those in the Global South? How do women resist certain cultural construction of identity which they see as oppressive?

To understand women's strategies of resistance and reinscriptions in diasporic spaces, we will have to first delve into the origins of the modern Indian diaspora, which lies primarily in the colonization of India by the British (See Surrinder Bhana and Bridglal Pachai, among others). South Africa has the largest population of Indians outside of India, yet not much is known or written about them. Apartheid policies made it certain that many people's stories and histories were denied access to the mainstream ideological spaces. In *South African Writings in English*, Rajendra Chetty states: "The state ... issues a long list of censorship laws resulting in writers fearing censorship and imprisonment.... The South African literary historiography has continuously silenced and marginalized the 'other' voice: the black voice" (12). Indians were categorized variously as "Coolies, Asian, politically as non-white or black people" (10); it is no wonder that Agnes Sam succinctly states in the introduction to her short story collection *Jesus is Indian*, "the history of Indians in South Africa was suppressed" (1). She writes that in 1860, her great-grandfather was "shanghaied" into indentureship as a child of nine and was brought to Durban on the *Lord George Bentinck II*. She continues:

> For as a schoolgirl in Port Elizabeth, I was taught a history beginning with a Portuguese sailor in the fifteenth century roughing the seas in search of a spice route to India. Bartholomeu Dias, Vasco da Gama, the Van der Stels, the Dutch settlers with Jan van Riebeeck, the 5,000 British settlers in 1820, even details about a tiny group of 150 French Huguenots fleeing religious persecution in France, all figured in history. But how and why the largest group of Indians outside the subcontinent came to be in South Africa was never accounted for. ("Introduction" 1)

These indentured labourers, little more than slaves, "confronted, adapted and won in various situations" (10) during moments of cultural conflicts. Sam adds that "South African Indians like myself have lost mother tongue, family name, religion, culture, history, and historical links with India. Cut off from India, apartheid has further separated us from other communities in South Africa, thereby exacerbating our isolation" (11). Yet many South Asians in South Africa manage to retain their tenuous link with what Salman Rushdie calls the "imaginary homeland." Their idea of Indianness and Indian womanhood will be problematized in this discussion to see how women in the diaspora negotiate cultural spaces for reinscription.

For the displaced peoples of Indian descent, then, alienation produced a hybrid culture. This hybridized cultural space is also the place to strategize resistance and generate counter-discursive practices. Women use this space to question gender identity constructions; their writings suggest that they no longer take the ideas of "Indian womanhood" as a given. In their hybridity, they try to represent new forms and new ideas of "Indianness"; the very idea of "Indianness" in transnational diasporic spaces is defined, redefined, contested, constructed, reconstructed, or reconstituted for different purposes and for different audiences by Indian women.

And as we can see in much of the literature, there is a constructed relationship between the diasporic community and "motherland" or "homeland." In such spaces, the question regarding woman and identity becomes complex. In order to understand how Indian women are defined in the diaspora, we must first understand the idea of "Indianness" within the Indian context and then examine the idea of Indian woman as it came to be defined during specific historical moments in India and abroad. While there are exhaustive studies available regarding gender and nationalism in India, let me reiterate, briefly, some seminal points which will situate the contexts of these studies during different periods.

Let us examine nationalism and its impact on identity formation in colonized India, particularly, for my purposes, gender identity formation. The group that came to redefine the Indian woman, based on traditional elements drawn from inherited caste ideologies modified and refined through contact with Western education, was the newly emergent middle classes. Nationalism deemed it necessary that women should be refashioned; however, their essential feminine qualities should not be changed. So, on the one hand, women had to be educated so that they would become more suitable for their Western-educated husbands, while on the other hand, patriarchal control of women's sexuality became an added concern at this time because of women's changing consciousness due to modernity (see Chapter 1).

The anxiety that modernization produced in the national consciousness is manifested in the reconstruction of women's identities. Women were becoming educated and were investigating public spaces, which had been previously closed off to them. Indian nationalists realized they were in need of modernizing reforms.

The result for nationalism turned out to be confusing and ambivalent for the new woman. On the one hand, her liberation was essentially just political propaganda, as reformation did not change the material or social position of the Indian woman (Mitra, "I Will Make Bimala" 245–64); however, it allowed the middle-class woman entry into the public sphere, and we will find Indian women writers belonging to this class, both at home and in the diaspora, exploring space which was previously prohibited to them. The ambiguity produced by nationalism can still be seen in cultural representations of modern-day women writers. While the construction of femininity during nationalism was limiting to women in terms of social and economic empowerment, middle-class women tried to become their own agents in defining their subjectivities, however limiting. This construction allowed the middle-class Indian woman, who is caught between two discursive ideological constructs, to negotiate her identity, even if it is within ambiguous and troubled territories.

Middle-class Indian women who are Western-educated are unable to change their social condition, which is then reflected in cultural representations produced by them. Moving back and forth from the public to the domestic sphere, she is unable, sometimes, to shed the other modes of thoughts and ideas. We see the protagonists of many Indian women writers resisting cultural constructions of gender identity; sometimes such resistance takes extreme forms, such as "madness"; in such cultural productions, one can see the implication of nationalism and its ambivalent outcomes for many Western-educated, middle-class Indian women writers in a postcolonial society. I locate my chosen texts in this postcolonial and transnational diasporic space from which postcolonial feminists, themselves the bearers of hybrid identity, translate and negotiate meanings and identities.

For Bhabha, the space of the "displaced," the "hybrid," is an empowered space which can produce counter-narratives of nations that challenge and displace fixed geopolitical boundaries. In "DissemiNation," Bhabha writes, "the boundaries that secure the cohesive limits of the western nation may imperceptibly turn into a contentious internal liminality that provides a place from which to speak both of, and as, the minority, the exilic, the marginal and the emergent" (Bhabha 149). This hybrid space is also the place to strategize resistance and generate counter-discursive practices for many displaced and diasporic women writers since this space presupposes difference without the concomitant oppressive hierarchy.

I argue that negotiation for cultural and national identity is rooted in gendered identity constructions. Women's subjectivities and the patriarchal interpretations of "Indianness" conflicted, and this conflict is reflected in women's writings that are shaped in resistance to this process both in India (home) and the diaspora (world).

Let us look at technology and multimedia and its impact on the forces of identity formation. For the diasporic subject, construction of national or ethnic identity, and specifically, gender identity construction and imposition in the diasporic community where notions of "Indianness" are constructed in imagined communities (Benedict Anderson) in a transnational or translocal space beyond the boundaries of the nation can be problematic and complex. As Appadurai argues, "Part of what mass media make possible, because of the condition of collective reading, criticism, and pleasure, is ... a 'community of sentiment'" (8). A group that has never come together in actuality can have group identity due to mass media and print capitalism.

As a child growing up in Burma, I remember watching "bioscope" in small, rural theatres; I spoke an antiquated form of Punjabi. The Hindi I spoke as a child is called "Bombaiya Hindi," which means it is a bastardized fusion of various Hindustani dialects I had picked up from the local working class Indian community to which I belonged. The elegant Hindi, or mostly Urdu, dialogues and songs from Indian films were mimicked by us, mostly to act out our "superior" Indianness in a Burmese-speaking country. In any case, we all flocked to the cinema halls every Sunday to learn about new fashions and keep India and Indianness alive in our memories, when none of us had ever seen India before, except my grandparents, who had left it as children to work as tailors and petty traders in Burma.

This Indianness was co-opted for nationalism during the Japanese occupation of Burma; my father's brother as well as my mother's brother became part of Subhash Chandra Bose's Azad Hind Fauj (army) that marched toward British India to liberate India, the "motherland," as well as Burma, which was part of British India. Azad Hind Fauj was mostly formed by the collective presence of the Indian diaspora in many parts of Asia. However, after the Japanese defeat, my Burma-born parents, wearied by the Japanese and British occupation of Burma, and encouraged by my grandmother to go back to their "*Mulkh*" (*desh*) and the ancestral land (with a well in it), journeyed to Chakwal (now in Pakistan) in 1946, but had to escape from there in one of the trains that narrowly escaped becoming a "ghost train" (their train was stoned and attacked, however) when India was partitioned in 1947. They escaped all the way back to their land of birth, Burma, and subsequently became Burmese citizens.

We, all my five siblings and I, were born in Burma and still raised Indians, taught to fear Pakistanis (in spite of the fact that many Muslim friends helped my parents' family escape the riots), and learned Punjabi (Gurumukhi) at the Sikh Gurudwara every evening while imbibing popular Indian culture through Hindi films. We also learned about Indian culture from our mother, who, though practising many Buddhist concepts, such as "right conduct" and "right speech" from Buddha's Eight-Fold Path to enlightenment, constantly reminded us about the modesty, honour, and shame befitting daughters of Indian descent. My mother's home truths plus the reinforcements from so forceful a medium as Hindi cinema constructed for my three sisters as well as for myself a certain hybrid idea of Indianness, while going to a Convent School run by European nuns taught us another form of shame – shame of our Indianness, seen as inferior by the nuns. That the nuns treated Indians with contempt and distaste, leading to self-contempt for many Indian children, adds to the ethos of Third World diasporic sensibilities. Thus, in these diasporic spaces, inhabited by the working classes, ideas of Indianness clashed with Western notions of enlightenment with ambiguous outcomes. Some are able to resist Western hegemony, some remain trapped within it, while a few others are able to embrace the ambiguities in complex ways. As a diasporic subject myself, I will compare my own ideas of Indianness to those that I see in parts of Africa on my periodic trips there, in order to critique notions of gender oppression and empowerment.

Let us investigate the diasporic communities and identity constructions in Uganda, South Africa, England, and the United States as represented in my chosen texts. I examine the transformation and dislocation of identities in the West, where notions of cultural diversity prevail; at the same time I look at diasporic Indians negotiating for and holding on to their ideas of "Indianness" in transnational spaces which become doubly oppressive for women due to the intersection of racist as well as sexist structures of social and cultural institutions.

Let us first examine *Mississippi Masala* as a new cultural form engendered in translocal or diasporic space. While this movie received its share of criticism in terms of racial stereotypes, it is worth bringing this film into our discussion, as it will lead to examinations of later inter-ethnic relationships in various locales. Harvard-educated Mira Nair, who was born in Orissa, India, directed this film, and it was released in February 1992. Nair herself is married to the Ugandan social scientist Mahmood Mumdani (Bose and Varghese 143). The film is partly shot in Nair's Ugandan home. *Mississippi Masala* is a story, in part, of Mina, the Uganda-born daughter of an Indian family living in Mississippi, and Demetrius, an American, of African descent. Mina works as a maid in a motel run by her relatives. Incidentally, in the United States, particularly in the southern states, motels have become closely associated with the Gujarati Patels (Lal *Manas*).[1] Demetrius runs his own carpet-clearing business. One of the interesting highlights of the narrative is that, as one character points out, Mina is of Indian descent and has never been to India and Demetrius is of African descent and has never been to Africa.

The story unfolds in 1972, with the expulsion of Mina's family from Uganda when she is a child. Her Ugandan-born parents are descendants of Indian labourers who were imported by the British to build the East African railway in the late 1800s. Mina's father, Jaymini Loha, is a prosperous Kampala lawyer who thinks of himself as an African first and Indian second (although in the United States, his "Indianness" re-emerges when he sees his daughter's romantic involvement with an African American man). But under the harsh rule of Idi Amin, he – like thousands of other Indian Ugandans – is forced to emigrate, first to England and then to the United States. Significantly, one of the complaints of the Amin government was that Indians kept themselves culturally isolated and did not intermarry with Ugandans. Such rhetoric is used by the ethnocentric government to deny citizens their rightful privileges.

The narrative then takes us to 1990, and to Greenwood, Mississippi, where Mina, now twenty-four, lives with her family. She meets Demetrius by accident, literally and figuratively, for while driving she collides with the back of his van. They start dating secretly. Her parents and relatives are shocked when they find out that Mina has actually spent a weekend away from home with Demetrius. Her father is upset, not only because Demetrius is Black but also because he still remembers the treatment meted out to him by Blacks in Uganda; Jay remembers the slogan "Uganda is for Africans – Black Africans" repeated to him by his childhood friend, Okelo.

It is at this point that the divisions of minority communities in the United States are highlighted. Demetrius, fighting for his dignity and pride as a Black man, tells Mina's father, "You and your folks come down from God knows where and be about as Black as the ace of spades, and as soon as you get here you start acting white and treating us like we're your doormats. I know you and your daughter ain't but a few shades from [mine], that I know." Thus the dislocation and alienation of Indians here are interwoven with that of the African diaspora, whose identity formation in the West is complicated with the history of slavery. Nationalism for African Americans and Indians takes on many layers, and the idea of an Indian and African diaspora and the cultural representations that they engender becomes complex.

What is of particular importance here, therefore, is the response of the other male members of the Indian community when they catch Mina, literally, making love to Demetrius at a seaside resort motel. They attack him physically and then have him arrested for assault and battery after indicating that Mina was somehow coerced into this state. Mina's cousin Anil shouts to Demetrius, "You leave our women alone." Their reaction is that of the clan taking control and restoring honour to the name of the family and thus maintaining patriarchal control and structure. Their idea of an Indian girl has been violated, and they will take any measures to remedy that.

While in earlier films and texts empowerment for Indian women, seen as upward mobility into the dominant community, was conceived in terms of Black/White, where a South Asian woman goes off with a white man (see Mukherjee's novels, for example), in *Mississippi Masala* it is within and across transnational ethnic diasporic spaces that change seems to be occurring. One does not see many textual representations of Indo-African sexual alliances. For example, Mina questions the notions of "Indianness" in such a space when she asks her parents, "What about me?" when they tell her that she must adhere to the Indian sensibility and not see Demetrius anymore. When they ask her where he is from and what his family background is, she answers, "This is America, Ma, nobody cares here," indicating the shifts in thinking in the new generations growing up in the diasporic spaces of the Global North. While in other texts, interracial relationships mean showing Black/White subjects, in this film, empowerment for women and interracial relationships are no longer so binary; such spaces are the transnational spaces where new cultural forms are engendered and where new hybrid identities are being formed. Filmed in both Mississippi and Uganda, *Mississippi Masala* features a soundtrack – Indian music, Delta blues, and African drums – that suggests that in diasporic spaces in the West, identities are being reconstructed and are evolving into a new hybrid reality for the new immigrants.

While discussing the work of the imagination in today's multimedia-influenced world, Appadurai states that the "creating of social imagination has moved from the realm of social life where forceful leaders used to implant their visions for great revolutions to ordinary people who deploy their imaginations in the practice of everyday life" (5). This fact, he adds, is "exemplified in the mutual contextualizing" of what he calls "motion and mediation" (5). By that he means people who are forced, at every level of social, national, and global life, to migrate or "choose" to migrate in order to make a living. "They move and must drag their imagination for new ways of living along with them" (6). Appadurai separates the groups into "diaspora of hope, diaspora of terror, and diaspora of despair" (6). African Americans as well as Indian Americans, among others, represent these groups – first as a diaspora of terror as slaves and indentured labourers, then a diaspora of despair in the early part of the twentieth century when they were expelled from many nations, and finally as a diaspora of hope in the twenty-first century as they chose to relocate around the globe. Appadurai elaborates:

> The differences between migration in the past and migration today is that now they create new mythographies for new social projects.... Those who wish to move, those who have moved, those who wish to return, and those who choose to stay rarely formulate their plans outside the sphere of radio and television, cassettes and videos, newsprint and telephone. For migrants, both the politics of adaptation to new environments and the stimulus to move or return are deeply affected by a mass-mediated imaginary that frequently transcends national space. (6)

While *Mississippi Masala* can be seen as the story of a diaspora of terror and despair, as is *Bhaji on the Beach* (as I will discuss later), there are moments in all these texts when we see characters moving toward empowering spaces or becoming part of the diaspora of hope.

Finally, Mina moves away with Demetrius to another city. While such representations become problematic in terms of postcolonial criticism, where Indian women leave "oppressive home cultures" for the liberating possibilities of others, in this instance, both characters appear to use the hybrid transnational space for empowerment. Many cities – for example, Los Angeles – have spaces that encompass multiple nationalisms, such as the Ethiopian community on Fairfax Street where one sees an intermingling of races. Such representations as *Mississippi Masala* reflect the reality of movements across racial lines in translocal diasporic spaces instead of upward into the dominant culture. As postcolonial diasporic subjects, Mina and Demetrius appear to be able to subvert the symbols of modernity. One can read Mina's and Demetrius' act as transnational diasporic subjects subverting the social authority imposed by modernity, pointing to "forms of social antagonism and contradiction that are not yet properly represented, political identities in the process of being formed, cultural enunciations in the act of hybridity, in the process of translating and transvaluing cultural differences" (Bhabha, "'Race', time and the revision of modernity" 252). Nair's narrative suggests that "cultural difference" of African American and Asian American as represented by Dimitrius and Mina are no longer integrating into the mainstream's definition of diversity; the meaning of this new Indo-African merging suggests intercultural transactions, where meanings are no longer "transparent." In the new cultural space, Demetrius and Mina are no longer seen as having left cultural and communal identity and support behind; they are, in what Bhabha calls, the "indeterminated" "Third Space," where meanings must be read anew. In transnational and translocal diasporic spaces, such cultural productions are giving new meanings to cultural, national, and gender identity formations. What is hopeful about "diasporas of hope" in terms of diversity and difference is that for the first time in the 2000 census in America, a new multiracial category was added. Additionally, and more importantly here, Mina and Demetrius do not come from elite privileged backgrounds, and therefore, their ideas of liberation and choice are not so blatantly and unproblematically couched in modernity's idiom.

Let us now look at other examples of transnational spaces and constructions of new imagination for immigrant communities who are forced to migrate. In 1992, a young woman from Britain named Gurinder Chadha directed her first feature film, *Bhaji on the Beach*, written by Meera Syal. Chadha was only twenty-four when she directed this film. The film explores the lives of nine South Asian women, spanning three generations, during one day at a seaside resort in Blackpool. (Bhaji is a popular Indian snack food in Britain.) The film traces, to a large extent, the stories of Ginder, who has taken refuge from her abusive husband at a women's hostel, and Hashida, who finds herself pregnant by her Black boyfriend.

Chadha herself grew up in Southall, a largely Punjabi neighborhood in West London, after her family was forced – the diaspora of despair – to move from Kenya when she was three. Indians who were taken to work on the railroads as indentured labourers by the British struggled to belong to the nation of domicile. Many, indeed, participated in anticolonial struggles. However, when they were eventually forced to move out of Kenya, many landed in the UK. Thus, ideas of diaspora are multilayered and multidimensional here. The cast of women characters includes three "aunties" – traditional, older Indian women; Ginder, who has fled with her five-year-old son from her handsome but abusive husband and his controlling family; Hashida, one of the community's "good girls" with a place in a medical school, but who, unbeknownst to the "aunties," is pregnant by her West Indian boyfriend, Oliver, a relationship she's kept secret from her parents; two giggly teenage sisters carrying a boom box and intensely interested in English boys (since, as they point out, Indian boys are too busy with White girls to notice Brown girls like them, anyway); Rekha, a modern, rich visitor from Bombay, who is dressed in fashionable Western clothes; and Simi, the trip's organizer, a feminist, wearing a leather jacket over a Punjabi salwar-kameez, who is part of the Asian community while being critical of many of its oppressive patriarchal roles.

The film touches on many aspects of gender identity formation and negotiation for women of Indian descent. Simi, who is a politically committed community worker and who talks about "the double yoke of racism and sexism," wants the women to just have a good old time at the Liverpool seaside resort away from their duties as women. Ginder is ready to go back to her spineless and abusive husband only if he leaves his oppressive family. She believes it is the in-laws who are the problem. Asha seems to be a sweet and friendly woman; however, she suffers severe headaches and escapes into fantasies, which are constructed like dream sequences from traditional Bollywood films. Though college-educated, Asha feels duty bound as a good wife, but there is a sense of dissatisfaction with life as she appears consumed in the act of serving her family and working in her husband's newsstand and video shop. Later in the narrative, as they go about having fun at the seaside, the "aunties" inadvertently discover Hashida's pregnancy with a Black man; they become instantly abusive toward her, calling the fetus *"Kala Kaluta Baigun Loota"* (Black as an eggplant). They act almost as one in renouncing her behavior as bad, except Rekha, who tells the English Indian women that they are twenty years behind in their social and cultural attitudes.

Let us look at what Appadurai calls the diasporic public spaces and the role of imagination in the reaction of the women toward Hashida's pregnancy. Appadurai maintains that "emotions are not raw, precultural materials that constitute a universal, transsocial substrate but in many ways, learned: what to feel sad or happy about, how to express it in different contexts, and whether or not the expression of affects is a simple playing out of inner sentiments (often assumed to be universal)" (147). He adds that emotions (as seen in films such as Chadha's or Nair's) are "culturally constructed and socially situated" (147). Thus, the reaction of the community toward Ginder and Hashida can be understood in such terms. Earlier in the narrative, we see Asha and the other women blaming Ginder for her husband's abusive behaviour toward her. She must have done something bad and brought the abuse upon herself, they muse.

Hashida's dishonour is complicated by the fact that her boyfriend is Black and mixed race relationships are taboo in the Indian community. Asians are also categorized as Black in Britain; however, Indians resist such simple definitions, although it has been a useful term for political mobilization against racism in specific historic periods. Also the term Black is often used for people of Afro-Caribbean descent. Here too we see the diasporic reality of Blacks from the Caribbean as a displaced and disenfranchised group in the UK becoming complicated with that of the Indian diaspora as discussed in *Mississippi Masala*. When the women inadvertently find out that Hashida is pregnant with Oliver's baby, they mourn their losses. They lament that not only have they lost their dignity as immigrants in the UK, but they also suffer due to loss of their culture.

As can be seen in the following example, women growing up in the West have to carry a double burden of being woman and Indian. When the

White proprietress of a café is being racist toward Pushpa and Bina, two middle-aged women, for bringing their own food into the café, Pushpa displaces her rage and racial oppression by turning against Hashida, calling her a "whore and a half," and grieves that England "has cost us our children." They want their children to be more Indian than the Indians themselves. Politics and culture complicates the outcome of such mediated events. Because Indians are seen as traditional and sexist, legal institutions can intervene in their cultural and communal spaces and enforce social change. On the one hand, it is because of such sentiments that the UK has now mobilized legal actions against Indians who are "forcefully" kidnapping their daughters and marrying them against their wishes to Indians in India or elsewhere. On the other hand, the pressure to remain Indian mounts as a reaction to such interference in the culture, and traditions become dearer to Indians due to racism and cultural colonization. As can be seen in the resurgence of fundamentalism in the past few years in the United States and in the UK, culture, with ideas of race, gender, and religion, become contentious and are used to foster narrow nationalism.

Imagination, especially collective, can fuel action. Appadurai explains the role of imagination in actions fuelled by cultural representations. "It is the imagination, in its collective forms, that creates ideas of neighborhood and nationhood, of moral economies, and unjust rule, of higher wages and foreign labor prospects. The imagination is a staging ground for action" (7). Imagination propels Pushpa and Bina to verbally assault Hashida for her "deviant" sexuality. Appadurai elaborates, "Part of what the mass media makes possible, because of the condition of collective reading, criticism, and pleasure.... [is] a community of sentiment ... a group that begins to imagine and feel things together" (8). Groups that have never seen each other start to imagine themselves Indian, or Sikhs, or Burmese, or Muslims, or as Indian women, Sikh women, or Burmese women. How does the phenomenon of collective sentiment occur? Appadurai explains the phenomenon of shared experiences further:

> They are communities in themselves but always potentially communities for themselves capable of moving from shared imagination to collective action.... They are often transnational, even postnational, and they frequently operate beyond the boundaries of the nation. These mass-mediated solidarities

> have the additional complexity that, in them, diverse local experiences of taste, pleasure, and politics can crisscross with one another, thus creating the possibility of convergences in translocal social action that would otherwise be hard to imagine. (8)

Appadurai provides the example of the Ayodhya temple incident in India in 1992, when huge sums of monies were raised in the United States and elsewhere to support the so-called "Hindu cause" against imagined Muslim aggression, where political leaders motivated local masses to action, while the mass media mobilized international solidarity and action.

More recently, the massacre of Muslims in Gujarat in 2002 is claimed to have been funded by fundamentalist Hindus in the United States. The other example is legal action against arranged marriages in the UK. Thus, while on the one hand, transnational spaces are oppressive in terms of translocal social action, as can be seen by the reaction of the "aunties" toward Hashida, there are also possible constructions of new mythologies for new social actions as can be seen by the resolution of the narrative in *Bhaji on the Beach*, discussed below.

Nair and Chadha show cultural construction and mass-mediated solidarity that can become the basis for social action; while the aunties are seen as enforcing oppressive cultural norms, they also appear to transcend and move toward new mythologies in this space as can be seen in the resolution of the film. The movie ends with the "aunties" understanding Hashida's decision to be with her boyfriend, if not completely accepting it. Asha finally stands up to Ginder's husband and berates him for his abusive treatment of his wife when he follows her to Blackpool and tries to abduct their son from her. In fact, she slaps Ginder's husband's face and protects her from his abusive actions. As the movie ends, we see the women returning to London while the silhouette of Hashida and Oliver against the setting sun portends hope as bhangra and reggae mixed music – which is a hybrid of English, Caribbean, and Indian pop Punjabi songs – plays on the soundtrack, highlighting the fusion and hybridity of cultural forms in transnational spaces. The new music in the diasporic spaces fuses styles and genres, representing the fusion of culture of East and West. For example, Chadha takes Cliff Richard's song "Summer Holiday" from the movie *Summer Holiday* and rewrites the lyrics in Punjabi, and adds

Bhangra beats to it. New cultural identities are being formed while the old ones still have a hold in such spaces, leading to hybridized sensibilities and representations.

While the ending of the film signifies female solidarity, what becomes abundantly clear is that although new identities are forming, the old ones are continually reinforced through the media and the viewing of the videos that Asha sells in her shop. We see examples of diaspora of despair as well as diaspora of hope in both the films that I have examined.

Both directors are careful in depicting Indians and Indianness in the diasporic spaces in the continuum of displacement and alienation. They realize that though Indians were dragged to many places of the world and had to live in abject poverty and in racist climes, through hard work and finding sustenance and strength in their own cultures, they have somehow managed to sustain themselves while giving their children a better future.

In the reconfiguration of identity for the diasporic Indian woman in a postcolonial space, the idea of an "authentic" Indian self is produced sometimes by the Indian community and sometimes by the dominant community (as in England, where Indians are seen as enforcing their cultural practices of oppressive "arranged marriages"). This reconfiguration occurs because Indians are situated in nation-states that pride themselves on having a homogenous national identity; such nation-states celebrate diversity and multiculturalism, yet the new space of empowerment, Bhabha's ambiguous "Third Space" of difference, is where new cultural ideas, forms, and identities are being articulated.

In the remaining paragraphs, I will discuss South African Indian writers, Agnes Sam and Farida Karodia, who form part of the Indian diaspora, having lived in both South Africa and the West. Let us examine Sam's short stories in *Jesus is Indian* in order to analyze how the author posits resistance and assimilation in some of her short stories. In the face of resurgent debates of national identity and national belongings in recent decades, such questioning of national identity and resistance as Sam's become doubly important. As we have seen in recent years since the attack on the World Trade Center and the Pentagon, and the wars in Iraq and Afghanistan, the urgent need to hold on to an essential national and cultural identity while at the same time celebrating diversity is becoming extremely problematic and contradictory in the Global North as well as in the South.

Sam's short stories are situated in South Africa and England; however, I chose those situated in South Africa for my purposes. Agnes Sam, who was born in 1942 in South Africa, is the great-granddaughter of an indentured labourer. She was brought up in Port Elizabeth, and attended university at Roma, Lesotho, and Zimbabwe. She was exiled from South Africa for political reasons and went to England, where she studied literature at the University of York. Many of her stories revolve round the theme of "love" and marriage for South Asians, although she does bring up the struggles Black South Africans faced under apartheid. However, as the author herself indicates in her introduction to the text, what is new about writers like her is that they are tackling issues of choice versus arranged marriages, which seem to be of profound and paramount importance in terms of what modernity promised the (post)colonized women. Sam writes, "Migration and exile are not new phenomena.... What is new reflects women's changed perception of themselves; it signals independence and status as individuals in society; the post-modern woman makes the decision to migrate – in her own right" (12). As she herself lives in England, she sees postmodern feminism as a space of liberation for women.

Comparing women's earlier "oppressed" status to her own, Sam further elaborates on her stance:

> Today's woman may decide to migrate or go into exile with or without dependents. If married, she may refuse to accompany a man into exile, or choose not to return to her native land when a man returns. She may even emigrate without her husband. Today's woman migrants may follow a profession, be skilled, and have her own capital. She may travel to a new country as an employee of a company, with a voluntary organization, for her own or a foreign government and then decide to remain where she is employed. (12)

While Sam's claim might appear simplistic in terms of choice for the diasporic woman, she does, however, complicate gender with the intersections of race, class, caste, religion in her work; her stories investigate the notion of choice vs. arranged marriage in complex ways. In her texts, there are no easy binaries to choose from. The hybrid space and hybridity of the postcolonial subjects who can move into transnational diasporic spaces in order to transcend national identity are problematized in terms of diasporas in the Global North and South.

In "A Bag of Sweets," for instance, Khadija, a Muslim woman, who marries a Christian out of choice and love – "wanting the right to choose whom she should marry" (40) – is seen as someone who has destroyed the family due to her actions. When Khadija comes to pay an unexpected visit to her sister, Khaltoum, in their family shop after three years of marriage, Khaltoum is unmoved by her sister's plea for understanding and forgiveness. While looking at her sister's hand resting on the glass counter, Khaltoum thinks of the "potential for unimaginable flights" that the hands were capable of. In fact, she sees them as hands that have given her sister freedom, but also "in doing so they destroyed the people we loved" (40). Thinking of the gossip and shame their family had to go through, she resents the natural way Khadija was acting with her, "as if she still belonged to us; as if she had done nothing to hurt us; as if her bid for freedom had not destroyed the family" (40). Khaltoum and her brothers could not forgive her for her actions; she remembers, "it was the consequences of that freedom that we could not forget. Our parents died within months of each other" (41). And although Khadija says she was married to a wonderful man and they have a beautiful baby, she still seeks to return to her family and community; her husband's community does not accept her because, although she married a Christian, she chose to remain a Muslim.

Sam's own stance is that one has freedom to make those personal choices; her stories reflect that even in the diaspora, which should be filled with hope for new beginnings and endings, old diasporic spaces, such as South Africa, remain diaspora of despair. Khadija leaves her sister's shop, never to return. Identity is constructed here in terms of religious nationalism; Khadija is unable to transcend her Muslim identity; she may have married a Christian, but as a Muslim woman, she really has no choice in terms of whom she can marry, particularly if she still wants to have social interaction with her "home" community. The idea of a "good Muslim woman" is strictly enforced in such spaces as religion takes on cultural undertones and women become bearers of cultural and national identities.

However, in "The Well-Loved Woman," Sam complicates gender oppression with the modern notion of love and choice by making it not only about religion but also about race. Most so-called love stories about choice are represented in terms of sexual relationships between Indian women and White men; if women could transcend nationalism, i.e., ideas of Indianness, it was because they were moving up in the hierarchical space where the hegemony of Whiteness prevails. When it comes to looking at racial intermixing in terms of Black and Indian, we have only recently started seeing the exploration of such spaces as spaces of empowerment or transcendence. What happens when an Indian girl falls in love with a Black South African Muslim man?

In this story, Chantal, a very young South African Indian woman, is falling in love with an African Muslim man, who "appeared one day as if from out of the blue to lean against a pillar" of the shop where he worked (45). Chantal thinks that not too many people know about this man: "How had she never seen him before? When had he come? Or had he always stood there without her noticing him? Where did he disappear to at night? Why did no one ever speak to him? And why did he stand there like that? As if he were waiting – without hope" (41). When her friends find out her interest in him, they admonish her with, "Don't *you* go falling in love with him! He's a skelm" (which in South Africa means someone who is dishonest, crooked, or a blatant liar) (46). Here we see racial biases – horizontal hostilities – against Black South Africans by Indians in a land oppressed by apartheid and race classification.

Most of Chantal's questions regarding the unknown Black African man remain unanswered as she fantasizes about him, until one day, her older sister, Kamilla, who has been married these last six years, returns from England with her new baby to visit. According to Chantal, her sister is the most loved woman in the community. She comes to South Africa to find someone to take care of her children while she studies at the university; while the community is shocked at her decision to go to school, they can do nothing about it because her husband endorses her decision, and everything rests on him (49). The young people in the community look up to her as she has status as a married woman, and she tells them they can be whatever they choose to be: "She suggest[s] the unmarried girls in the family should have a chance to go to university, college, run the family business, be mechanics – whatever the goals – they should pursue it" (49). Such ideas create a "rumpus" in the community. "The women trembled to leave their daughters alone with her" (49). However, no one in the community dares to ignore or ostracize her, as she is a "well-loved woman."

Women in the community discuss the merits and pitfalls of educating the girls; they are afraid men will not marry educated women. Kamilla suggests finding husbands who do not wish to be the head of households and who want to marry educated women. While she makes bold statements such as "Let our girls choose their husbands. Instead of sitting at home while brave young men come forward with proposals, let our girls come home with a young man and say – this is the man I want to marry" (50), Chantal wonders why Kamilla speaks in such a way when her marriage was arranged, or so she thinks.

Chantal asks Kamilla about love, and her sister assures her that she will know when she falls in love because she would want to touch the man. When finally she acts on her impulses and speaks to the African man, the community is shattered by the news, and it sends "shock waves through the community" (50). It is not that she has talked to a man; it is that he is an African man. By that, they mean a Black African man. They still consider themselves Indian, of course. As I explained earlier in my discussion of *Mississippi Masala*, one of Idi Amin's many complaints against Indians was that they kept to their idea of racial purity and superiority by not marrying Black Ugandans; in fact, in that film, Jay acknowledges Indians' preoccupation with material wealth rather than with taking a meaningful role in Uganda. He says, "Most people are born with five senses. We are left with only one, sense of property." Indians' preoccupation with "making it," either in Africa, the United States, or South Africa, while trying to maintain their cultural and national identity is amply demonstrated in these texts. While the preoccupation with materialism is a stereotype regarding Indians, and is used to whip up anti-nationalist sentiments, these texts buy into the dominant myths regarding Indians as being non- or anti-nationalist. The Indian community's response to Chantal's action is, "No one in this city will marry you now! We'll have to send for a husband from India for you!" (50). They are emphatic that she not marry him, and when she asks, "Can't an African marry an Indian?" her brothers beat her and ask her where she will live if she marries an African man. She'll have to go and live in the coloured area. Here the narrative points to the Race Classification and Group Area Acts of South Africa. As Chetty points out in *South African Indian Writers in English*, "Totalitarian politicisation meant that virtually no realm of personal relationship was left free of politics" (11). Race, of course, plays a major role in the formation of prejudices. The idea of national and cultural identity here is implicitly and explicitly expressed. He is African and she is Indian. She cannot marry him.

Kamilla explains that the earlier generations had it hard as they had to conform to societal roles, but as they challenge the roles more and more, changes are occurring. She suggests that sometimes, in order to gain freedom, one will have to marry, as she did to someone from England, and move away where a woman can "choose" to go to school. However, rather than see the move as an economic necessity – the fact that she goes back to school to gain a better-paying job – she posits it as a matter of choice. She does not see it as a Third World/First World issue, where economic prosperity as well as the demand for workers in the corporate labor force has opened up "choices" for jobs.

When Kamilla mediates between her parents and her brothers on behalf of Chantal regarding her fitting punishment for speaking to a Black African man, Chantal is amazed that she can talk in such a way: "How could she speak so intimately of an African man and not be divorced by her husband?" (52). It is only later that Chantal understands that Kamilla is rewarded with acceptance and love for her sacrifice. Kamilla takes her newest baby to town and walks into the shop where the African man works, and Chantal sees the wordless communication between them and her sister's touches on his face as she simply says, "Maqhmoud, this is my son, Maqhmoud" (52). The readers as well as Chantal simultaneously realize that Kamilla had sacrificed her love for her family's and community's honour.

In fact, one is reminded here of the adulation of Chatterjee's "new women" in India with "spiritual" qualities of "self-sacrifice, benevolence, devotion, religiosity ..." (233). Such ideas are regularly disseminated throughout the world via Bollywood films. Additionally, the "Divide and Rule" policy of the colonial government and its aftermath is clearly demonstrated here. Therefore, while she hopes for new choices for the new generation, and hopes that with education they, i.e., choices, will come, the Indian way of life, which has stood unchanged for decades, persists in terms of what it means to be an Indian woman in the diaspora, particularly in the Global South; Kamilla, presently as a privileged immigrant in the West, tries to impose her views regarding choice in South Africa. She does not see women's oppression being complicated by race and class struggles, but visualizes it purely in gendered terms.

While Kamilla's story is situated in the earlier decades and shows that change in term of gender roles is problematic in transnational diasporic spaces of the Global South, in Farida Karodia's "Crossmatch," we see translocal and multiple migrations impacting gender and national identity formation for women and gay men of the South Asian diaspora in metropolitan centres of the Global North *and* South.

Farida Karodia, a South African writer, born in 1942, grew up in a small town called Aliwal North in the Eastern Cape. Karodia's father was a Gujarati Indian who had settled in South Africa in 1920 and married a Coloured woman. Karodia, however, considers herself an Indian in spite of her mother's multiracial background (Versi 39). Her idea of herself as Indian is further reinforced by her comment that she feels most at home in India (Versi 40). She taught school in Johannesburg and in Zambia. In 1969, exiled from South Africa due to the apartheid régime, she immigrated to Canada, where she worked as a teacher and as a radio writer. What is of special interest about Karodia is that although she writes predominantly about strong women, she does not consider herself a feminist. "Women, I feel, always had the power to change and create," states Karodia. She adds, "For me, they are the most important elements in the story. I come from a family with very strong women … It was a natural progression to write about strong women" (Chetty, "Exile and Return" 146). However, "she strongly refuses to be categorized as a feminist" and does not see it as a "feminist tendency" to write about strong women characters (Chetty, "Exile" 146). Yet all her strong women are located abroad, even though she acknowledges that even during apartheid, it was women that kept the families together (Chetty, "Exile" 147).

Let us turn our attention to the story "Crossmatch." Situated in Lenasia, an Indian township just outside Johannesburg, the story revolves around the younger Makhanji daughter, Sushila, a successful stage actress residing in London. She is back home to visit her parents and older, unhappily married pregnant sister, Indira. Her father is a successful businessman and her mother an elegant stay-at-home mom. The subtext of the plot shows a post-apartheid South Africa, with its new rich, of which the Makanjis are one, and the rampant poverty and crime in the larger community. Mrs. Makanji complains that she has to wear fake jewellery and not her substantial stash of diamonds and gold, as "Thugs just walk by and yank them right off. If they come off easily, you are lucky, otherwise they drag you by the chain until they break either the chain or your neck" (171). Instead of seeing the larger socio-economic impact of apartheid and post-apartheid policies and legacies, many Indians remain locked in the binary logic of the oppressors, seeing Black Africans simply as *tsotsis*/gangsters, which the author showcases well.

The story begins with Sushila reading a script for a play called *Love under the Banyan Tree*, in which a young wife is trapped in a loveless marriage. Sushila looks at her older sister and realizes that her sister is unhappy in her marriage. Indira has a little daughter and is expecting again. Her mother insists that she loves her first grandchild, even though it is a girl, but would definitely hope for a son from this pregnancy (174). It is only later that Sushila finds out the reasons for her sister's unhappiness; her mother-in-law as well as her husband had insisted that she get an amniocentesis procedure to ascertain the sex of the child; if it was a female, Ravi, Indira's husband told his mother that he would persuade her to abort it in the United States. Indira had refused; hence his abandonment of her while "he's jetting around" the UK and India in order to punish her. The idea of female daughters as a curse seems to follow Indians into the far reaches of the diaspora.

In the next episode, the two sisters are having a discussion regarding Sushila's relationship with Kevin, an Englishman. Indira had found a picture of her sister and her English boyfriend, and declares that, "there'll be hell to pay" if their parents saw the two of them "practically doing it for the camera" ("Crossmatch" 164). Sushila realizes that the "mere thought of her living with a man, let alone an Englishman, would drive her parents crazy" (164). She was particularly certain of her parents' reaction, as at this time, her parents are trying to arrange her marriage with a suitable boy, Dilip Vasant, a chemical engineer teaching at Stanford University in California, who also happens to be visiting his parents in South Africa. Sushila is twenty-eight years old and Dilip is thirty-six. While living in Africa, the Makanjis and the Vasants have constructed their cultural identities as Indian through maintaining what they consider Indian cultural traditions. Mrs. Makanji decries the fact that they have lost Sushila, a good Hindu girl, to a decadent life in England. She asks her husband about her work on the London stage, "What kind of life is that for an Indian girl from a good home?" (169). How do they keep the idea of Indianness alive in the diaspora? Mr. Makanji brings his wife the "finest silk saris money could buy" from his trips to India and Taiwan. Their house is decorated with pictures of Hindu deities: "prints of Krishna playing the flute with the *gopies* dancing around in their colorful skirts, pictures of Lakshmi and Ganesha" on the walls (171); listening to "*The Ghazals*," a Hindi music tape of popular Indian singer, bought by Mrs. Makanji in London (172); and "consulting with an astrologer to fix an auspicious date and time for the meeting" (175) with a suitable boy are all part of the imagination that they had "dragged" (Appadurai) with them across continents to create their imagined Indian community. This imagination is complicated in the post-apartheid era for the affluent Indians who cross cultural and national boundaries and borders of nation-states as and when they please.

Mrs. Vasant, "a traditional Indian woman who always wore a sari," serves traditional Indian food at home – "relishes, chutney, pickles" (176). Mr. And Mrs. Vasant expect their son to carry on the Indian tradition by having an arranged marriage. Mrs. Vasant had cried when she had found out that Dilip, a Hindu boy, was eating meat (177). His mother is portrayed as a simple traditional Indian woman, whose "too tight a bodice ... exposed the upper rise of her breasts. Around her midriff, pinched folds of skin were visible. Her hair hung loose to her waist" (176). How could one refuse to accommodate such parents, who seem to have sacrificed so much for the children's future? He had even taken out his ear stud to appease his parents; now, to appease his parents further and through "guilt," he agrees to meet the girl (177).

Sushila, too, agrees to see the boy to get her parents off her back, although she refuses to wear a sari to the meeting; Mrs. Makanji is afraid that Sushila would turn up in her usual garb of "[t]hose tight, tight, pants.... You can see the shape of everything. Has she no shame to go around in public like that (166)? She declares that "a nice Hindu girl" should not dress in such indecent clothes (166).

However, as Sushila and Dilip are introduced to each other, they realize that they are putting on a show for their parents and are quite comfortable in each other's company and chat easily regarding their parents' "crazy" expectations. Sushila later tells her sister that Dilip is gay; Indira is confused, as she cannot imagine a gay Hindu boy. Later that night, Mrs. Makanji gets up to get a glass of milk and inadvertently discovers the photo of Kevin and Sushila in an embrace, with the words, "To Shushi. My lips, my heart and all those important parts, love you forever! Kevin" (192). She is devastated as she moans, "Such a curse! ... Oh, my God! ... Oh, my God," and clasping her breasts with both her hands, writhes in agony on the floor (192). In the meantime, Sushila wonders how Dilip is ever going to tell his parents about his gayness; she would eventually have to tell her parents about Kevin, but she wants to do it slowly, slowly. Sushila and Dilip can transcend their Indianness in the diasporic spaces of the Global North in San Francisco and London due to their cosmopolitanism; Indira is unable to transcend ideas of gender and nationalism because she is in Johannesburg, which should imply cosmopolitan privilege but simply remains local in some sense, as it is located in the Global South. In such representations of Indians abroad, one can see art and the media (for example, paintings of Indian gods and goddesses, or taped Indian music for London) helping the "complex cultural politics of reproduction in an overseas Indian community" leading to "an understanding of the globalization of Hinduism" as well as Indianness (Appadurai 57) to combat social and cultural colonization.

What is the role of the imagination in transnational, in some sense deterritorialized world (for example, the South Asian gay community in San Francisco) for the "complex, partly imagined lives" of the South Asian diaspora (Appadurai 54)? According to Appadurai,

> The link between the imagination and social life ... is increasingly a global and deterritorialized one. Thus, those who represent real or ordinary lives must resist making claims to epistemic privilege in regard to the lived particularities of social life. Rather, ethnography must redefine itself as that practice of representation that illuminates the power of large-scale, imagined life possibilities over specific life trajectories. This is thickness with a difference, and the difference lies in a new alertness to the fact that ordinary lives today are more often powered not by the givenness of things but by the possibilities that the media (either directly or indirectly) suggests are available. (55)

The South Asians in South Africa are not Indian less because of "natural facts" such as "language, blood, soil, or race – and more out of quintessential cultural product, a product of the collective imagination" (161). Sushila, in her quest for identity, is incapable of thinking beyond what it means to be Indian; her refusal to wear a sari or her thoughts about oppressive loveless arranged marriages are tied to the idea of Indianness that she gets from such texts as *Love Under the Banyan Tree*; she seems "to embrace the very imaginary [she] seeks to escape" (Appadurai 116), for although she seeks to escape one kind of oppression (gender), as a Black woman in England, she cannot very well escape gender and racial oppression. She cannot avoid exoticism and eroticism, as she most certainly will play the loveless wife of the script she is reading.

Appadurai suggests that because of changes or flux in the global conditions of life-worlds, there is no longer a givenness about place; place or locality "has to be painstakingly reinforced in the face of life-worlds that are frequently in flux" (Appadurai 56). It seems that Sushila and Dilip can move to a transnational diasporic space – "the journey from the space of the former colony to the space of the postcolony" – that Appadurai calls the "heart of whiteness" (159). This place is, for Dilip, America, a "postnational space marked by its whiteness but marked too by its uneasy engagement with diasporic peoples, mobile technologies, and queer nationalities" (159). This space is in flux due to global conditions, and negotiations for empowering identity for the migrants or non-Westerns become problematic because of the emphasis on assimilation through multiculturalism, which ultimately reinforces the authority of the centre (Bhabha, *Nation and Narration*? 252). If one imagines that Sushila and Dilip are empowered due to the privileged social status and transnational mobility, and can ignore community and cultural identity, there is also a price to pay. As Appadurai puts it,

> But while we make our identities, we cannot do so exactly as we please. As many of us find ourselves racialized, biologized, minoritized, somehow reduced rather than enabled by our bodies and our histories, our special diacritics become our prisons, and the trope of the tribe sets us off from an other, unspecified America, for from the clamor of the tribe, decorous, civil, and white, a land in which we are not yet welcome. (171)[2]

Appadurai's contention is truer in the post–9/11 Global North. Though Sushila makes her identity as a woman who has choices in terms of love and marriage in England, she remains "Indian" as a stage actress, performing stereotypical roles of loveless Indian women who is "forced into marrying someone [she] despised" (163). While it appears that Sushila and Dilip might be privileged in their hybridity and hybridized space of the metropolitan centres, the reality, as Appadurai posits, and Bhabha points to, is that pluralism in such spaces is premature (Bhabha, "DisseміNation" 139).

While it is true that there is a large visible South Asian gay community in the San Francisco Bay area, it too, as a community, has to combat racial and other forms of oppression and marginalization. In other words, while they celebrate their sexuality as South Asian gays, which they may not be able to do in India as a group, they realize that they are not quite "American" as the absolute acceptance of racial minorities in America as a pluralistic society has still not materialized.

The problems of being racialized as a minority that is not quite accepted into mainstream American society can be seen by the murders of Sikhs and assaults on South Asians immediately following the attack on the World Trade Centre and the Pentagon in September 2001.[3] Too, the imprisonment without due process of terror suspects who look "Muslim" in the Global North reinforces my earlier statement. In such spaces, the dominant ideology of multiculturalism and pluralism finds ways to minimize the challenges posed by the minority communities in order to construct the "host" nation as normative, which also preserves the hegemony of the centre. If in this hybrid stage Dilip and Sushila appear to erase difference through their sexuality, the reality in the Global North is that it has not been able to come to a point where East/West binaries, as Appadurai explains, are no longer deployed. Yet because of the multiple positionings of the characters in Sam's and Karodia's texts, we are seeing new beginnings, as Sushila hopes, while the old are dying, which we see in Mrs. Makanji's piteous moans of defeatism. A new beginning may be a curse to some, while it may be a blessing to others. As Bhabha notes: "Designations of cultural difference interpellate forms of identity which, because of their continual implication in other symbolic systems, are always 'incomplete' or open to cultural translation" (Bhabha, "DissemiNation" 163). Because of the shifting contexts and the dynamic relationship between old and new, between what is considered traditional and modern, there are new possibilities for articulation of identity in transnational diasporic spaces during processes of change.

Thus, even though cultural identities are seemingly unalterable or bound within culturally constituted categories, there is hope for diasporic groups in reconstructing identity along lines of political and social choices. Placed as many diasporic Indians are in an in-between space, they may be the ones to reconstruct and renew as we have seen in these cultural productions. As Appadurai posits, diasporic public spaces are the postnational political order, although "In the short run, as we can already see, it is full of increased incivility and violence" (23), in the long run, free from the constraints of the nation-state, this postnational political order is an exciting space as it portends cultural freedom and sustainable justice (23). Nevertheless, the question of who can inhabit these postnational diasporic spaces for empowerment must be examined for a critical and political understanding of identity construction and representation.

9

Queering Diaspora in Shani Mootoo's *Cereus Blooms at Night*, Nisha Ganatra's *Chutney Popcorn*, and Deepa Mehta's *Fire*

To investigate the politics of location for transnational feminist critical theory and practice, to examine their various uses, and to study the ramification of such practices, we must pay special attention to the politics of production and reception of feminist texts in diasporic cultural spaces (Grewal and Kaplan 2). In an era of globalization and transnational cultural flow, gender representation and construction in the Global North and throughout the world remain problematic, leading us to ask some important questions: How are transnational women's texts theorized and received in the Global North? How do multicultural/diasporic South Asian women construct cultural, national, and gender identity? How do they define gender in cross-cultural spaces of both the Global North and South where ideas of identity take on special meaning? How are hybrid identities and sexualities represented and received in the Global North?

Indian women who construct a separate sexual self from that of the idealized and essentialized notion of "pure" womanhood struggle to depict their identities in troubled territories and diasporic locales. Given resurgent debates on nationalism and gender since 9/11 and the subsequent wars in Iraq and Afghanistan, moreover, it has become difficult for certain diasporic Indian women to negotiate identity even in the "liberal" Global North, where ideas of individualism are seemingly encouraged. Thus, the necessity for transformational creative work for transnational feminist critical theory and practices is urgently needed. At the same time, however, as academics and critics, we need to be extra-vigilant about female writers' representational texts and the politics of their location, particularly their reception and their continued use of modernist assumptions regarding gender in a troubled globalized world.

While looking at the "transnational cultural production and reception" of texts by postmodern and postcolonial feminists, Indrapal Grewal and Caren Kaplan critique "certain forms of feminism [that] emerge from [the feminists'] willing participation in modernity with its colonial discourse and hegemonic First World formations that wittingly or unwittingly lead to the oppression and exploitation of many women" (2). Many so-called feminists support agendas of globalization, thereby misrecognizing and failing to resist "Western hegemonies" (2). Many cosmopolitan women writers see themselves as feminists, and come to inhabit privileged spaces. They then assume to speak for what they come to see as oppressed Indian womanhood, leading to a resumption of "form[s] of feminist cultural imperialism" (137).

How, then, can we read texts such as Shani Mootoo's novel *Cereus Blooms at Night*, Nisha Ganatra's film *Chutney Popcorn*, and Deepa Mehta's film *Fire*? Are these artists perpetuating Western feminism's imperial rescuing mission, or are they too navigating between various heteropatriarchal and feminist concerns (Grewal and Kaplan) which are necessarily depicted through narratives of global modernity (Arif Dirlik)? Or, are their sensibilities so Westernized, as seen by the Western audiences' responses to their work, that white feminists are "[embracing] them as those who 'finally learned their lessons'" (Shohat 12) and can be finally admitted to the ranks of liberated and modern subjects?

For example, in Ganatra's *Chutney Popcorn*, Reena, who is a headstrong and independent lesbian, constantly struggles with her Indian mother's idea of good Indian girls. Once again, we are faced with representation of backward Indian cultural practices clashing with notions of liberal sexualities in diasporic Indian communities in the Global North. Whereas *Chutney Popcorn* suggests hybridized identity constructions in diasporic spaces of the Global North, where arbitrary designs of Indianness prevail, *Fire* portrays ideas of "oppressive" arranged marriages vying with love and lesbianism for liberation and choice in postcolonial India. Of the three texts, Mootoo's literary exploration of alienation and dislocation – sexual as well as national – is more nuanced and multidimensional than the filmic narratives, and provides excellent material for my extensive textual analysis. However, I will show that even an artist as savvy as Mootoo betrays fragmentation of her psyche when she bows down to Western and Westernized sensibilities of her audience in the Global North.

Let us examine *Chutney Popcorn*. Directed and acted by the Canadian-born Ganatra, the film received many awards.[1] The film opens with the gaze of the camera lingering on young female bodies being decorated with what are popularly known as henna tattoos. Just as the film's title connotes Asian Americanness, henna tattoos construct Indian culture as a commodity for American consumption. Born into a Punjabi American family, Reena, the lesbian protagonist of the film, works in a beauty salon in New York and struggles to define her sexual and racial identity in a hybrid space. This diasporic identity is conflicted as Reena negotiates between the transnational social spaces represented by the multicultural beauty salon and the traditional home space provided by Reena's mother, Meena, and the diasporic Indian community. Empowerment for both Reena and her sister, Sarita, comes from constructing independent identities separate from seemingly Indian ones – Sarita marries a white man, Mitch, while Reena dates a white woman. While Sarita's choices are sanctioned by her mother due to her heterosexuality – she is trying to become pregnant – Reena's lesbian sexuality and the presence of her girlfriend are either seemingly ignored or glossed over by Meena (played by Madhur Jaffrey) or become a site for hilarity.

While the film revolves around a gay and a straight sister, the intergenerational conflict takes centre stage. The Indian mother, no matter how long she resides in the West, must try to arrange a marriage for her daughter with a suitable boy. In one scene, she invites Reena's male agemate to the house for tea, knowing Reena will have to talk to this very "nice young man." In yet another scene, when Reena attends her sister's wedding, she stands on the sidelines, dressed in an odd assortment of Indian and Western clothing, unable or unwilling to join members of the Indian community Bhangra dancing to loud Punjabi music. Her mother introduces her lesbian partner, Lisa, as Reena's roommate. Thus, the home space for Reena is rendered inhospitable and unsafe. While the dilemma of racial and sexual identity for young Asian Americans is explored in this film, the immigrant community is rendered as illiberal, only interested in progeny and religious impositions.

When Reena insists that she is a lesbian, her mother seemingly ignores her declaration. Sunaina Marr Maira suggests that "for second generation Indian Americans, ideas about gender roles and sexuality are constructed in both local and global contexts, shaped not just by the expectation of youth cultures and mainstream media, but also by the norms held by immigrant parents and the ethnic community" (153). Maira discusses dating and sexuality in the Indian American community, particularly for girls, and the problems of naming such desires. She suggests that debates regarding arranged marriages, sexuality, and dating among second generation Indian Americans, "with its underlying erotic fantasies, are ... fraught with the politics of not only gender and sexuality but also of nation, generation, and belonging" (153). As can be seen from Maira's discussion, in immigrant communities, sexuality is implicated in the idea of nationalism and in the sense of belonging to the nation. Reena feels at home with all her white women friends in her shared apartment, as well as in the beauty salon, but not in her mother's house or in the Indian community, where she cannot name herself or her sexuality. Naming will make her modern and American. She will belong to a modern nation-state. She will be safe.

Ganatra shows the Indian American community in problematic ways in order to bring the taboo subject of lesbianism to the fore, while the Canadian-based Deepa Mehta's *Fire* shows construction of gender and sexuality through two sisters-in-law's lesbian love for each other. *Fire* also received much critical acclaim in the West.[2] The Western audience's admiration for these films is not to be negated. As Gayatri Gopinath points out in "Local Sites/Global Contexts: The Transnational Trajectories of Deepa Mehta's *Fire*," this film was "funded largely with Canadian money [and] had circulated from 1996 to 1998 mostly at international film festivals in India, Europe, and North America and had a lengthy art house release in major U.S. cities" ("Local Sites" 149). As noted, the film was first released mostly at international film festivals as well as at art houses in the U.S. and abroad, but because of its controversial representations, it erupted into mainstream cultural and urban spaces in India and other diasporic spaces of the Global North.

The film's narrative portrays the lives of two sisters-in-law in a middle-class New Delhi neighborhood who are oppressed or ignored by their respective husbands. Radha (Shabana Azmi) and Sita (Nandita Das) – named after mythic heroines who are supposedly self-sacrificing, pure, and idealized wives – provide most of the labour for the family business as well as for the household. Radha's husband experiments with sexual asceticism because she cannot procreate, while Sita's newly wedded husband continues his sexual liaison with an Americanized Chinese hairdresser. Sita's husband views arranged marriages as backward and oppressive, but still tries to impregnate her as his duty, which is carried out in a distasteful and callous manner. He literally rapes her. Eventually, the sisters-in-law turn to each other for support and comfort. That this support and community takes the form of sexual expression – lesbian love – between two sisters-in-law is the focus of much controversy – in fact, becoming a "Hindu dilemma" in India.[3]

While critiquing this film, one has to be mindful of the right-wing Hindu government's reaction to it. The film does bring a taboo topic to the fore, and the director must certainly be lauded for her considerable effort so that needed social and cultural transformation can occur. However, it does so at the cost of demonizing Indian patriarchy and fetishizing oppression in monolithic terms. Additionally, in a culture where same-sex expressions of affection are not seen as deviant, the portrayal of Sita and Radha, as two typical middle-class wives who enjoy community and show affection in sexualized terms might have long-term detrimental effects on same-sex support (see Madhu Kishwar's discussion). How many sisters-in-law oil each other's hair on a regular basis in India – or Burma, where I was born and raised, for that matter-- and are never considered deviant? I saw such acts on a daily basis within my own family. However, in this film, Sita and Radha eventually leave the "oppressive" household – after Radha miraculously escapes being burned alive by her husband (shades of Sita's *Agni Pariksha)* – portending a life of love, liberty, and independence. In one scene in *Fire*, Sita comments to Radha about lesbian love and notes that there is no word in their language to describe what they feel for each other. Western critics view the narrative in terms of the Indians' inability to "articulate lesbianism, which in turn signifies the failure of the non-West to progress toward the organization of sexuality and gender prevalent in the West" (Gopinath 153). For example, in *Chutney Popcorn*, for Reena's mother, not naming Reena's sexuality does not mean that she negates her lesbianism; she does not see the need for it, as many first generation immigrants do not see the need to name their children's sexuality, hetero or homo. Gopinath suggests that non-disclosure regarding dating and sexuality in the Indian immigrant community harkens back to India, but for Reena, naming this identity appears paramount because "within the dominant discursive production of India as anterior to the West, lesbian or gay identity is explicitly articulated as the marker of full-fledged modernity" (Gopinath 153). Both Ganatra and Mehta fall into the category of writers who favour modernity and therefore have become complicit with Western ideology by showcasing oppressed Indian women in simple binary constructions. However, when we as transnational feminists critique the showcasing of gender oppression in such simple binaries as limiting, there is a danger of us being labelled fascists or as being in cahoots with right-wing heteropatriarchal fundamentalists in perpetuating gender and sexual oppression. Monica Bachmann, for example, demands the right to "choose ... the ability to be open with the world about intimate relations" for homosexual Indians (237). Again, the word "choice" becomes conflated with liberty and liberation in Western terms, as though homosexual people are not persecuted in the Global North. Bachmann's article implies that we, who dare critique *Fire* for its limitations, are trying to silence and censor lesbians. Bachmann claims that for political and social change to occur, sexual oppression must be articulated, for "analysis has shown that separating [the personal and the political] is impossible, linked as they are to kinship and economic structures that encompass both the most intimate and the most public relations" (240). Bachmann's assertion appears valid, for paradigms do shift, leading to expansion and social change; however, we must engage political structures strategically, and toward that end, work with majority groups by forming coalitions within a given paradigm. Otherwise, feminist voices simply become a fashion statement, as seen in many parts of the Global North.

Modernity and the construction of liberated sexuality are also showcased in Shani Mootoo's writing. Mootoo, who was born in Ireland and grew up in Trinidad, is a filmmaker and visual artist who now resides in Canada. Her first novel, *Cereus Blooms at Night* (1996), is set in a fictional Caribbean island called Paradise, in Lantanacamara. Mootoo, a product of four cultures – India, Ireland, England, and Trinidad – shows her characters negotiating in and out of many different and difficult spaces. Her novel focuses on homosexual and transsexual identity construction for the transnational subject.

Mootoo focuses her attention on the members of the Indian diasporic community in the Caribbean and their painful search for personal and sexual identities. She portrays the struggles and pain of the displaced and dispossessed Indo-Caribbeans who, due to severe colonial oppression and postcolonial/neocolonial conditions, become alienated, and in their alienation we see the internal and external violence of the subjects shaped in this troubled space taking extreme forms. Abused, they either become abusers, or find escape – in the in-between spaces, through a maddening descent into the void, or through displacement, physical or metaphoric, to the "liberating" spaces of the West. Yet beyond madness in Bhabha's "Third Space" ("DissemiNation" 149), there is transformation for Mootoo's characters; through healing, there is hope, there is an idealized space for all creatures, mad, queer, or the nervous, and this space too is predominantly located in the Global North. How do we provide a postcolonial criticism of Mootoo's seemingly hopeful text? I examine Mootoo's politics of location to provide an analysis of the novel's characters, and show how they can be misread and (mis)interpreted by mainstream readers.

The narrative begins with the arrival of Mala Ramchandin, a madwoman suspected of murder, to the Paradise Alms House. The circular narrative reveals the story of Mala's family, which spans about sixty years, to the present time. The narrator of the story is Nurse Tyler, whose own story of sexual ambiguity is interwoven with Mala's sexual abuse, as well as with her mother's lesbian love for Lavinia, a white woman her father used to be in love with. The subplot of the story revolves around Ambrosia, or Otoh, the "son" of Mala's childhood friend, Ambrose (or Boyee). Otoh is born a female but convinces everyone that she is male. Such characterizations of madness and sexual ambiguity are linked to colonialism's oppression and exploitation.

We see colonialism's oppressive practices and their effect on the Indians in the Caribbean. Mala's father, Chandin Ramchandin, the son of indentured labourers, who is "adopted" by a white missionary, Reverend Thoroughly, eventually becomes so alienated from himself due to English education that, in the end, he perpetrates the worst kind of sexual and physical abuse on his own family members. As Frantz Fanon explains about the colonized in *The Wretched of the Earth*, colonialism uses extreme violence to keep the colonized oppressed, and when the oppressed subject reaches the limits of tolerance, he/she either explodes in revolt, or implodes (61). Since violence is also cyclical, the abused then becomes the abuser. Many postcolonial/neocolonial economies, such as Zimbabwe, Uganda, South Africa, many parts of the Caribbean, Burma, just to provide a few examples, attest to the theory of cyclical violence. This "nervous condition" of the postcolonial subject is amply represented in Mootoo's narrative. We see madness in Chandin – who ultimately constructs his masculinity in opposition to the abused body of his daughter, Mala – exploding in the text.

Chandin's soul is imprisoned by colonial ideology, as can be seen from his tutelage by Reverend Thoroughly. According to Ngugi, "the bullet was the means of the physical subjugation [of the colonized]. Language was the means of spiritual subjugation" (5). If, as Ngugi claims, the introduction of the colonizer's language is like a "cultural bomb" that changes the psyche of the victim, we can see such cultural violence represented in Chandin's character. Ngugi asserts that language was the most important vehicle by means of which the colonizers kept the soul of the colonized imprisoned; we see such examples when Chandin, as a young boy, is torn from his family. Imperceptibly, the boy's psyche begins to shift. He starts to believe in the superiority of the White man: "In his innocence he felt that his people's lack of these things (the chandelier, the fine cabinets, carved chairs and side tables and lamps with fancy shades in the Reverend's house) was a result of apathy and a poverty of ambition. He thought of his parents' mud house and the things there [and] felt immense distaste for his background and the people in it" (30–31). The outsider's viewpoint is really well put by the author, who can see the dismal quality of life in the Indian homes. However, the outlook appears more dismal than it should, for, having spent only a few days in the Reverend's home, it seems unlikely that Chandin could become so aware of the stark difference between the two homes. However, Mootoo, who lived in the Caribbean until the age of nineteen and now resides in Canada, could and did see the immense disparity between the two lifestyles and so can write it with such clarity, yet in simple binaries, for the Western audience. One must be aware of the metropolitan privilege of such writers who can negotiate two territories with relative ease; although she herself is still a minority in the West, Mootoo's accounts of the dismal lifestyles of the Indo-Caribbean, though not unfounded, are highly exaggerated. However, for Western readers, the Indo-Caribbeans appear gloomy and dreadful; there is no heterogeneity in their representations and they appear homogeneously oppressed and oppressive, leading truncated lives.

Chandin, who painstakingly copies the Reverend's mannerisms, practises for the power to change. His love for Lavinia, the Reverend's daughter, presents additional pressure to "improve." However, he soon realizes that Lavinia can never belong to him because the Reverend, who surmises his intense feelings for his daughter, expressly forbids the liaison on the grounds that she is his sister, even though Chandin is "adopted." Because of the Reverend's treatment of him, and because Lavinia, suddenly relocated to the West, is now out of his reach, Chandin turns to Sarah, "a woman from his background," for security (45). Chandin, who still mourns the loss of Lavinia, is an indifferent and "dispassionate" (49) husband to Sarah, and the two seldom speak to each other unless it is strictly necessary. Soon, Lavinia returns, raising Chandin's hopes. However, Lavinia returns only to elope with Sarah, whom we now know to be her lover, to the West where they can be "safe" as a family (59). What is of considerable importance here are ideas of sexualities which are seen as deviant in the Caribbean but are seen as perfectly acceptable in the West. Knowing the persecution and discrimination members of the gay community suffer in the West, one wonders at such utopic representation of the West in many Westernized Indian texts.

Tragically and inadvertently, however, they leave Sarah's two daughters behind, and soon, Lantanacamarans come to know that "Chandin pick up with [his] older daughter" (47).

Later, when Ambrose (Boyee), Mala's childhood friend, returns from the West, educated and gentrified, he finds Mala leading a truncated life as her drunken father's caretaker; Asha has eventually run off to the West and to liberty from her father's abuse. Ambrose starts to woo Mala again. As their love for each other blossoms, the increased threat from Chandin becomes imminent. One day, when he discovers the romance, his incest and increased sexual and physical brutalization of Mala's body shove her into madness. Years later, when Otoh, Ambrose's son, comes to deliver some food for Mala, her delusional mind misrecognizes him as Boyee, leading him to her father's skeleton in the basement. In his panic, he inadvertently leads the police to her house, becoming the instrument of Mala's incarceration at the Paradise Alm House. Tyler, the male nurse – "who was neither properly man nor woman but some in-between, unnamed thing" (71) – could identify with Mala because "she has secrets and I had secrets" – the secret of Mala's incest (124). He could also eventually become a lover to Otoh, or Ambrosia, the "son" of Ambrose. The circular narrative allows us to see Mala's sexual oppression, and gives us an insight into Chandin's tormented soul, fractured by colonialism, manifesting in cyclical violence and eventual madness.

Even though colonialism's violence is contextualized well in Mootoo's text, many Western and Westernized critics show Indo-Caribbean Hindu patriarchy and masculinity as ultimately monolithically oppressive and violent. Take Brinda Mehta's analysis of Mootoo's *Cereus Blooms at Night*, for example, where she *does* provide a careful historical perspective of Indian plantation indentured servitude and colonial violence, leading to further violence in the post-indenture period, *but* she too eventually falls prey to imperialist feminist ideology when she sees the *Hindu* household as *inherently* violent, "especially in terms of their control over women" (194).

What is flawed in many so-called feminist critical analyses is the valorization of the West as a liberatory space. While pondering deviancy and its definition, Tyler thinks about his own "perversion" and concludes that his desire to go abroad has less to do with his wish to study there than with wanting to be in a place where his sexuality will not be seen as perverse, only his "foreignness" (47). When Tyler and Otoh stroll in the garden arm in arm, Hector, the gardener, wishes that his gay brother, who left town (presumably for the liberating West!) never to be seen again, could meet the two of them. When Elsie, Otoh's mother, declares that there are always a "handful of people like you in every village" (238), Otoh evinces surprise at her mother's knowledge of her sexuality, at which Elsie claims, "You think because I never say anything that I forgot what you are" (237), very much in the manner of Reena's mother, Meena. The idea of naming is Western and is then monolithically imposed on to all communities. For Mootoo, who dwells in the West, queerness is "conceptualized in motion," and she suggests queerness will suddenly be proclaimed and named in the Caribbean, for she deploys "nostalgia" as "a means by which to imagine [herself] within those spaces from which [she] is perpetually excluded or denied existence" (Gopinath, *Impossible* 186). Additionally, the narrative points to a liberatory space in the egalitarian West, where "deviant" sexualities can be proclaimed loudly, leading one to modernity and to belonging to the modern nation-state, which in itself is a myth for many gays and lesbians in a nation that continues to discriminate against and brutalize many minorities, including, of course, homosexuals. What is problematic in this text is that once the fluid sexualities of the Third World spaces begin to be defined by First World ideology, misreadings occur, sometimes purposefully. It is not that queerness is suddenly going to be accepted in Lantanacamara; as Elsie declares, there have always been people like Otoh around. As Shohat suggests, Westernized "elites have absorbed the binaristic sexual norms of their colonizers, even in the Middle East/North Africa [and I add, South Asia], where a kind of informal bisexuality had sometimes been tacitly accepted" (20). It is only when Western ideas of gayness and patriarchal oppressions are imposed onto the cultural spaces of the Global South that the problem takes on a new face.

Take India, for example. In a land of fluid sexualities (and unofficial bisexuality) where women have had solidarity and community in domestic spaces for centuries without it being termed feminist, womanist, or lesbian/gay, it is only with the modernist agenda and recent movies such as Deepa Mehta's *Fire*, as well as the Hindu fundamentalists' reactionary politics, that discussion of such practices as deviant are coming into popular discourse. Even with that, the majority of India remains disconnected. In Paradise, if Tyler and Otoh find acceptance as a couple, it is because of the previously mentioned sensibilities and not because in the new millennium we are stepping into an idealized and utopian New World Order. On the other hand, representing mythical spaces, such as Ireland and Canada, where gay sexualities are accepted as normal, as seen by Sarah's and Lavinia's example, and where only race matters for immigrants as Tyler suggests (48), distorts the reality of minority and gay oppression, particularly for gays of colour. While there are urban centres and spaces where there is more visibility for gays of colour, they are still extremely marginalized and often exploited members of the gay community. In many gay film festivals, for example, films of or by gays of colour are tokenized and fetishized, as are gays of colour themselves.

Therefore, in reading *Cereus Blooms at Night*, one must not forget the location of the writer, the text, and the reception of it in the Global North or in privileged diasporic spaces in the Global South. In addition, and regarding race, while the text is located in the Caribbean, there is no Afro-Caribbean presence in the novel. While the narrative too is reflexive of the Black/White dualism, and where the Caribbean is represented as dismal, abusive, and oppressive, and where freedom, liberty, and happiness are located in the West, one wonders at the absolute absence of Afro-Caribbean or mixed-race elements; if any are present, one is hard pressed to find them. Even the Indo-Caribbean identity is ambiguous for the most part. That remains incidental. We are always only sure about the White presence. Mootoo becomes complicit in the exploitation of Afro- and Indo-Caribbean landscapes by "supporting the agenda of modernity" as she "misrecognize[s] and fail[s] to resist Western hegemonies" (Grewal and Kaplan 2). She, along with Ganatra and Mehta, falls prey to the "conventional belief in travel as transformation" as she resides, works, and publishes in the West (Grewal and Kaplan 141). It is the utopic space that these diasporic writers, along with the Westernized feminist critics, point to that is so disturbing, particularly due to neocolonialism and transnationalism in a globalized and post–9/11 world.

Vijay Mishra defines two types of diasporas – the diaspora of early and late capital. The early capital diaspora is the working class or the diaspora of plantation labour, while the diaspora of late capital is "distinguished by movements of economic migrants ... into the metropolitan centers of the former empires" (234). Mehta, Ganatra, and Mootoo, as well as their viewers and critics, belong to the diaspora of late capital, "generally referred to as NRIs (non-resident Indians) and largely seen as upwardly mobile" (Mishra 234). A diasporic imaginary growing out of a sense of marginality, of being rejected outright, desperately "try to hang on to values that mark their differences from the rest of the nation-state" (Mishra 234), such as tradition, community, and family, while the attraction for the hybridized selves, such as Ganatra, Mehta, and Mootoo, is to love, sexuality, and liberty. My point is that while artists as socially responsible critics must bring oppressive practices to the forefront of debates in order for social and structural change to occur, they must not replicate imperialist feminists' agendas, particularly during these troubled times where violence shadows the everyday existence of many minorities, including members of the gay community. We must also be careful how we critique Indian female-authored texts. As Kirsten Holst Petersen pointed out so long ago, it is an oversimplification that a "woman's view is always bound to be more valid than a man's" in the discussion of women's oppression (251), and similarly, it is an oversimplification to think that an Indian woman's opinion regarding Indian women's monolithic oppression is always going to be legitimate.

The audiences of such films and texts are often the Euro-interpellated elite. Ganatra, Mehta, and Mootoo (very much like the Nigerian Buchi Emecheta whom Petersen critiques), can recreate the situation and difficulties of women with authenticity and give valuable insights into their thoughts and feelings. [Their] prime concern is not so much with cultural liberation, nor with social change. To [them] the object seems to be to give women access to power in the society as it exists, to beat men at their own game. [They] lay claim to no ideology, not even a feminist one. [They] simply ignore the [Indian] dilemma. (Peterson 254)

Years later, Ketu H. Katrak's "Decolonizing Culture," as well as Mohanty's "Under Western Eyes," echoed Petersen's stance. To be truly empowering models for feminist pedagogy, our readings of *Fire* and *Chutney Popcorn* must contextualize both the upwardly mobile middle-class milieu of Sita and Radha's families and the metropolitan spaces of Reena's and Sarita's lived worlds, as well as the directors'. These artists are modern and show modernity as a marker for equality.

As multicultural and transnational postcolonial feminists, we must see that resistance is not merely posited in gendered terms for a politically engaged pedagogy; it requires multicultural as well as postcolonial concerns. These three diasporic texts are marked by the artists' metropolitan as well as nationalist sensibilities; the reception of their texts suggests that the debate regarding individual vs. communal identity is still being posited in modern terms, long after debates regarding the modern moment should have passed, leading to a skewered perception of Indian culture, Indian womanhood, Indian masculinity, and Indian patriarchy. In institutions of higher learning, where issues of multiculturalism, transnationalism, and feminism are taught interchangeably in efforts toward curriculum diversification, dissemination of stereotypes leading to discrimination against ethnic and sexual minorities continues to occur in dangerous ways.

Due to the increased racism and violence that many ethnic minorities have been recently facing in the Global North, we must ask: Are feminist political concerns separate from multicultural concerns? More importantly, how can we, as transnational feminists, continue to critique and teach postcolonial texts that represent 'oppressed and powerless Indian women' brutalized by a monolithic indigenous patriarchy – be it in the 'First' or 'Third World' diasporic spaces – for a Westernized and Western audience? In hierarchical social and political spheres, can transnational feminists focus only on feminist concerns – for all women, homosexual or heterosexual – ignoring racism, elitism, and globalism? According to Shohat, "the mutual embeddedness between transnational and multicultural struggles" must be highlighted, and feminists must pay special attention to "the political intersectionality of all ... axes of stratification" (1), be it class, race, gender, or sexuality. Shohat argues that "even with the best of intentions, a fetishized focus on African female genital mutilation or on Asian foot-binding ends up as complicit with a Eurocentric victimology that reduces African or Asian agency and organizing" (9).

Gender issues must be theorized within a "conflictual community" in complex and strategic ways, where oppression in certain practices does not "perpetuate the false dichotomy of savagery versus civilization or tradition versus modernity" (Shohat 9); otherwise, social and structural change, the goal of all feminist writing and organizing, becomes just empty rhetoric. Thus, as global, postcolonial/transnational/multicultural feminists, we must not duplicate the colonial narrative of a rescuing mission. Instead, we must share the "critique of hegemony and the burden of representation" (9). Our work, especially with resurgent global debates on nationalism and national belongings in recent years, and particularly regarding the politics of location for transnational critics like us who continue to read and teach postcolonial literature and theory in the West, has just begun.[4]

10

Transnationalism and the Politics of Representation in the Texts of Meena Alexander, Gurinder Chadha, Zainab Ali, and Samina Ali

PART ONE:
EXILE, MEMORY, AND TRAUMA IN MEENA ALEXANDER'S TEXTS

How does Meena Alexander construct an American identity for herself through her fragmented, traumatized diasporic consciousness and "postcolonial memory" (*Shock* 1)? She attempts to write about women who are not only mad, but who through madness rewrite themselves in maddening diasporic and transnational spaces produced by violence through "global modernity" (Arif Dirlik). She doesn't write only about women who jumped into wells to drown; the women she attempts to write about are the "well jumped women" – women with "saris swept up shamelessly, high above the ankles, high above the knees, women well jumping: jumping over wells," (*Shock* 206), even if the Western audience only wants to hear about "palm trees and back waters" (206) of Kerala. Yet, Alexander is finally unsuccessful in negotiating the First World academic and privileged territories in order to bring "well jumping women" to the Western audience, for she falls into the trap of fetishizing "oppressed Third World Women" for a Western audience, leading to repetition compulsion and to voyeurism.

Alexander's *Manhattan Music* examines cultural border crossing and diasporic experience, commenting on interracial relationships and marriage and ideas of cultural and national belongings. In her autobiographical novel, *Fault Lines*, Alexander writes: "I am a woman cracked by multiple migrations. Uprooted so many times I can connect nothing with nothing" (2). Alexander, a poet and a novelist, was born in Allahabad, India, has lived in Sudan and England, and now lives in the United States. In *The Shock of Arrival*, she writes, "The shock of arrival is multifold – what was borne in the mind is jarred, tossed into new shapes, an exciting exfoliation of the senses.... What the immigrant must work with is what she must invent in order to live" (3). This shock shows that the questions of race, ethnicity, gender, and nationality are all arbitrary signs to be contested and revised, so that one can reconstruct one's subjectivity anew.

Alexander reclaims the memory of oppressed "Third World Women" to reconstruct her subjectivity anew in the First World. Is that memory "heteropathic" or "idiopathic" (Silverman 185), and what does that mean? In "Projected Memory: Holocaust Photographs," Marianne Hirsch elaborates on Kaja Silverman's terms by explaining that in "heteropathic" identification, the remembering subject identifies with the victim at a distance, whereas in "idiopathic" identification, it identifies overappropriately, where "distances disappears, creating too available, too easy an access to [a] particular past," thereby creating an "appetite for alterity" (408). The artist who remembers the painful events in the lives of victims must "resist appropriation and incorporation, resist annihilating the distance between self and other, the otherness of others" (Hirsch 407), otherwise, due to the "appetite for alterity" and "overappropriation," the remembering subject will construct itself as a "surrogate victim" (Hirsch 414).

Alexander's poetry shows her fragmentation in interesting ways. For example, in "Alphabets of Flesh," the poet writes: "My back against the barbed wire/snagged and coiled to belly height.... Slow accoutrements of habits/and of speech/the lust of grief/the savagery of waste/flicker and burn.... Come ferocious alphabets of flesh/splinter and raze my page/that out of dumb/and bleeding part of me/I may claim my heritage

... to cacophony" (*Shock* 15). Postcolonial poets such as Alexander use Bhabha's hybridized "Third Space" to reconstruct and re-turn to "claim [their] heritage" after the trauma of alienation. While analyzing Cesaire's poetry, for example, Michael Dash asserts that "he re-enacts the need to reintegrate the exiled subject in the lost body [and] imagines the journey of the disembodied subject across the estranging waters and the eventual reintegration of the body with the *pays natal*" (332). Dash suggests that for the subject to be reintegrated, it must first "overcome the initial revulsion ... [and] must radically redefine notions of time, space, beauty and power before return becomes possible, and must strip away all illusions ... empty consciousness of all pretensions" (332). Male writers have used "verbal muscularity" for the "spiritual awakening expressed in images of revitalized physicality" (334). To feel whole, to be reintegrated, to be "fulfilled is a *ceaseless* task of the psyche," claim Petersen and Rutherford (189).

Alexander, too, explores the "liberatory space" found through nationalism in the Global South as well as in the diaspora in order to question, reconstruct, and reinscribe the "mutilated and dismembered" female body (Dash 334), not only of her own but also of many oppressed "Third World" women. However, Alexander's attempt at reintegration appears incomplete as she seems unable to overcome her revulsion for her disembodied self. For reanimation of the castrated and dismembered male body, poets use the liberatory space found in revolutionary movements. For Alexander, diasporic cultural spaces created by border crossings are used to rewrite herself. How far can we take intertextuality in terms of writing on the "mutilated" body of the displaced and alienated subject? This question is particularly important for the diasporic writer, such as Alexander, who by her own testimony was never wrenched from her home but crossed the ocean out of choice. How is it that this artist who belongs to the "diaspora of hope" uses the words of subjects who belong to the "diaspora of despair" and "terror" (Appadurai, *Modernity at Large* 6)?

Alexander argues that the female Indian body, after nationalism, had to "bear the pitiful burden of repressed desire and the pain of withdrawn sexuality" (*Shock* 182). Here, of course, Alexander gestures toward the "new women" of nationalist discourse. All the repressed sexuality of women in India is in Alexander's memory, for she says, "The voice that is other grows great. It bursts through the body. It sings. The world that [women writers] wrote from is not far from me. I bear it within. It becomes part of the memory I need for knowledge of this new world, part of a migrant music" (*Shock* 192). Alexander's idiopathic identification with the sexually repressed and oppressed collective female Indian bodies constructs for us a pastiche of the Indian woman body, be it in India or the diaspora, as she rewrites herself anew in the new world through "projection ... [and] over-appropriation" (Hirsch 411) at the expense of the real victims of oppression in the U.S. nation-states and in other postcolonial spaces. While her images are powerful and she shows that rewriting and reimagining can occur through violence and the Foucauldian limit experience, she does not belong to Appadurai's "diaspora of despair" as she would like her audiences to believe. I argue that because of her privileged background the author is unable to "address the concerns of women around the world in the historical particularity of their relationship to multiple patriarchies as well as to international economic hegemonies" (Grewal and Kaplan 17).

Let us explore some examples of Alexander's "idiopathic identification" and her easy construction of a *pays natal* that for many Indians, born in Burma (Myanmar), or Uganda, or what is now Pakistan, for example, was brutally wrenched from them. In the *Shock of Arrival*, Alexander calls "history a mad, mad joke" (119). She is a person of the diaspora of hope, in Appadurai's terms, as "[she] did not leave [her] motherland because of terror or political repression. [She] was not torn away from [her] ancestral home by armed militants" (*Shock* 116). Instead, her story is that her well-educated and well-to-do father wanted to teach in another country, "far away ... across an ocean and a sea ... a country in North Africa" (*Shock* 116).

Brought up in a well-to-do Syrian Christian family in Kerala, Alexander recalls her childhood of plenitude even though traumas of sexual abuse are hinted at, yet repressed. When she was four or five, her father took the family to Sudan, where she grew up, and at the young age of thirteen, attended the University of Khartoum. Eventually, she studied in England at the University of Nottingham for her Ph.D. She taught at Delhi University, Central Institute of Hyderabad, Hyderabad University. Now, she is a professor at Hunter College and the Graduate Center of the City University of New York. Yet despite of all these possibilities, she writes,

> What might it mean to look at myself straight, see myself? ... My voice splintered in my ears into a cacophony: whispering cadences, shouts, moans, the quick delight of bodily pleasure,

all rising up as if the condition of being fractured had freed the selves jammed into my skin, multiple beings locked into the journeys of one body. (1)

So how does her splintered body write herself back into wholeness? What are her traumas, besides going through multiple migrations? Her repressed sexual abuse by her grandfather (Alexander, *Fault Lines* 302) splintered her sexuality, but her fragmented identity, which she claims is due to her multiple migrations, and which she "sutures" back with the "thread of memory," seems flawed, constructed as it is for First World voyeurism. For in spite of belonging to the diaspora of hope, she continues to ask, "am I a creature with no home, no nation? And if so, what new genus could I possibly be" (*Shock* 116)? What genus, exactly? And what of people who are part of these diasporic sensibilities, who for one reason or another, whether they acknowledge it or not, are interpellated due to "modernity at large" (Appadurai) belonging to the diaspora of hope, and yet appropriate idioms of the diasporas of despair, or sorrow? Do these three dwell in separate spaces, or do these spaces collide, intermingle, and cross-fertilize?

In spite of the awareness that no one forced her out of India, in Alexander's fragmented psyche, "Words [recoil] back into a vacant space ... [which is a] place of waste, dingy detritus of a life uncared for, no images to offer it hospitality" (*Shock* 116). As a woman, this fragmentation has led her toward "tale telling" where she has to "unlearn the fixed positioning she was taught" (*Shock* 117). Unlearning takes place in many parts of the world that she travels to. Alexander cites the tipsy houses that she dwells in, "houses to be born in, houses to die in, houses to make love in wet, sticky sheets, houses with the pallor of dove's wings, houses fragrant as cloves and cinnamon ground together," yet she is unable to name any of the houses as empowering, for "her tongue has grown thick" (*Shock* 119). This thickness occurs due to the suffering she witnesses. In Sudan, the acrid smell of tear gas invades her shivering body. In England, she writes a thesis about memory, "while [her] mind cuts loose from her body and circles empty space" (*Shock* 120). In Palghat, in her ancestral home, she "becomes mute," wrapped in "reams of paper" and shit (*Shock* 120). In New York, where her house is "split through, a fault in the ground where she stands, [her] soul is auctioned off," and this split and fragmented psyche, looking for its home, calms down through the remembered road between "Tiruvella and Kozhencheri," and the feeling of home this road provides (*Shock* 121). The alienated subject remembers an idealized space for reconstruction.

Still, whenever she crosses a border, she dies a little (*Shock* 93), and out of this death, a new life emerges, "tearing up the old skin" toward a new consciousness (*Shock* 93), which includes a desiring sexualized subject. Alexander states that when the body turns into a "brutal instrument" in the "surreal theater of cruelty that fractures identities, [leading] to the sudden eruptions of sexual desire [and] small explosions of pleasure, the second language of violence serves to force into visibility the longing for love" (*Shock* 86). The body becomes the site for cruelty, the site of passion and longing and the site for sexuality. When the body sinks into nothingness, into a void, it forces "us back into the fraught compact between body and language," and it is only "in the teeth of violence that we can speak the unstable truths of our bodies" (*Shock* 78). Alexander interchanges the meaning of the body and the soul, as she sees woman as "prisoner of her sex" (*Shock* 67), like her imaginary "mad" aunt Chinna (*Shock* 52).

The new consciousness born of violence leads Alexander into marrying a White American man and moving to the United States of America and eventually making it to the Ivory Tower in New York. Here, in this new space, eruptive and volatile, she can name herself and even her sexuality anew. She states, "And the possibilities for female expressivity becomes multifarious, even verging on the explosive" (*Shock* 83). She must translate herself anew in these conflicted spaces. Sexuality or the lack of it becomes the trope of modernity and cultural belonging for her. Even though in *The History of Sexuality*, Foucault envisions a space for "bodies and pleasures" that go beyond "sex desire," he laments that for the modern person, "truth" is inscribed in the body and soul and can only be recovered "through sex" (155). Each person, argues Foucault, must pass through sex "in order to have access to his own intelligibly (since it is simultaneously the hidden element and the productive principle of sense), to the totality of the body (since it is a real and menaced part of it, and symbolically constitutes the whole), [and] to his identity (since it joins to the force of an impulse the singularity of history" (155–56). He adds that while in earlier times it was love that the West discovered and deployed, [bestowing] on it a value high enough to make death acceptable ... nowadays, it is sex that claims this equivalence, the highest of all. And while the deployment of sexuality permits the techniques of power to invest life, the fictitious point in sex, itself marked by that deployment, exerts enough charm on everyone for them to accept hearing the grumble of death within it. (156)

Examples of such investments in sexuality, even through the "grumble of death within" the subject as it comes into words, are abundantly present in Alexander's texts.

In America, Alexander sees modern and sexualized subjects who reclaim their bodies, sexualities, and souls as "the [women] who [were] permitted everything" (*Manhattan Music* 2) and compares them to the "Third World" women "whose veins were etched with centuries of arranged marriages, dark blue blood pouring through" (4). For example, Sandhya, the protagonist of *Manhattan Music*, could point to a "plot of land bounded by granite walls and name ancestors who had owned land for generations.... Then too, she remembered the cemeteries where her grandparents were buried, the houses that held them, the rites under which they were married" (*Manhattan* 4). Draupati, the hybridized and diasporic subject, permitted everything, must bring Sandhya, the oppressed Indian women, into her sexuality and identity as defined by her Westernized intellectual self.

Fault Lines is full of references to the suffering masses and oppressed "Third World" women, with their arranged marriages and abusive husbands, and the romanticized space of plenitude which is Tiruvella. And while the author herself roams the earth as if it belongs to her – "Allahabad, Tiruvella, Kozencheri, Pune, Khartoum, Cairo, Beirut, Jerusalem, Dubai, London, New York, Minneapolis, Saint Paul, New Delhi, Trivandrum," she claims to be suffering the trauma of exile and its consequent fragmentation, while trying to rewrite herself back into a whole through memory. She calls herself "a nowhere creature," who has no "home, no fixed address, no shelter" (30). When she left India, she writes: "My life shattered into little bits and pieces. In my dreams, I am haunted by thoughts of a homeland I will never find. So I have turned my lines into a different aesthetic, one that I build up out of all the stuff around me, improvising as

I go along" (27). She is an improviser, she can rewrite herself anew, from fragments to wholeness, from nothing – "a woman cracked by multiple migrations [who] can connect nothing to nothing" (2) – to all the privileges of the First World!

Alexander's prose is full of descriptions of places she has travelled to, the well-known people she's met along the way; it is also liberally peppered with vignettes of the suffering masses and oppressed women for whom she suffers. But first, her own pain is reflected in comments in her Khartoum journal that she provides as witness to the misery she went through: "If you want me to live as a woman, why educate me?" "Why not kill me if you want to dictate my life?" "God, why teach me to write?" (*Fault* 208). She suggests that these lines are not really aimed at God, but at her mother. "The fault," she writes, "lay in the tension I felt between the claims of my intelligence – what my father had taught me to honor, what allowed me to live my life – and the requirements of a femininity my mother had been born and bred in. Essential to the latter is an arranged marriage" (*Fault* 102). While it would appear that she finds, as an educated woman in Sudan attending co-ed parties, meeting boys, and sensing her sexual desires, that the idea of arranged marriages might not appeal to her, in actuality she finds fault with the very institution of arranged marriages. In fact, she admits to her mother, "Amma, those dreams of an arranged marriage almost destroyed me" (*Fault* 208). She cannot understand why her mother settled for one. Even her imaginary maternal grandmother had married a "man of her choice" (*Fault* 208)! She asks her mother bluntly, "So how did you feel when your own marriage was arranged" (*Fault* 206)? She seems to indicate that she married David Lelyveld to escape such a fate. In between the narrative, we read about bride burning:

> As adult women we were facing the reality of women in arranged marriages – housewives and government workers, college lecturers and doctors, all young women married in accordance with their parents' wishes – who were being burnt to death when their families of origin could not meet the demands of extra dowry. An exploding stove here, a burst can of kerosene there, matches that mysteriously caught flame when held to a dupatta or a pallu. (*Fault* 209)

While such crimes as dowry deaths are a vital issue and need to be addressed, her conflation of arranged marriages with crimes against women suggests that if arranged marriages were to be replaced with "love" marriages or marriages of choice, crimes against women would disappear. Additionally, when such crimes are explained away as a "Punjabi thing" by her mother, and not much to do with poverty or the scramble for material goods in the social climbing milieu of New India, Alexander persists in her exposé of the oppressed "Third World" women: "In your days," she states, "there were women wells. Women jumping into wells" (*Fault* 209), pregnant and unmarried women jumping into wells à la Maxine Hong Kingston's "No Name Woman" in *The Woman Warrior*.

In Khartoum, she thinks about the possibility of marrying the rich Samir and being driven around in a car, living in the large house in Khartoum North, and as other married Sudanese women do, she would indulge in shopping trips to

> Alexandria and Beirut for slippers and cosmetics, even Rome and Paris every now and then; I could have the sweet-scented halava run over my legs and arms ripping off the small hairs, so my skin felt as smooth as a newborn baby; I could place cotton balls with rose attar or Chanel No. 5 on my skin. (*Fault* 134)

But something gives her pause: "But what would become of me, my mind, myself?" Positing the "traditional" lifestyle of married Sudanese women as mindless, and in order to escape the "web of traditional life" in India, she chooses an exhilarating life of "adventure" – "go to England, young woman, they all said. Then you can return to India" (*Fault* 135).

As a woman of the diaspora, what can she do to empower herself? She can "make herself up, and this," she says, "is enticement, the exhilaration, the compulsive energy of America. But only up to a point. And the point, the sticking point," she continues, is her "dark female body" (*Fault* 202). This dark female body is yet again conflated with the dark female bodies of oppressed women in the "Third World", those who are cliterodectomized in Sudan, the bodies that jumped into wells in Kerala, the Punjabi women who are burned for dowry, even the women picking up "shards of glass" in the aftermath of the 1973 flood in Pune: "women picking up bottles, wire, paper, anything but stones, to recycle them for a few paise, this with the right hand while the left scrounged around for scraps of food that might have been thrown out of the houses nearby: rice, dal, chapattis, half-cooked vegetables" (144). Her idiopathic identification and "appetite for alterity" enters her body, making her a surrogate victim. She writes, "Seeing all this, I could not eat and grew very thin" (144). External violence resonates with internal violence, leading to irruptions, allowing the narrator to construct a history through identification, but not "at-a-distance" (Silverman 185). In the United States, her fragmentation and exile come in forms such as the dirty subway system and the homeless man wandering the cold night air in Manhattan – her identifications with the "Third World" in the First World. "My life was so torn up into bits and pieces of the actual that depended on the poems, irruptions of the imaginary to make an internal history for me" (125). In this new history, Alexander is the surrogate, oppressed "Third World" woman, who, through her own individual endeavour, has liberated herself from oppression.

The reception and consumption of such texts in the Global North has been the subject of an ongoing critique within postcolonial studies, particularly in this era of global capitalism. Dirlik argues that the intellectual brain drain from the Global South to North is the outcome of global capitalism, although the "beneficiaries" conceal their class privileges by appropriating subaltern sensibilities and locations" (581). Alexander's voice becomes a metonym for the oppressed and marginalized Indians and Indian women in India as well as in the United States of America, thus eliding her many privileges. She was part of the First World in the Third World, and plays the part of the Third World in the First World.

Dirlik elaborates upon the common cultures of such people who share in privileges, regardless of where they are located:

> The globe has become as jumbled up spatially as the ideology of progress has temporally. Third Worlds have appeared in the First World and First Worlds in Third. New diasporas have relocated the Self there and the Other here, and consequently borders and boundaries have been confounded. And the flow of culture has been at once homogenizing and hydrogenising: some groups share in a common global culture regardless of locations even as they are alienated from the cultures of the hinterlands. (Dirlik 581)

As a postcolonial artist and intellectual who teaches at an elite institution in the United States of America, Alexander's claim to marginality is troubling. "To put it bluntly," states Dirlik, "postcoloniality is designed ... to cover up origins of postcolonial intellectuals in a global capitalism of which they are not so much victims as beneficiaries" (Dirlik 581). Allowing writers such as Alexander space within the West and particularly within the American Academy actually reinforces Eurocentrism, and "for this hegemony to be sustained, its boundaries must be rendered more porous in order to absorb alternative cultural possibilities that might otherwise serve as sources of destructive oppositions" (Dirlik 582). Hence space is created for the likes of Alexander, who, while seemingly critiquing colonial and neocolonial power structures, are actually helping in reinforcing them.

Rey Chow critiques the postcolonial intelligentsia writing about the "oppressed third world woman," suggesting that when we write and discuss such oppression, we need to "unmask ourselves through a scrupulous declaration of self-interest," because our acts are "tied less to the oppressed women in [Third World] communities 'back home' than to our own careers in the West" (603). Can Alexander face up to her "truthful relationship to those 'objects of study' behind which [she] can easily hide" (Chow 603)? She is a voyeur, posing simultaneously as a "fellow victim," and as "self-appointed [custodian]" (605). Says Chow, "It is necessary to write against the lure of diaspora: Any attempt to deal with 'women' or the 'oppressed classes' in the 'third world' that does not at the same time come to terms with the historical conditions of its own articulation is bound to repeat the exploitativeness that used to and still characterizes most 'exchanges' between 'West' and 'East.'" (605).

Because of her "idiopathic identification," distances seem to disappear; within this desire, past and present, self and other, East and West, appear to merge. Because of Alexander's "overappropriate identification" with the other, distances disappear, creating a too available and easy access. In such a scenario, she is unable to work through her sexual abuse and racial oppression and only ends up displacing and "acting out" the trauma through her rhetoric of otherness, which leads to retraumatizing – for example, her nervous breakdown in England (*Fault* 141) – due to her lack of self-reflexivity and critical distance from the Other. When one lacks critical distance from the Other, one represses what is real and turns instead to idealization (Silverman 74–75). Alexander's glorification of her "choices" – her marriage to David Lelyveld, her writing, her work, and so forth, allows for "libidinal" affirmation of what is culturally accepted due to the "normative nature of [her] unconscious idealization" (Silverman 75). She tells her mother she married David so that she could come home (*Fault* 208). Idiopathic identification allows for such affirmation. Although Alexander does not "depoliticize" the relationships of self and other, of First World exploitation and Third World oppression, she "[masks] the pleasure" (JanMohamed, "The Economy of the Manichean Allegory" 23) she derives from her position in the Western academy, and indeed in the Global North.

Thus, I argue that in Alexander's text, alterity is fetishized (JanMohamed, "The Economy" 20) as she is unable to keep the distance from the oppressed and fetishized objects she gazes at and interweaves into her own history. She ends up "acting out," rather than "working through" her trauma of sexual abuse, exile, and alienation (Hirsch 414). Throughout this reading, I have shown Alexander's "appetite for alterity" (Silverman 188) wherein she is unable to separate the pain of the Other from her own, and in her overidentification, her attempted critical analysis of neocolonialism and neo-imperialism are rendered ineffective.

I suggest that Alexander's fractured gaze becomes complicit with the West's desire for its Other as she lives in the First World and functions "not only as [native] but spokespersons for 'native' (and I add native women) in the 'third world'" (Chow 589). This is because in the Western academy, many intellectuals of colour achieve a particular status due to their positions "as cultural workers/brokers in diaspora" (Chow 589). Such intellectuals and writers take their "'raw materials' from the suffering of the oppressed," and become "exotic minors" (Chow 601).

In addition, because Alexander is unable to identify at a distance with the oppressed and suffering Third World people and women, her appetite for alterity, which assumes a sympathetic cast, only manages to exploit the fetishized Other. The discussion of the oppressed Third World women in the First World academy is "tied less to the oppressed women in [Indian] communities 'back home' than [the Indian] intellectual careers in the West" (Chow 603).

Thus, to be truly critical, Alexander must "retroactively" read Indian women to "painstakingly reverse the processes through which [she has] arrogated to [herself] what does not belong to [her], or displaced onto another what [she] did not want to recognize in [herself]" (Silverman

118). Otherwise, she will end up repeating the scenario of oppression, and acting out. "Such a re-viewing can have only a very limited efficacy ... it is a necessary step in the coming of the subject into an ethical or nonviolent relation to the other" (Silverman 3). Alexander is unable to acquire that distance from India and is unable to "respect the otherness of the [Third World] bodies" (Silverman 2) and hence her gaze simply confirms "dominant values" of Western desires. She must consciously acknowledge that she is the agent of representation; otherwise, her ideals of marriage and love, of freedom and choice, oppression and liberation "congeal into a tyrannizing [exoticizing] essence" (Silverman 2). In spite of moments of critique of colonialism, neocolonialism and globalization, her representations and her position as a Western intellectual allow her to continue to exploit the marginalized and fetishized Others due to her positionality, which destabilizes and subverts the political possibilities of *The Shock of Arrival* and *Fault Lines*. If Alexander declares her self-interest in her representations of the oppressed Third World woman, if she "unmasks" herself, will her texts be rendered any less problematic and voyeuristic? Chow claims that

> Such declaration does not clean our hands, but it prevents the continuance of a tendency, rather strong among "third world" intellectuals in diaspora as well as researchers of non-Western cultures in "first world" nations, to sentimentalize precisely those day-to-day realities from which they are distanced. (603)

Such distances lead either to idealization or to re-remembering, the outcomes of which are "competing narratives" of "'development' or 'underdevelopment' – one of celebration, [and] the other of crisis" (Gikandi 609). Additionally, and ultimately, as postcolonial intelligentsia and artists in the West, what we, as women of colour "can do without is the illusion that, through privileged speech, [we are] helping the wretched of the earth" (Chow 605).

PART TWO:
POLITICS OF REPRESENTATION IN GURINDER CHADHA'S *BEND IT LIKE BECKHAM*, ZAINAB ALI'S "MADRAS ON RAINY DAYS," AND SAMINA ALI'S *MADRAS ON RAINY DAYS*

In this section, I will examine Gurinder Chadha's film *Bend it Like Beckham*, Samina Ali's novel *Madras on Rainy Days* and Zainab Ali's short story "Madras on Rainy Days" in order to provide the trajectory of hybridized identity constructions and representations of Indian womanhood in diaspora spaces of the Global North. While in these texts, traditional notions of "oppressive" arranged marriages vie with ideas of love and sexuality, where the latter is posited as liberation and choice, neocolonial and racist contexts are either ignored or elided, thereby creating monolithic ideas of oppressive Indian patriarchal structures and their cultural practices. Are "counter hegemonic representations" possible in these texts, or are they impossible, framed as they are by "developmental narratives" and "liberal humanist discourses within both India and the diaspora" (Gopinath 140)?

Let us examine Samina Ali's *Madras on Rainy Days*, revised completely after her illness when she went into a coma during childbirth, reflected in the fragmented quality of the narrative as well as the protagonist. Additionally, and more importantly, her attempts to recover ideas of identity formation and representations, particularly of the passive and feminized Indians of her short stories and essay, published more than a decade earlier than the novel, are noted; however, the thrust of my argument is that her attempts are ultimately unsuccessful as the fragmented narratives expose the protagonist's split psyche, leading to contradictions within the texts.

After she recovered from her coma, Ali admits "I did not remember writing the book. I could have simply gone to a bookstore and picked out any book ... that's how foreign the book was to me.... It was not mine. I could not put my name on it" (qtd. in Hughes, *Poets and Writers* 46). This title appeared as a short story in the anthology *Our Feet Walk the Sky* (1993) when she published as Zainab Fatima Ali. Her short essay "Becoming the Agents of Our Destiny," appearing in the same anthology, provides the autobiographical elements which are incorporated in *Madras on Rainy Days*. In her essay, Ali writes about the terror of not belonging to America, which led her to reinvent and to lie: "This terror forced me to overcompensate – to lie – in order to express universality in customs and practices" (*Our Feet* 239).

In the novel, the hybridized nature of Layla's psyche and identity is ever present: "Stitch my tongue together, stitch my body together, the two women jostling inside the one frame no longer tearing the skin by the seams" (80). Carolyn Hughes asserts that the novel is about "Layla, a first generation Muslim Indo-American woman, who bristles under the constraints of an arranged marriage" (46). Layla, as her own arranged marriage to an Indian Muslim man approaches, ruminates about her aunt's arranged marriage and her wedding night ritual of the "two-by-two white sheet that would give more validity to this union than her wedding necklace or their vows" (*Madras* 3) – a blood-soaked proof of virginity and sexual consummation. "The next morning, [her uncle] hung the red-spotted cloth on the clothesline and it fluttered in the wind for all to see, a white flag of her surrender and his victory" (*Madras* 3).

In the short story, American-raised Samena, who, "forced by arranged marriage to become intimate" with Mohsin, "recoils from this stranger" and "was repulsed by him, and [her] repulsion was so strong [she] was unable to surrender to Allah's will for [their] union.... That night, [she] could not submit to Allah's will nor to her husband" (156). Later, we learn that he "hopelessly [pants] over [her] until three in the morning, rolling off [her] stomach" only to be woken by her mother-in-law at six in the morning to do the washing with "rocks and brittle soap ... alongside black cockroaches" (158). Both husbands (of the novel and short story) are unable to consummate the marriage, Mohsin, in spite of his intense efforts, and Sameer, because he is *repelled* by Layla's body, due, as we finally find out, to his being homosexual.

In both cases, an Alim is involved, touching the bride in intimate places to help the couple consummate their marriage. In the short story, however, Samena doesn't want the Alim to heal her because, feeling nervous, she is uncomfortable with his presence. "For some reasons, my mind allowed me to feel comfortable in a crowd of drunken men at the First Avenue bar in Chicago, but not while alone with one Muslim holy man" (157). In the novel, the Alim asks to be alone with Layla, touching her breasts, thighs and other intimate places, but she seems to think that it will be ultimately helpful. However, in her earlier short story, the Alim asks Samena: "Can you undo your pants?" and "Spread your legs a little, please" (159). Finally, she feels "his hand lightly caress [her] vagina" (159), his "kurta [becoming] wet with sweat" (159). As he is about to leave, the Alim "set his arm on my shoulders and smiled. 'What a shame about your husband. You're such a pretty, pretty girl.' He bent down, and kissed the side of my mouth as his hand cupped my right breast" (160). Eventually, her husband and the Alim leave the room, with [her] husband's arm around the Alim's wet back, portending the gay relationship Layla's husband has with his "friend" Naveed in the novel.

While the novel attempts to move beyond the earlier binary representations, it betrays many moments of such binary Manichaeism (JanMohamed, "Economy" 18). For example, India is still a place of demons and devils. Layla thinks, "Something about India, its collapse of walls between spiritual and the material, the mundane and the profane, made anything possible. Even devils. Especially devils" (45). The narrator is always aware of her Western and Westernized reader, explicating every cultural practice, especially regarding sexuality – "Men did that here, openly caressed one another, and no one was sure what those touches really meant, not even the men themselves … or their brides-to-be" (8). And because in India, Islam does not sanction homosexuality, states Layla, Sameer wants to escape to the liberal West: "America's freedom, from religious riots and curfew, from tainted water and hiring practices, and from whatever personal demons each was escaping" (223) appears liberating. That this myth is deconstructed after every racist moment and the murders which abounded and abound after 9/11 (which is not to say that racism has not occurred on a daily basis for most of the minorities in the United States even before the terrorist attacks) seems clear, yet such unproblematic representations of the "Promised Land" litter postcolonial "feminist" literature.

In the short story "Daddy," Ali creates a character very similar to that of Layla in *Madras*, who, when she sees her father treating her mother like "his whore," admits that she will never accept such treatment from a man, saying, "perhaps it's because I grew up in America where it's unacceptable. No, I admit, it may be more acceptable for Hydrabadi Muslims, like Amee" (*Our Feet* 9). And Amee, Layla's mother in the novel, is seen as shrill, gaudy, and one-dimensional (67–68), as is Chadha's Mrs. Bambra in *Bend it Like Beckham*. States Layla, "My mother's flashy sari and jewels [are] glowing more brightly than the wedding lights," exposing "the loose flesh of her belly" (85); in another part, she appears like an "angel," standing alone in her "ethereal splendor," praying to Allah (73). Her mother is never real to the diasporic subject, and like herself, she is just another "[woman] brought up knowing we would be sold, and looking forward to it" (230).

Labelling an arranged marriage a "Pagan ritual of sacrifice" (246), she eventually leaves her husband and her in-laws, but has nowhere to go. "Where will these streets lead me?" she muses as the novel ends. Empowerment for the diasporic Indian woman comes from leaving the home space and Indian cultural practices, replicating the "binarist logic and representations of early Third World Feminists' modernist agenda" (Shohat 12).

Leaving the "oppressive" home space is also reflected in *Bend It Like Beckham*, and even though Chadha touches upon the neocolonial component in critiquing what is considered male domination in postcolonial and transnational women's texts, her attempts, too, ultimately lead to failure, as I discuss in the remainder of this chapter. The director tries to show a complex set of oppressions operating in Jasminder's father's seemingly harsh behaviour toward his daughter's ambition to play soccer – he explains that he faced racism and rejection as a Black man and an immigrant from Kenya – and therefore, his earlier, seemingly unreasonable, actions in denying his daughter permission to play football ultimately make sense. However, such moments, too, seem forced and inserted, for the resolution of the film belies Bambra's sentiments.

The model of empowerment that Chadha provides throughout the film is limited, in that it involves a "white man [and women] saving a brown woman from a brown man" (Spivak, "Can the Subaltern Speak?" 120). Jasminder is persuaded by her white friend, Juliette, to try out for football, and ultimately, it is the white coach who persuades her to follow her dreams and desires; he also becomes her love interest. Jasminder's mother, Sukhi, too, is rendered voiceless and oppressive, only interested in teaching her daughter how to make "round, round *chappatis*" and "*alu gobi*," and even though she appears as a fierce and strong Punjabi woman, she is shown as the castrator of her seemingly meek husband, who can only speak out against her after getting "Dutch courage" by consuming whiskey. Sukhi, the hysterical Indian woman, yelling and shrieking, becomes a marker of Indian womanhood and culture, obviously to be avoided at all costs!

Thus, Westernization couched in terms of choice will bring freedom and happiness to Jasminder, while the *alu gobi* will bring spiritual and cultural sustenance! In this era of global capitalism, U.S. Orientalists view India, according to Prasad, as "pure fantasy," and to get away from materialism, they cultivate their souls through an "engagement with this thing called India" (20), and certain forms of exotic cultural enthusiasms, such as the resurgent popularity of yoga and Indian fashion and films in the past decade, attest to such claims.

In all these films and texts, the Indian household is constructed as oppressive for the next generation, while Indianness is fetishized in the form of colourful Indian weddings. Racism and neocolonialism are elided, and the audience is only sympathetic to the modern subject. In *Bend It*, for example, when Jasminder is mistakenly perceived by the would-be in-laws of her sister as kissing an English boy on the streets of London, Sukhi's sense of communal belonging, which is extremely important for Indians in a racist country, is threatened. She explains how transgressive women bring shame upon their families, who are then ostracized from the community. Yet, because Sukhi is seen as a stereotypical and traditional Indian woman, the Western audience's sympathy is with Jasminder.

Thus, even though artists and writers may try to provide nuanced portrayals of oppression, they do not "warn us to examine the limits and pitfalls of easy sympathy" (Kumar 193). Such easy sympathy by the Western audience ignores and represses the appalling "complicity between oppressive, dominant forces" in India and the West (Kumar 190). While Chadha attempts to show English households as equally oppressive for English girls by representing Juliette's bumbling mother, she actually comes across as a likeable character, as compared to Sukhi.

And while some of the oppressions of patriarchal structures are uncovered, such as Jasminder's "mate" Tony's closeted homosexuality, it becomes just a fetishized moment for displacing the anxieties and conflicts of discursive constructions of identities within the First World diaspora for postcolonial subjects (Gopinath, "Local Sites" 159). While Jasminder's father looks the monster of racism in the eye, and calls it by name, it is the enforced resolution, where Jasminder leaves the oppressive Indian community for more liberal climes in the United States, with the promise of romantic love that the narrative gestures toward, that is ultimately troubling. The fact that this film was a hit in the West shows the too easy acceptance of such commodified and fetishized versions of oppression and Indianness constantly being circulated.

Regarding the diaspora in the West, Dirlik agues that for Eurocentricism and its "cultural hegemony to be sustained, its boundaries must be rendered more porous in order to absorb alternative cultural possibilities that might otherwise serve as sources of destructive oppositions" ("Postcolonial Aura" 582). The boundaries are rendered porous by so-called postcolonial artists, writers, and intellectuals representing the "soul," tormented or otherwise, for the West to consume, comfortable in their "knowledge" of themselves as superior. These artists, "beneficiaries" of "global capital," are then commodifying victimhood and oppression for a Western neo-Oreintalist audience.

Chadha and Ali are unable to write "against the lure of diaspora" because they are "made to speak uniformly as minors and women to the West," reinforcing the hegemony of the centre, and are unable to "break alliance with this kind of official sponsorship of 'minority discourse'" (Chow 599). Their fractured gaze becomes complicit with the West's desire for its Other as they live in the First World and function as spokespersons for native woman in the Global South (Chow 589). They therefore function as "exotic minors" unable to "fight the crippling effects of Western imperialism and [Third World] paternalism" (601).

These artists cannot face up to their "truthful relationship to those 'objects of study' behind which [they] … easily hide – voyeurs, as 'fellow victims,' and as self-appointed [custodians]" (605). Chow claims that "It is necessary to write against the lure of diaspora: Any attempt to deal with 'women' or the 'oppressed classes' in the 'third world' that does not at the same time come to term with the historical conditions of its own articulation is bound to repeat the exploitativeness that used to and still characterizes most 'exchange' between 'West' and 'East.'" (605). In spite of moments of critique of colonialism and globalization, these writers are unable to politicize the relationships of self and other, of the Global North's exploitation and the Global South's oppression, for they "[mask] the pleasure" (JanMohamed, "Economy" 23) they derive, allowing them to exploit the Other, which ultimately undermines the very possibility latent in these texts.

Conclusion: The Politics of Location and Postcolonial/Transnational Feminist Critical Practices

To read postcolonial women's texts, then, we have to keep in mind why they write about oppressive cultural practices and for which audience. For the dislocated subject, "The discontinuities, the fragments, and fractures become the implied substance of ... short stories and novels. Multiplicity and contradiction, rather than totality and harmony, become constitutive of identity" (Kanaganayakam 3). The politics of location of these artists and writers have to be taken into consideration when conducting a postcolonial, multicultural and transnational feminist critical reading.

Many of these writers move across "time and space, invoking multiple communities, in ways that subvert 'national' readings of literature" (Kanaganayakam 4). These writers and artists hope to undermine and subvert dominant and oppressive national and indeed, global, cultural scripts. Françoise Lionnet claims that

> [l]iterature, as a discursive practice that encodes and transmits as well as creates ideology, is a mediating force in society: it structures our sense of the world since narrative or stylistic conventions and plot resolutions serve to either

> sanction and perpetuate cultural myths, or to create new mythologies that allow the writer and the reader to engage in a constructive re-writing of their social context. Women writers are often especially aware of their task as producers of images that both participate in the dominant representations of their culture and simultaneously undermine and subvert those images by offering a re-vision of familiar scripts. (132)

However, not many women writers are successful in subverting myths and recasting female subjectivity; they participate in naming structures of oppression in manners that appear Orientalist, or they inadvertently betray their internalization of dominant mythologies through implicit reinforcement of the binaries, categories, and logic of the West.

These writers then inadvertently or strategically (depending on the location of the reader) carry on imperialism's mission by becoming agents of globalization. This last accusation becomes particularly relevant when the ideas of gender oppression disseminated by these postcolonial women writers are co-opted by structures of globalization in the capitalist world economy.

Therefore, when postcolonial women writers participate in dominant representations of their culture, they must offer a possible revision of cultural texts; the answer does not lie simply in dismantling oppressive structures (assuming that such a thing is possible) or relocating to the "liberating" West. Fortunately, rewriting and renaming does occur. Women writers such as Sen, Dangarembga, or Chadha (here I mean her earlier film), are trying to recast female subjectivity and agency by allowing women to name the structure of oppressions in order to resist patriarchal oppression within the postcolonial and global framework. They do not provide an enforced resolution but instead show an alternate vision within interstitial spaces of all ideological constructs where identities can be refashioned.

This empowering space is found within patriarchal and capitalist ideological spaces, as there is no "elsewhere" that is not tainted by dominant power structures; the authors do not suggest dismantling existing social structures or displacement to another space; instead, they look for a liminal or "Third Space" (Bhabha) for rearticulation and refashioning for empowerment, even if the choices are limited at first. These female writers dramatize inequalities so that women readers can share in their views and help raise consciousness and work toward institutional changes.

In interpreting and revising these texts, women must read them, like Tambu reads Nyasha's story or Hélène reads Juletane's, to form a community where they read women's "madness" and pain as constructing an alternate space, an alternate and empowering identity. Women do not simply exchange one set of oppressions for another; instead, they work toward social change and expansion, where multiple identities can be incorporated and embraced into old ones, where one is no longer cast in binaries but can be multiple and inclusive, and where the domestic and public spheres blur, as Hélène, Tambu, or Parama demonstrate.

Thus, even though cultural identities are seemingly unalterable or bound within culturally constituted categories, there is hope for national or diasporic groups in reconstructing identity along lines of political and social choices. Placed as many diasporic Indians are in an in-between space, they may be the ones to reconstruct and renew as we have seen in these cultural productions. As Appadurai posits, diasporic public spaces are the postnational political order, although "[i]n the short run, as we can already see, it is full of increased incivility and violence" (23). However, in the long run, free from the constraints of the nation-state, this postnational political order is an exciting space, as it portends cultural freedom and sustainable justice (23). Hopefully, in the new millennium, we are headed into some form of cultural freedom leading into sustainable justice for all women – within nation-states and within translocal diasporic spaces. It can be maddening to accomplish this task, but as we have seen, it may be only in maddening or contradictory spaces that re-articulation and re-vision of a changing consciousness seeking empowerment can take place.

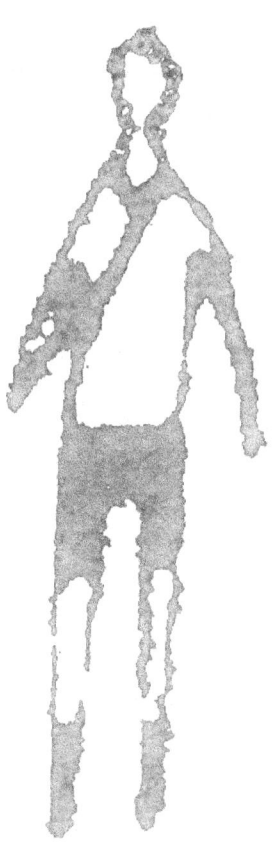

Notes

1: POSTCOLONIAL WOMEN WRITERS AND THEIR CULTURAL PRODUCTIONS

1. For a more detailed discussion on the use of the Mother Africa trope by male writers, see Florence Stratton's "The Mother Africa Trope," in *Contemporary African Literature and the Politics of Gender* (New York: Routledge, 1994), 39–55.

2. Kathleen McLuskie and Lynn Innes, "Women and African Literature," *Wasafiri* 8 (1988), p. 4.

3. In Jean Paul Sartre's introduction to Fanon's *The Wretched of the Earth*, he explains the colonial condition as a nervous condition, in which the subject formed by colonialism and nationalism is conflicted and destabilized (Frantz Fanon, *The Wretched of the Earth*. trans. Constance Farrington (New York: Grove, 1963)). I discuss gender and madness, or nervous condition, at some length in Chapter 2.

4. Also, for more discussion on the complexities and ambiguities of postmodernity in a postcolonial nation, see Jawaharlal Nehru's discussion of development in *The Discovery of India* (New Delhi: Penguin, 2004).

5. "In the United States, there is no dissent from the prevailing orthodoxy that gross inequality between nations (and individuals) is one of the unavoidable facts of history; nor does the plight of the sub-Saharan Africa, where real incomes have been *declining* for the last decade, attract any attention except when its genocides, child soldiers, droughts, and wars force themselves upon the world's conscious" (Lal, *Empire of Knowledge* 148).

2: DOMINANT EPISTEMOLOGIES AND ALTERNATIVE READINGS: GENDER AND GLOBALIZATION

1. For a more detailed analysis of the feminization of Indian culture and males, see Indrani Mitra's dissertation entitled "Colonialism, Nationalism and the Cultural Construction of Woman: Ideological Tensions in the Works of Three Indo-English Women Writers," Kent State University, 1992.

2   For a more detailed analysis of this film, see Indrani Mitra's "'I will Make Bimala One with My Country': Gender and Nationalism in Tagore's *The Home and the World*," *Modern Fiction Studies* 41.2 (1995): 243–64.

3   *Devi* was not approved for showing outside India until Nehru approved.

4   The Brahmo Samaj, which was formed by enlightened Bengalis in 1828, drew inspiration from many religions and aimed at changing the debased form of Hinduism (such as *sati* and prohibition of widow remarriage) that prevailed. The "Brahmos" challenged all forms of obscurantism and ritual, as well as female oppression associated with orthodox beliefs. Many later activists who worked to end women's oppression in India were from this group of reformers (Jayawardena, *Feminism and Nationalism* 82).

5   Tagore, according to Jayavardena, while attacking traditional practices which kept women oppressed, was, at the same time, a "believer in the unique contribution of women, through her special qualities, to the harmonious continuance of human society" (Jayawardena, *Feminism and Nationalism* 85).

6   Bharati Mukherjee, "American Dreamer" *Mother Jones Magazine*. January/February 1997 issue. <http://www.motherjones.com/commentary/columns/1997/01/mukherjee.html>

3: THE INDIAN DIASOPRA AND CULTURAL ALIENATION IN BHARATI MUKHERJEE'S TEXTS

1   Sita is the loving and dutiful wife of Lord Rama from the Hindu mythological epic *Ramayana*. When she is abducted by Ravana, the king of Lanka, and is later rescued, she has to walk through fire to prove her purity.

2   See, for example, Joseph E. Stiglitz's *Globalization and Its Discontents* for his discussion on the widening divide between the "haves" and the "have-nots" in the Global South due to the forces of globalization.

4: POSTCOLONIALITY AND INDIAN FEMALE SEXUALITY IN APARNA SEN'S FILM *PARAMA*

1   For a more detailed discussion on *Bhadramhila* (female member of the *Bhadralok*), see Sumanta Banerjee, "Marginalization of Women's Popular Culture in Nineteenth Century Bengal," in *Recasting Women: Essays in Indian Colonial History*, ed. Kumkum Sangari and Sudesh Vaid (New Brunswick, NJ: Rutgers UP, 1990), 127–79.

2   For a more detailed idea of this silence brought on by madness, see Michel Foucault, *Madness and Civilization* (New York: Vintage, 1988).

3   See Deepa Mehta's *Fire* (1996), for example. While this film was initially banned in India, its eventual release created a radical space for Indians to confront female sexuality and identity politics for women.

4   For more discussion on Shohat's theoretical position, see *Talking Visions: Multicultural Feminism in a Transnational Age* (New York: MIT Press, 1998).

7: MADDENING INSCRIPTIONS AND CONTRADICTORY SUBJECTIVITIES IN TSITSI DANGAREMBGA'S *NERVOUS CONDITION*

1   Tsitsi Dangarembga has recently published another novel, *The Book of Not* and has also released a film, *Kare Kare Zvako*. For more discussion on the film, see Flora Veit-Wild's *Writing Madness: Borderlines of the Body in African Literature* (Oxford: James Currey, 2006).

8: GLOBALISM AND TRANSNATIONALISM: CULTURAL POLITICS IN THE TEXTS OF MIRA NAIR, GURINDER CHADHA, AGNES SAM AND FARIDA KARODIA

1   Vinay Lal, *Manas: India and Its Neighbours.* <http://www.sscnet.ucla.edu/southasia/index.html>

2   For a discussion on the trope of the tribe used to describe successful Indians in the West, see Appadurai's *Modernity at Large*. The author states, "As I oscillate between the detachment of a postcolonial, diasporic, academic identity (taking advantage of the mood of exile and the space of displacement) and the ugly realities of being racialized, minoritized, and tribalized in my everyday encounters, theory encounters practice" (170). He then goes on to elaborate on the theory of Joel Kotkin, whose book *Tribes: How Race, Religion, and Identity Determine Success in the New Global Economy*, published by Random House in 1993, includes Indians along with the Jews, the Chinese, the Japanese, the British, and connects ethnicities to business successes. Appadurai posits that "however, diasporic we get, like the Jews, South Asians are doomed to remain a tribe, forever fixers and dealers in a world of open markets, fair deals, and opportunity for all" (170).

3   For a detailed account of hate crimes against Sikhs and other South Asians, see The Sikh Mediawatch and Resource Taskforce (SMART), a national Sikh advocacy group founded in 1995. A SMART press release from Sunday, September 16, 2001, immediately following the hate crimes against Sikhs and other South Asians can be found in the article, "Sikh Americans Condemn Hate Crimes and Urge Nation to Unite; Demand Protection from Police and Public Officials," *Amerasia Journal* 27.3 (2001)/28.1 (2002): 283–85.

was voted Favorite Foreign Film. <http://www.umiacs.umd.edu/users/sawweb/sawnet/news/fire.html>

3   Hindu Fundamentalist and Shiv Sena members wrecked the theatres that screened the film in India. <http://www.umiacs.umd.edu/users/sawweb/sawnet/news/fire.html>

4   See, for example, the call for papers for the 59th Annual Convention of the 2005 RMMLA, "Imaginary Dangers: Postcolonial Literature and the U.S. National Security." For many diasporic subjects, the desire to belong has never been so urgent. <http://cfp.english.upenn.edu/archive/Postcolonial/0231.html>

9: QUEERING DIASPORA IN SHANI MOOTOO'S *CEREUS BLOOMS AT NIGHT*, NISHA GANATRA'S *CHUTNEY POPCORN*, AND DEEPA MEHTA'S *FIRE*

1   The awards included the Audience Award at both the 1999 Newport Film Festival and the Provincetown Film Festival, and the Best Feature Film Award at the 1999 San Francisco Film Festival. <http://www.asiasource.org/arts/Nisha.cfm>

2   At the Vancouver Film Festival, *Fire* won the Federal Express Award for Best Canadian Film chosen by the audience. At the Chicago International Film Festival, it won Silver Hugo Awards for Best Direction and Best Actress. In Mannheim, it won the Jury Award, and in Paris it

Bibliography

Achebe, Chinua. *No Longer at Ease*. New York: Anchor, 1960.

Ahmad, Aijaz. "Jameson's Rhetoric of Otherness and the 'National Allegory.'" *The Postcolonial Studies Reader*. Ed. Bill Ashcroft, Gareth Griffith, and Helen Tiffin. London: Routledge, 1995. 77–82.

Alexander, Jacqui M. and Chandra T. Mohanty. *Feminist Genealogies, Colonial Legacies, Democratic Futures*. New York: Routledge, 1997.

Alexander, Meena. *Fault Lines*. New York: Feminist Press, CUNY, 1993.

———. *Manhattan Music*. San Francisco: Mercury House, 1997.

———. *The Shock of Arrival*. Boston: South End Press, 1996.

Ali, Samina. *Madras on Rainy Days*. New York: Picador, 2004.

Ali, Zainab. "Becoming Agents of Our Destiny." *Our Feet Walk the Sky: Women of the South Asian Diaspora*. Ed. The Women of the South Asian Descent Collective. San Francisco: Aunt Lute Books, 1993. 237–41.

———. "Daddy." *Our Feet Walk the Sky: Women of the South Asian Diaspora*. Ed. The Women of the South Asian Descent Collective. San Francisco: Aunt Lute Books, 1993. 4–11.

———. "Madras on Rainy Days." *Our Feet Walk the Sky: Women of the South Asian Diaspora*. Ed. The Women of the South Asian Descent Collective. San Francisco: Aunt Lute Books, 1993. 155–60.

Anderson, Benedict. *Imagined Communities: Reflections on the Origin and Spread of Nationalism*. New York: Verso, 1991.

Appadurai, Arjun. *Modernity at Large: Cultural Dimension of Globalization*. Minneapolis: U of Minnesota P, 1996.

Arora, Poonam. "The Production of First World Subject for First World Consumption: *Salaam Bombay!* and *Parama*." *Multiple Voices in Feminist Film Criticism*. Ed. Diane Carson, Linda Dittmar, and Janice R. Welsch. Minneapolis: U of Minnesota P, 1994. 293–304.

Asia Source. June 14, 2005 <http://www.asiasource.org/arts/Nisha.cfm>.

Ashcroft, Bill, Gareth Griffiths, and Helen Tiffin, eds. *The Empire Writes Back: Theory and Practice in Post-Colonial Literatures*. London: Routledge, 1989.

Bâ, Mariama. *So Long a Letter.* Trans. Modupé Bodé-Thomas. Oxford: Heinemann, 1981.

Bachmann, Monica. "After the Fire." *Queering India: Same-Sex Love and Eroticism in Indian Culture and Society.* New York: Routledge, 2002. 234–44.

Banerjee, Sumanta. "Marginalization of Women's Popular Culture in Nineteenth Century Bengal." *Recasting Women: Essays in Indian Colonial History.* Ed. Kumkum Sangari and Sudesh Vaid. New Brunswick, NJ: Rutgers UP, 1990. 127–79.

Bend it Like Beckham. Dir. Gurinder Chadha. 20th Century Fox, 2003.

Bhabha, Homi. "DissemiNation: Time, Narrative and the Margins of the Modern Nation." *The Location of Culture.* New York: Routledge, 1994. 139–70.

———. *Nation and Narration.* New York: Routledge, 1990.

———. "'Race', time and the revision of modernity." *The Location of Culture.* New York: Routledge, 1994. 236–56.

———. "The Commitment to Theory." *The Location of Culture.* New York: Routledge, 1994. 19–39.

Bhaji on the Beach. Dir. Gurinder Chadha. Columbia Tristar, 1994.

Bhana, Surendra, and Bridglal Pachai, eds. *A Documentary History of Indian South Africans 1860–1982.* Stanford, CA: Hoover Institution Press, 1984.

Boehmer, Elleke. *Stories of Women: Gender and Narrative in the Postcolonial Nation.* Manchester: Manchester U P, 2005.

———. "Stories of Women and Mothers: Gender and Nationalism in Early Fiction of Flora Nwapa." *Motherlands: Black Women's Writing from Africa, the Caribbean and South Asia.* Ed. Susheila Nasta. New Brunswick, NJ: Rutgers UP, 1992.

Bose, Purnima, and Linta Varghese. "*Mississippi Masala*, South Asian Activism, and Agency." *Haunting Violations: Feminist Criticism and the Crisis of the "Real."* Ed. Wendy S. Hesford and Wendy Kozol. Urbana and Chicago: U of Illinois P, 2001. 137–68.

Brennan, Tim. "Cosmopolitans and Celebrities." *Race and Class* 31 (1989): 2.

Broe, Mary Lynn, and Angela Ingram, eds. *Women's Writing in Exile.* Chapel Hill: U of North Carolina P, 1989.

Brown, Anne E., and Marjanne E. Grooze, eds. *International Women's Writing: New Landscapes of Identity.* Westport, CT: Greenwood, 1995.

Bruner, Charlotte H. *African Women's Writing.* Oxford: Heinemann, 1993.

Burton, Antoinette. "The White Woman's Burden: British Feminists and the 'Indian Woman', 1865–1915." *Women Studies International Forum* 13 (1990): 295–308.

Butler, Judith. *Bodies that Matter: On the Discursive Limits of Sex*. New York: Routledge, 1993.

———. *Subjects of Desire: Hegelian Reflections in Twentieth-Century France*. New York: Columbia UP, 1999.

Carson, Diane, Linda Dittmar, and Janice R. Welsh, eds. *Multiple Voices in Feminist Criticism*. Minneapolis: U of Minnesota P, 1994.

Cazenave, Odile. *Rebellious Women: The New Generation of Female African Novelists*. Boulder, CO: Lynne Rienner, 2000.

Chatterjee, Partha. "Colonialism, Nationalism, and Colonized Women: The Contest in India." *American Ethnologist* 16 (1989): 622–33.

———. "The Nationalist Resolution of the Women's Question." *Recasting Women: Essays in Indian Colonial History*. Ed. Kumkum Sangari and Sudesh Vaid. New Brunswick, NJ: Rutgers UP, 1990. 233–53.

———. *The Nation and Its Fragments: Colonial and Postcolonial Histories*. Princeton, NJ: Princeton UP, 1993.

Chetty, Rajendra, and Pier Paolo Piciucco, eds. *Indians Abroad: The Diaspora Writes Back*. Johannesburg: STE, 2004.

Chetty, Rajendra. "Exile and Return in Farida Karodia's *Other Secrets*." *Indians Abroad: The Diaspora Writes Back*. Ed. Rajendra Chetty and Pier Paolo Piciucco. Johannesburg: STE, 2004. 143–50.

Chetty, Rajendra. *South African Writings in English*. Durban, South Africa: Madiba Publishers, 2002.

Chow, Rey. "Against the Lures of Diaspora: Minority Discourse, Chinese Women, and Intellectual Hegemony." *Postcolonialism: An Anthology of Cultural Theory and Criticism*. Ed. Desai, Gaurav and Supriya Nair. New Brunswick, NJ: Rutgers UP, 2005. 589–607.

Chutney Popcorn. Dir. Nisha Ganatra. Mata Films, 2002.

Condé, Mary. "Introduction." *Caribbean Women Writers: Fiction in English*. Ed. Condé, Mary, and Thorunn Lonsdale. New York: St. Martin's, 1999. 1–10.

Connell, Michael, Jessie Greason, and Tom Grimes, "An Interview with Bharati Mukherjee." *Iowa Review* 20.3 (1990): 7–32.

Dangarembga, Tsitsi. *Nervous Conditions*. Seattle: Seal, 1988.

Dash, Michael. "In Search of the Lost Body: Redefining the Subject in Caribbean Literature." *The Postcolonial Studies Reader*. Ed. Bill Ashcroft, Gareth Griffith, and Helen Tiffin. London: Routledge, 1995. 332–35.

Davies, Carole Boyce. *Black Women, Writing and Identity: Migrations of the Subject.* London: Routledge, 1996.

Davies, Carole Boyce, and Anne Adams Graves, eds. *Ngambika: Studies of Women in African Literature.* Trenton, NJ: Africa World, 1986.

Desai, Gaurav, and Supriya Nair, eds. *Postcolonialism: An Anthology of Cultural Theory and Criticism.* New Brunswick, NJ: Rutgers UP, 2005.

Devi: The Goddess. Dir. Satyajit Ray. 1960.

Dimitris, Eleftheriotis. "Cultural Difference and Exchange: A Future for European Film." *Screen* 41.1 (2000): 92-101.

Dirlik, Arif. *Global Modernity: Modernity in the Age of Global Capitalism.* Boulder, CO: Paradigm, 2007.

———. "The Postcolonial Aura: Third World Criticism in the Age of Global Capitalism." *Postcolonialism: An Anthology of Cultural Theory and Criticism.* Ed. Desai, Gaurav and Supriya Nair. New Brunswick, NJ: Rutgers UP, 2005. 569-88.

Eng, David L., and Alice Y. Hom. *Queer in South Asia.* Philadelphia: Temple UP, 1998.

Fanon, Frantz. *A Dying Colonialism.* Trans. Haakon Chevalier. New York: Grove, 1965.

———. *The Wretched of the Earth.* 1963. Trans. Constance Farrington. New York: Grove, 1963.

Fayad, Mona. "Cartographies of Identity: Writing Maghribi Women as Postcolonial Subjects." *Beyond Colonialism and Nationalism in the Maghrib: History, Culture, and Politics.* Ed. Ali Abdullatif Ahmida. New York: Palgrave, 2000.

Fire. Dir. Deepa Mehta. Zeitgeist Films, 1997.

Foucault, Michel. *The History of Sexuality, an Introduction: Volume 1.* New York: Vintage, 1990.

———. *Madness and Civilization: A History of Insanity in the Age of Reason.* New York: Vintage, 1988.

Gandhi, Leela. *Postcolonial Theory: A Critical Introduction.* New York: Columbia UP, 1998.

Gandhi, Mohandas Karamchand. Vol 14. 1918. *The Collected Works of Mahatama Gandhi.* Delhi: Government of India, 1969. 207-8.

Ghosh, Kalpana. "*Parama*: Aparna Sen's fight against male chauvinism." *Screen* July 1984:10-17.

Gikandi, Simon. *Postcolonialism: An Anthology of Cultural Theory and Criticism.* Ed. Gaurav Desai and Supriya Nair. New Brunswick, NJ: Rutgers UP, 2005. 608-34.

Gilbert, Sandra M., and Susan Gubar, eds. *The Madwoman in the Attic: The Women Writer and the Nineteenth-Century Literary Tradition*. New Haven, CT: Yale UP, 1979.

Gopinath, Gayatri. *Impossible Desires: Queer Desire and the South Asian Public Culture*. Durham, NC: Duke UP, 2005.

———. "Local Sites/Global Contexts: The Transnational Trajectories of Deepa Mehta's Fire," *Queer Globalizations: Citizenship and the Afterlife of Colonialism*. New York: New York UP, 2002. 149–61.

Grewal, Gurleen. "Born Again American: Immigrant Consciousness in Jasmine." *Bharati Mukherjee: Critical Perspectives*. Ed. Emmanuel Nelson. New York: Garland, 1993. 183–94.

———. *Transnational America: Feminisms, Diasporas, Neoliberalisms*. Durham, NC: Duke UP, 2005.

Grewal, Inderpal. *Transnational America: Feminisms, Diasporas, Neoliberalisms*. Durham, NC: Duke UP, 2005.

Grewal, Inderpal, and Caren Kaplan, eds. *Scattered Hegemonies: Postmodernity and Transnational Feminist Practices*. Minneapolis: U of Minnesota P, 1994.

Guha, Ranajit. *Subaltern Studies: Writings on South Asian History and Society*. Oxford: Oxford UP, 1989.

Gunew, Sneja. "Questions of Multiculturalism." *Women's Writing in Exile*. Ed. Mary Lynn Broe and Angela Ingram. Chapel Hill: U of North Carolina P, 1989. 419–32.

Harrell-Bond, Barbara. "Interview with Mariama Bâ." *African Book Publishing Record* 6.3–4 (1980): 209–14.

Hirsch, Marianne. "Projected Memory: Holocaust Photographs in Personal and Public Fantasy." *Ways of Reading*. Ed. David Bartholomae and Anthony Petrosky. Boston: St. Martin's, 2002. 400–427.

Hughes, Carolyn T. "Five Fiction Writers Debut with Notable Books." *Poets and Writers*. July/August 2004. <http://www.pw.org/mag/0407/contents.htm>.

Iqbal Rashid, Ian. "Introduction to the Videos of Shani Mootoo." *Wide Angle: A Film Quarterly of Theory, Criticism, and Practice* 17 (1995): 341–42.

JanMohamed, Abdul R. *Manichean Aesthetics: The Politics of Literature in Colonial Africa*. Amherst: U of Massachusetts P, 1983.

———. "The Economy of the Manichean Allegory." *The Postcolonial Studies Reader*. Ed. Bill Ashcroft, Gareth Griffith, and Helen Tiffin. London: Routledge, 1995. 18–24.

Jayawardena, Kumari. *Feminism and Nationalism in the Third World.* London: Zed, 1986.

Jussawalla, Feroza. "Chiffon Saris: The Plight of the South Asian Immigrant in the New World." *Massachusetts Review* 29 (1988–89): 583–95.

Kafka, Phillipa. *On the Outside Looking In(dian): Indian Women Writers at Home and Abroad.* New York: Peter Lang, 2003.

Kakar, Sudhir. *Intimate Relations: Exploring Indian Sexuality.* New Delhi: Viking Press, 1989.

Kanaganayakam, Chelva. *Moveable Margins: The Shifting Spaces in Canadian Literature.* Toronto: TSAR Publications, 2005.

Katrak, Ketu H. "Decolonizing Culture: Toward a Theory for Post-colonial Women's Texts." *The Postcolonial Studies Reader.* Ed. Bill Ashcroft, Gareth Griffith, and Helen Tiffin. London: Routledge, 1995. 255–58.

Karodia, Farida. "Crossmatch." *No Place Like Home and Other Stories by Southern African Women Writers.* Ed. Robin Malan. New Delhi: Sterling, 1999. 163–92.

Khanna, Tarun. *Billions of Entrepreneurs: How China and India are Reshaping Their Futures and Yours.* Boston: Harvard Business School, 2007.

Kingston, Maxine Hong. *The Woman Warrior.* New York: Vintage, 1989.

Kishwar, Madhu. "Naïve Outpourings of a Self-Hating Indian: Deepa Mehta's *Fire.*" *Manushi* 109 (March-April 1999): 6.

Kotkin, Joel. *Tribes: How Race, Religion, and Identity Determine Success in the New Global Economy.* New York: Random House, 1993.

Kumar, Amitava. *Passport Photos.* Los Angeles: U of California P, 2000.

Lal, Vinay. *Empire of Knowledge: Culture and Plurality in the Global Economy.* London: Pluto, 2002.

———. *Manas: India and Its Neighbours.* September 7, 2007; <http://www.sscnet.ucla.edu/southasia/index.html>.

Landy, Marcia. *Imitation of Life: A Reader in Film and Television Melodrama.* Detroit: Wayne State UP, 1991.

Lashgari, Deirdre. *Violence, Silence, and Anger: Women's Writings as Transgression.* Charlottesville: UP of Virginia, 1995.

Liddle, Joanna, and Rama Joshi, eds. *Daughters of Independence: Gender, Class and Caste in India.* London: Zed, 1986.

Lionnet, Françoise. "Geographies of Pain: Captive Bodies and Violent Acts in the Fictions of Myriam Warner-Vieyra, Gayle Jones, and Bessie Head." *Callaloo* 16.1 (1993): 132–52.

Loomba, Ania. *Colonialism/Postcolonialism*. London: Routledge, 2005.

Loomba, Ania, Suvir Kaul, Matti Bunzl, Antoinette Burton, and Jed Esty, eds. *Postcolonial Studies and Beyond*. Durham: Duke UP, 2005.

Luhr, William, ed. *World Cinema Since 1945*. New York: Ungar, 1987.

Maachis. Dir. Gulzar. 1996.

Macaulay, T. B. *Selected Speeches*. London: Oxford UP, 1952.

Macherey, Pierre. *A Theory of Literary Production*. Trans. Geoffrey Wall. London: Routledge, 1978.

Maira, Sunaina Marr. *Desis in the House: Indian American Youth Culture in New York City*. Philadelphia: Temple UP, 2002.

Mama, Amina. Editorial. *Feminist Africa: Intellectual Politics* 1.1 (2002): 1–8.

———. "Sheroes and Villains: Conceptualizing Colonial and Contemporary Violence Against Women in Africa." *Feminist Genealogies, Colonial Legacies, Democratic Futures*. Ed. Jacqui Alexander M. and Chandra T. Mohanty. New York: Routledge, 1997. 46–62.

Mayo, Katherine. *Mother India*. New York: Blue Ribbon, 1927.

McLuskie, Kathleen, and Lynn Innes. "Women and African Literature." *Wasafiri* 8 (1998): 4–12.

Meer, Ameena. "Bharati Mukherjee." *Bomb* 29 (1989): 28.

Meer, Fatima. *Prison Diary: One Hundred and Thirteen Days, 1976*. Cape Town: Kwela, 2001.

Mehta, Brinda. *Diasporic (Dis)locations: Indo-Caribbean Women Writers Negotiating the Kala Pani*. Kingston: U of West Indies P, 2004.

Memmi, Albert. *The Dominated Man: Notes Toward a Portrait*. London: Orion, 1968.

Menon, Nivedita. "Between the Burqa and the Beauty Parlor? Globalization, Cultural Nationalism, and Feminist Politics." *Postcolonial Studies and Beyond*. Eds. Ania Loomba, et al. Durham: Duke UP, 2005. 206–32.

Mill, James. *The History of British India*. Originally published 1817. New York: Chelsea, 1968.

Miller, James. *The Passion of Michel Foucault*. New York: Simon and Schuster, 1993.

Minh-ha, Trinh T. "No Master Territories." *The Postcolonial Studies Reader*. Eds. Bill Ashcroft, Gareth Griffith, and Helen Tiffin. London: Routledge, 1995. 215–18.

———. *Women, Native, Other*. Bloomington: Indiana UP, 1989.

Mishra, Vijay. *Bollywood Cinema: Temples of Desire*. New York: Routledge, 2001.

Misrahi-Barak, Judith. "Beginners' Luck among Caribbean-Canadian Writers: Nalo Hopkinson, Andre Alexis and Shani Mootoo." *Commonwealth Essays and Studies*. 22.1 (1999 Autumn): 89–96.

Mississippi Masala. Dir. Mira Nair. Mirabai Films, 1992.

Mitra, Indrani. "Colonialism, Nationalism and the Cultural Construction of Woman: Ideological Tensions in the Works of Three Indo-English Women Writers." Diss. Kent State University, 1992.

———. "'I Will Make Bimala One With My Country': Gender and Nationalism in Tagore's *The Home and the World*." *Modern Fiction Studies* 41.2 (1995): 243–64.

Mohanty, Chandra Talpade, Ann Russo, and Lourdes Torres, eds. *Third World Women and the Politics of Feminism*. Bloomington: Indiana UP, 1991.

Mohanty, Chandra Talpade. "Feminist Encounters: Locating the Politics of Experience." *Copyright* 1 (1987): 31–44.

———. "Under Western Eyes: Feminist Scholarship and Colonial Discourse." *The Postcolonial Studies Reader*. Ed. Bill Ashcroft, Gareth Griffith, and Helen Tiffin. London: Routledge, 1995. 259–63.

Mootoo Shani. *Cereus Blooms at Night*. New York: Avon, 1996.

———. *Out on Main Street*. Vancouver: Press Gang, 1993.

Mukherjee, Bharati. "American Dreamer." *Mother Jones*. January/February 1997. <http://www.motherjones.com/commentary/columns/1997/01/mukherjee.html>.

———. "An Invisible Woman." *Saturday Night* 96.3 (1981): 36.

———. "Immigrant Writing: Give Us Your Maximalists!" *The New York Times Book Review* 28 Aug. 1988: 28.

———. *Jasmine*. New York: Fawcett Crest, 1989.

———. *The Tiger's Daughter*. 1971. London: Penguin, 1987.

———. *Wife*. New York: Fawcett, 1975.

———. *Desirable Daughters*. New York: Theia, 2003.

Mukherjee, Bharati, and Clark Blaise. *Days and Nights in Calcutta*. Garden City, NY: Doubleday, 1977.

Mukherjee, Meenakshi. *Realism and Reality: The Novel and Society in India*. New Delhi: Oxford UP, 1985.

———. *Realism and Domestic Fiction: A Political History of the Novel*. New York: Oxford UP, 1987.

Naipaul, V. S. *A House for Mr. Biswas*. London: Penguin, 1961.

Narasimhan, Shakuntala. *Sati: Widow Burning in India.* New York: Doubleday, 1990.

Nasta, Susheila, ed. *Motherland: Black Women's Writing from Africa, the Caribbean and South Asia.* New Brunswick, NJ: Rutgers UP, 1992.

Nehru, Jawaharlal. *The Discovery of India.* 1946. New Delhi: Penguin, 2004.

Newell, Stephanie. *Writing African Women: Gender, Popular Culture and Literature in West Africa.* London: Zed, 1997.

Ngugi wa Thiong'o. *Decolonizing the Mind.* London: James Curry, 1986.

Obiechina, Emmanuel. *An African Popular Literature: A Study of Onitsha Market Pamphlets.* Cambridge: Cambridge UP, 1973.

Ogunyemi, Chikwenye Okonjo. *African Wo/Man Palava: The Nigerian Novel by Women.* Chicago: U of Chicago P, 1996.

Oyêwùmí, Oyèrónké. *Postcolonialism: An Anthology of Cultural Theory and Criticism.* Ed. Gaurav Desai and Supriya Nair. New Brunswick, NJ: Rutgers UP, 2005. 339-61.

———. *The Invention of Women: Making an African Sense of Western Gender Discourses.* Minneapolis: U of Minnesota P, 1997.

Parama. Dir. Aparna Sen. Perf. Rakhee Gulzar and Mukul Sharma, 1985.

Patel, Geeta. "On Fire: Sexuality and Its Incitements." *Queering India: Same-Sex Love and Eroticism in Indian Culture and Society.* New York: Routledge, 2002. 222-31.

Parker, Andrew, et al., eds. *Nationalism and Sexualities.* London: Routledge, 1992.

Patel, Sujata. "Constructions and Reconstructions of Women in Gandhi." *Economic and Political Weekly* 20 Feb. 1988. 377-87.

Pereira, Charmaine. "Between Knowing and Imagining: What Space for Feminism in Scholarship of Africa?" *Feminist Africa Intellectual Politics* 1.1 (2002): 9-33.

Petersen, Kirsten Holst. "First Things First: Problems of a Feminist Approach to African Literature." *The Postcolonial Studies Reader.* Ed. Bill Ashcroft, Gareth Griffith, and Helen Tiffin. London: Routledge, 1995. 251-54.

Petersen, Kirsten Holst, and A. Rutherford. "Fossil and Psyche." *The Postcolonial Studies Reader.* Ed. Bill Ashcroft, Gareth Griffith, and Helen Tiffin. London: Routledge, 1995. 185.

Petty, Sheila J. "(Re)Presenting the Self: Identity and Consciousness in the Feature Films of Safi Faye." *International Women's Writing: New Landscapes of Identity.* Ed. Anne E. Brown and Marjanne E. Gooze. Westport, CT: Greenwood, 1995. 22-35.

Pratt, Mary Louise. "Arts of the Contact Zones." *Ways of Reading*. Ed. David Bartholomae and Anthony Petrosky. Boston: St. Martin's, 1996. 528-34.

Radhakrishnan, R. *Theory in an Uneven World*. Oxford: Blackwell, 2004.

Rashid, Ian Iqbal. "Introduction to the Videos of Shani Mootoo." *Wide Angle: A Film Quarterly of Theory, Criticism, and Practice*. 17. 1-4 (1995): 341-42.

Ratti, Rakesh. *A Lotus of Another Color: An Unfolding of the South Asian Gay and Lesbian Experience*. Los Angeles: Alyson, 1993.

Rich, Adrienne. *Blood, Bread and Poetry: Selected Prose 1979-1985*. London: Virago, 1986.

Rodowick, David N. "Madness, Authority, and Ideology in the Domestic Melodrama of the 1950s." *Imitation of Life: A Reader on Film and Television Melodrama*. Ed. Marcia Landy. Detroit: Wayne State UP, 1991. 237-47.

Roy, Anindyo. "The Aesthetics of an (Un)willing Immigrant: Bharati Mukherjee's *Days and Nights in Calcutta* and *Jasmine*." *Bharati Mukherjee: Critical Perspectives*. Ed. Emmanuel Nelson. New York: Garland, 1993. 126-39.

Rushdie, Salman. *Imaginary Homelands: Essays and Criticism, 1981-1991*. New York: Penguin, 1991.

Said, Edward. *Orientalism*. London: Vintage, 1979.

Sam, Agnes. *Jesus is Indian and Other Stories*. Berkshire: Heinemann, 1989.

Samuelson, Meg. *Remembering the Nation, Dismembering Women?: Stories of the South African Transition*. Durban: University of KwaZulu Natal P, 2007.

Sangari, Kumkum, and Sudesh Vaid, eds. *Recasting Women: Essays in Indian Colonial History*. New Brunswick, NJ: Rutgers UP, 1990.

Sarkar, Lotika, and Vina Mazumdar. "A Note of Dissent." *Towards Equality: Report of the Committee on the Status of Women in India*. Government of India. Department of Social Welfare. New Delhi: Government of India, 1974.

Sarkar, Sumit. *Swadeshi Movement in Bengal, 1903-1908*. New Delhi: People's Publishing, 1973.

Sarkar, Tanika. "Nationalist Iconography: Image of Women in 19th Century Bengali Literature." *Economic and Political Weekly* 21 Nov. 1987: 2011-55.

Seidel, Michael. *Exiles and the Narrative Imagination*. New Haven, CT: Yale UP, 1986.

Sen, Maya. *Death by Fire: Sati, Dowry Death, and Female Infanticide in Modern India*. New Brunswick, NJ: Rutgers UP, 2001.

Senghor, Léopold Sédar. *African Report* 33 (May-June 1988): 70-71.

———. *Léopold Sédar Senghor: Prose and Poetry*. Trans. and Ed. John Reed and Clive Wake. London: Oxford UP, 1965.

Shohat, Ella, ed. *Talking Visions: Multicultural Feminism in a Transnational Age*. New York: MIT Press, 1998.

"Sikh Americans Condemn Hate Crimes and Urge Nation to Unite; Demand Protection from Police and Public Officials." The Sikh Meidawatch and Resource Taskforce (SMART). *Amerasia Journal* 27.3 (2001)/ 28.1 (2002): 283–85.

Silverman, Kaja. *The Threshold of the Visible World*. London: Routledge, 1996.

Smyth, Heather. "Sexual Citizenship and Caribbean-Canadian Fiction: Dionne Brand's 'In Another Place, Not Here,' and Shani Mootoo's *Cereus Blooms at Night*." *Ariel: A Review of International English Literature* 30 (1999 Apr.): 141–60.

Spivak, Gayatri Chakravorty. "Can the Subaltern Speak? Speculations on Widow Sacrifice." *Wedge* 7/8 (Winter/Spring 1985): 120–30.

———. *In Other Worlds: Essays in Cultural Politics*. New York: Routledge, 1987.

———. *The Post-colonial Critic: Interviews, Strategies, Dialogues*. New York: Routledge, 1990.

———. "Three Women's Texts and a Critique of Imperialism." *Race, Writing, and Difference*. Ed. Henry Louis Gates, Jr. Chicago: U of Chicago P, 1985.

Stiglitz, Joseph E. *Globalization and its Discontents*. New York: Norton, 2002.

Stratton, Florence. *Contemporary African Literature and the Politics of Gender*. New York: Routledge, 1994.

Sturgess, Charlotte. "Dionne Brand: Writing the Margins." *Caribbean Women Writers: Fiction in English*. Ed. Mary Conde and Thorunn Lonsdale. New York: St. Martin's, 1999. 202–19.

Subramanyam, Radha. "Compromising Positions: Class, Caste, and Gender in Indian Women's Film." Diss. Northwestern, 1996.

Sunder Rajan, Rajeshswari. *Real and Imagined Women: Gender, culture and postcolonialism*. London: Routledge, 1993.

Tagore, Rabindranath. *The Home and the World*. Trans. Surrendranath Tagore. New York: Macmillan, 1919.

The Home and the World. Dir. Satyajit Ray. 1984.

Vaidyanathan, T.G. *Hours in the Dark: Essays in Cinema*. Delhi: Oxford UP, 1996.

Vanita, Ruth, ed. *Queering India: Same-Sex Love and Eroticism in Indian Culture and Society*. New York: Routledge, 2002.

Vanita, Ruth, and Saleem Kidwai, eds. *Same Sex Love in India.* New York: Palgrave, 2000.

Veit-Wild, Flora. *Writing Madness: Borderlines of the Body in African Literature.* Oxford: James Currey, 2006.

Versi, Anver. "Not At Home, At Home: Novelist Farida Karodia." *New African* 318 (1994): 39–40.

Wallerstein, Immanuel. *Alternatives: The United States Confronts the World.* Boulder, CO: Paradigm, 2004.

———. *The Capitalist World Economy.* Cambridge: Cambridge UP, 1979.

———. *Unthinking Social Science: The Limits of Nineteenth-Century Paradigms.* Cambridge, UK: Polity, 1991.

Warner-Vieyra, Myriam. *Juletane.* Trans. Betty Wilson. Oxford: Heinemann, 1987.

Water. Dir. Deepa Mehta. 2005.

Zeleza, Paul. "African Universities and Globalization." *Feminist Africa: Intellectual Politics.* Issue 1: Nov./Dec. 2002. 64–86.

Index

A

abortion, 69, 156. *See also* "rejection of motherhood"
    act of "madness" to Indian audience, 74
abuse of women, 145, 183. *See also* violence against women
    blaming the woman, 146
    bride burning, 184–85
Afghanistan, 2, 10, 34, 149, 164
Africa, 15, 36. *See also* individual African countries
'African culture and traditions,' 7
African diaspora, 115
African feminism, 10–12
African universities and intellectual communities, 55
African woman, 1, 103
    as the Great Mother Africa, 4, 104
    participation in nationalist movement, 104
    revolt against social and familial pressures, 9
African Women's Writing (Bruner), 106
African writers, 19, 103
Afro-American literature, 17
Ahmad Aijaz, 64
Alexander, Meena, 6, 177–89
    "Alphabets of Flesh," 178
    appetite for alterity, 178, 186, 188
    exposé of oppressed "Third World" women, 178, 185–86
    Fault Lines, 178, 183, 189
    glorification of her "choices," 187–88
    identification with "Third World" in the First World, 186
    idiopathic identification, 180, 186–88
    Khartoum journal, 184
    Manhattan Music, 178, 183
    marriage to White American man, 182, 184, 188
    nervous breakdown, 187
    overappropriate identification, 178, 180, 187
    privileged background, 180, 186
    sexual abuse, 181, 187
    The Shock of Arrival, 178, 180, 189
    token representative of oppressed Indian Womanhood, 21
    use of Bhabha's hybridized "Third Space," 179
    use of madness, 177
    as voyeur, 187
Algeria, 34–35, 48
Ali, Samina (a.k.a. Zainab Ali), 6, 195
    Madras on Rainy Days, 190
Ali, Zainab Fatima
    "Becoming the Agents of Our Destiny," 190
    "Daddy," 192
    "Madras on Rainy Days," 190
    Our Feet Walk the Sky, 190
alienation, 48, 115, 120
    from home culture, 62–63, 66, 79, 84
"Alphabets of Flesh" (Alexander), 178
alternate mythology, 121, 198
alternate spaces, 126, 199
alternative readings to dominant knowledge systems, 56–57
ambivalence, 50, 58, 108
    postcolonial notion of, 58
Amin, Idi, 141
anorexia, 129–30, 132
apartheid, 136, 150, 155

Appadurai, Arjun, 23, 139, 158–59, 161, 180, 199
  on *Bhaji on the Beach,* 146
  on mass-mediated solidarities, 147–48
  Modernity at Large, 179
  "motion and mediation," 143
appetite for alterity, 178, 186, 188
Arora, Poonam, 91–92, 100
arranged marriage, 72, 147–50, 156–57, 166, 183–84, 191
  legal action against, 147–48
  "Pagan ritual of sacrifice," 193
  Westernized upper-class women, 62
arranged marriage *vs.* choice, 81, 190
Ashcroft, Bill, *The Empire Writes Back,* 115
Asian foot-binding, 24, 176
assimilation, 66, 70, 159
Azad Hind Fauj (army), 139

B

Bâ, Mariama, 6, 48
  critique of polygamy, 111, 117
  ideological crisis of tradition and modernity, 105, 107
  So Long a Letter, 103–14
Bachmann, Monica, 168
"A Bag of Sweets" (Sam), 151
Banerjee, Sumanta, 38
"Becoming the Agents of Our Destiny" (Ali), 190
Bend it Like Beckham (film), 190, 192, 194
  leaving "oppressive" home space, 193
Bhabha, Homi, 52, 160
  "The Commitment to Theory," 15
  "DissemiNation," 53, 138
  Nation and Narration, 159
  "Third Space" of, 87, 91, 100, 144, 149, 169, 179, 198
Bhadra lok, 83
Bhadra mahilla, 83
Bhadramhil, 202n1
Bhaji on the Beach (film), 135, 145
  female solidarity in, 149

fusion and hybridity of cultural forms, 148
Blaise, Clark, 63, 73
Bodies That Matter (Butler), 75
Boehmer, Elleke, 4–5, 8, 10, 36
Bollywood films, 96–97, 146, 154
Bose, Subhash Chandra, 139
Brahno Samaj, 202n4
brain drain, 186
"brain gain," 55
Brennan, Tim, 53
  "Cosmopolitans and Celebrities," 52
bride burning, 184–85
Britain. *See* United Kingdom
British colonialism, 30
British colonization of India, 136, 140
Bruner, Charlotte, 4
  African Women's Writing, 106
Buddhism, 80–81, 140
Burma, 170
  Indian culture through Hindi films, 139–40
  Indianness co-opted for nationalism, 139
burqa, purdah, and the veil, xii, 2, 33–34, 46
Burton, Antoinette, 32
Butler, Judith, *Bodies That Matter,* 75

C

"Can the Subaltern Speak?" (Spivak), 30, 77, 193
capitalist world-economy, 18–20, 57–58. *See also* global capitalism
Caribbean, 170
  aftermath of colonialism, 115–16
Caribbean Blacks
  displaced and disenfranchised group in UK, 146
Caribbean women writers, 116
Cazenave, Odile, 4, 9–10, 122
censorship, 136
Cereus Blooms at Night (Mootoo), 164, 172–73

homosexual and transsexual identity, 168
Césaire, Aimé, 6, 179
Chadha, Gurinder, 6, 135, 145, 148, 190, 192-93, 195, 198
Chatterjee, Partha, 39, 42, 44, 94, 154
   "Colonialism, Nationalism, and the Colonialized Woman," 7, 33
   "The Nation and its Women," 83
   "The Nationalist Resolution of the Women's Question," 43
Chetty, Rajendra, 24
   South African Writings in English, 136, 153
Chow, Rey, 187, 189
Christianity, 19
   monogamous romantic love, 109
Churchill, Winston, 20
Chutney Popcorn (film), 164, 166
   critical acclaim, 165
   Indian culture as commodity, 165
   intergenerational conflict, 165
   lesbianism, 164, 167
civilization, 5, 24
   colonial ideology of, 30, 32, 35
   "enduring 'civilizations'," 20
class, 15
   emergent middle class, 29, 38, 137
   English-educated, middle-class elite, 93
   upper and middle classes, 21, 41
   upper class and upper-caste, 38, 63
   working classes, 17
cliterodectomies. *See* Female Genital Mutilation (FGM)
co-optation, xi, 1, 19, 21, 27, 57
   unveiled woman, 34
collective imagination, 158. *See also* "community of sentiment"
colonialism, 4-5, 13, 29, 34, 126, 132
   aftermath, 115-16, 126
   complicity with elite native patriarchy, 128, 130
   cultural, 26, 147
   cyclical violence and madness, 172
   destructive powers in the Caribbean, 115-16

   French, 34
   lasting and ambiguous impact, 16
   lowered women's social standing, 31, 130
   madness and sexual ambiguity linked to, 169
   rhetoric of civilization, 30
"Colonialism" (Mitra), 33
"Colonialism, Nationalism, and the Colonialized Woman" (Chatterjee), 7, 33
colonized nations
   represented as feminine, 30
colonizers' language, 16, 29. *See also* English language; French language
"cultural bomb," 18, 170
colonizers' need to "unveil" native woman, 34-35
"The Commitment to Theory" (Bhabha), 15
commodification of ethnic cultures, 15, 53, 165, 194-95
common global culture of privilege, 186
"community of sentiment," 139, 147. *See also* collective imagination
community of women, 120, 123, 149, 173. *See also* sisterhood
   empowerment from, 133
companionate marriage, 67
   accommodation of traditional roles, 94, 109
   patriarchal control, 41
"competing universalism," 26
Condé, Mary, 116
Contemporary African Literature and the Politics of Gender (Stratton), 104
"controversial marriage"
   choosing one's mate, 109, 150-51
   marriage for love, 107
cosmopolitanism, 1, 52, 164. *See also* metropolitan centres
   transcending Indianness, 158
"Cosmopolitans and Celebrities" (Brennan), 52
"counter hegemonic representations," 190
"Crossmatch" (Karodia), 135, 154-55

cultural and psychological madness, 19
"cultural bomb," 18, 170
cultural colonization, 26, 147
cultural construction, 148
cultural diversity, 140
cultural emancipation, 25
cultural freedom, 199
cultural fusion, 148
cultural hierarchy and oppression internal to modernity, 21
cultural imperialism, 20
cultural oppression through language, 16, 18
cyclical violence theory, 169–70

D

"Daddy" (Ali), 192
Dangarembga, Tsitsi, 6, 13, 26, 198
   Nervous Conditions, 125–34
Dash, Michael, 179
Davies, Carole Boyce, 4, 11–12, 116
   on African feminism, 10
Days and Nights in Calcutta (Mukherjee), 63–65, 72, 79
decolonization. *See also* nationalism
   Fanon on, 48–49
   women's oppression and exploitation, 130
"Decolonizing Culture" (Katrak), 175
democracy, 19, 21
Deshpande, Shashi, 24
Desirable Daughters (Mukherjee), 79–88
despair and despondency, 18, 25
Devi: The Goddess (1960), 9, 39
deviant sexuality, 147, 157, 171
   homosexuality, 155, 157–58, 191–92, 194
   lesbianism, 173
diaspora of despair, 143–45, 149, 151, 179–81
diaspora of early capital, 174
diaspora of hope, 143–44, 149, 179–81
diaspora of late capital, 174
diaspora of terror, 143–44, 179
diasporic community, 22
   alienation, 115
   hope for reconstructing identity, 160
   nervous condition, 23
   relationship to motherland or homeland, 137
   strategies of resistance and reinscriptions, 136
diasporic Indian men
   racialized and feminized in America, 92
Dirlik, Arif, 177, 186–87, 194
The Discovery of India (Nehru), 41
"DissemiNation" (Bhabha), 53, 138
diversity and multiculturalism, 149. *See also* pluralism
"Divide and Rule" policy, 154
divine love, 100
divorce and remarriage, 89
double oppression, 13
dowry deaths, 73, 184–85
dreams, 8, 69, 146
   redreaming, 10

E

East/West exploitativeness, 115, 187, 195
"ecology of plurality," 26
"The Economy of the Manichean Allegory" (JanMohamed), 188
education for women, 5, 46, 110, 128. *See also* Western education
   "choice" in marriage, 109
   conservative influence, 36
   debates in French West Africa, 107
   for educated husband, 94
   essential feminine qualities should remain, 38
   good wives and mothers, 36
   strengthening marriage institution, 35
   suitable for Western-educated husbands, 38, 98, 137
   Victorian England, 35, 38
   women to be both modern and traditional, 36
education of women
   pitfalls of educating girls, 152
emergent middle class, 29, 38, 137

Empire of Knowledge (Lal), 20–21, 56
The Empire Writes Back (Ashcroft), 115–16
England. *See* United Kingdom
English language, 16, 55, 63
    Indian culture and, 64
    official language in India, 65
'Englishness,' 130
"escape" through education and "expansion," 127. *See also* leaving "oppressive" home space
essentialism (gender), 38–39, 44–45
    Gandhi's belief in, 46
essentialized notion of Indianness, 61
"essentially" African, 125
Ethnic Studies, 19
Eurocentrism, 187, 194
European education. *See* Western education
European languages. *See also* colonizers' language; English language; French language
    supporting capitalist ideology, 18
exile, 79, 116, 122, 150, 155, 179, 183, 186, 188
"exotic minors," 188, 195

F

fame, 52
Fanon, Frantz, 34–36, 49, 130
    notion of "occult instability," 49
    The Wretched of the Earth, 48, 126, 169
Fault Lines (Alexander), 178, 183, 189
female body, 44, 46, 179–80
    as diseased or contaminated, 125
    impure due to Westernization, 126
    indecent clothes, 157
female children seen as curse, 156
female circumcision, 26
Female Genital Mutilation (FGM), 131, 176, 185
    fetishized focus on, 24
    used by women to empower themselves, 132
female sexuality, 102, 129–30
    patriarchal control of, 38, 41
    seen as evil by traditional males, 132

female solidarity. *See* community of women
feminism, 12, 24
    international feminism, 10
    postcolonial African feminism, 120
    postcolonial feminism, 10, 12, 50
    postcolonial/transnational/multicultural feminism, 3, 12–15, 23–24
    postmodern feminism, 150
    transnational feminism, 10, 15
    transnational feminists, 15
Feminisms 2 (Grewal), 54
feminist and gender studies, 6
feminist cultural imperialism, 14, 164, 172, 174
'feminist emancipation,' 25
feminists
    global, postcolonia/transnational/multicultural feminists, 176
    "Third World Feminists" so-called, 7
feminists' participation in modernity
    Grewal and Kaplan's critique, 164
Fire (film), 164, 173
    arranged marriages, 165
    critical acclaim in the west, 166
    demonizing Indian patriarchy, 167
    lesbianism, 165
First World voyeurism, 178, 181. *See also* Western audience
Foucault, Michel, 98–99
    on dominant discourse, 19
    History of Sexuality, 182
    "limit of madness," 49
Francophone African literature, 9
French colonialism, 34
French language, 9, 119
French West Africa, 103
Fuentes, Carlos, 52

G

Ganatra, Nisha, 164–66
    complicity with Western ideology, 168
    diaspora of late capital, 174
Gandhi, Leela, 25

Gandhi, Mahatma
   another language of dissent, 20
   use of non-violence and passive resistance, 41
   woman-in-the-home ideology, 46–47
Gandhian nationalism, 46–47
gay men, 155, 157–58, 191–92
"gender and globalization"
   literature on, 55
gender and madness, 15
gender and violence, 15
gender identity, 1, 139
gender identity in minority communities (US), 75
gender oppression, 1, 5, 10, 15, 104, 130, 172. *See also* abuse of women; Indian woman; violence against women
gender politics, 53
gender roles, 67
Ghanatra, Nisha, 6
Gilbert, Sandra, 48
   The Madwoman in the Attic, 50
global, postcolonia/transnational/multicultural feminists, 176
global capitalism, 187, 193. *See also* capitalist world-economy
   alternate spaces within, 126
   increased subordination of women, 130
Global North, 55, 57–58, 69, 149, 169. *See also* United States; West
   dating and sexuality, 87, 164, 166
   East/West binaries still apply, 160
   ethnic ghettos, 82
   increased racism and violence, 58, 175
Global North diasporic spaces
   shifts in thinking in new generation, 142
Global South, xi, 2, 25, 55, 58, 64, 88, 149
   disempowerment, 1
   "enduring 'civilizations'", 20
   oppressive and limiting, 54
   raw material producing area, 57
Global West, 88

globalization, 10, 48, 174. *See also* global capitalism
   access to English and egalitarian knowledge systems, 55
   alternative visions and values, 55
   in cultural realm, 54
   in economic sphere, 54
   "engendering" of, 55
Gopinath, Gayatri, 168
   "Local Sites/Global Contexts," 166
Grewal, Gurleen, 66, 70–71
Grewal, Indrapal, 13, 16, 24–25, 66, 73, 164, 174
   Feminisms 2, 54
Griffiths, Gareth, 115
group identity, 139, 175
Gubar, Susan, 48
Gujarati Patels, 140
Gulzar, Rakhee, 89–102
Gunew, Sneja, 68–69

H

"heteropathic" identification, 178
Hirsch, Marianne, "Projected Memory," 178
History of Sexuality (Foucault), 182
The Home and the World (Tagore), 19, 37, 41
homeland
   "imaginary homeland," 117, 136
   return to, 116–17
homosexual and transsexual identity, 168
homosexuality, 155, 157–58, 191–92, 194
Hughes, Carolyn, 191
hybrid culture, 137
hybrid idea of Indianness, 140
hybrid identities, 23, 52, 59, 132, 143, 191
hybrid spaces, 30, 53, 87, 138
hybrid tradition (Afro-European literature), 17
hybridized sensibilities and representations, 149, 174

I

"I Will Make Bimala One with My Country" (Mitra), 37–38, 41, 138
idealization of woman
    as Earth Mother/Motherland, 26
    masking subordination of women, 105
    as pure and self-sacrificing wife, 26
idealized domestic sphere
    symbol of national regeneration, 46–47
identity construction, 69
    gendered, 139
    Global North vs. Global South, 135
    limitations, 159
    in terms of religious nationalism, 151
    in transnational diasporic space, 79
identity politics, 23, 63
idiopathic identification, 178, 180, 186–88
Ilaiah, Kancha, 54
"imaginary homeland," 117, 136
imagination
    collective, 158
    staging ground for action, 147
imagined Indian community, 157
imperialism, 65
imperialist feminist ideology, 14, 164, 172, 174
incest, 171
India, 21
    British colonization of, 136, 140
    English education, 18, 93
    English language, 64–65
    place of demons and devils, 192
    social reform movement in, 36
    supposed equal rights for women, 43
    unofficial bisexuality, 173
Indian cinema, 95, 139. *See also* Bollywood films
    Hindi films, 139–40
Indian culture, 175
    backwardness, 62, 164
Indian diaspora, 65, 135, 141
    dating and sexuality, 166
    ethnic ghettos, 82
    in-between space, 199
    negotiating for and holding on to ideas of "Indianness," 140
    origins of, 136
    traditional femininity still imposed, 87
Indian diaspora (South Africa), 136
Indian diaspora (Uganda)
    forced migration, 140
    kept to themselves, 153
Indian diaspora (UK)
    seen as enforcing oppressive "arranged marriages," 149
Indian diaspora in the Caribbean, 169
Indian diaspora in the West, 136. *See also* Global North; United States
    double burden (woman and Indian), 146
Indian masculinity, 172, 175
Indian men
    as inferior and oppressive of women, 30
    programmed to provide for wives and children, 86
    racialized and feminized in America, 86
    stereotyped as unfeeling, 86
    as unfit for self-rule, 31
Indian patriarchy. *See* patriarchy
Indian woman, 180
    centre of national culture, 43
    darker, inferior "other" of the Victorian gentlewoman, 31
    disillusionment, 67
    empowerment through gender roles, 95
    lower status after colonial intervention, 31
    middle class, 90, 95
    postcolonial/transnational/ multicultural/diasporic, 23
    repressed sexuality, 96 (*See also* sexuality)
    seen as passive victim of patriarchal oppression, 30–31, 166–68, 175
    shrill, gaudy, one-dimensional, 192–93
    unable to change social position, 47, 138

Indian womanhood, 62, 135, 137, 175, 193
  justification for colonial penetration of
    India, 30–34
  token representatives, 21
Indianness, 135, 137
  "authentic" Indian self, 149
  constructed in imagined communities, 139
  shame of, 140
  transcending, 158
individual vs. communal identity, 120, 175
individualism, 22–23, 26, 95
  in Hindu philosophy, 91, 93
international feminism, 10
interracial sexual relationships, 157, 182, 194
  in Alexander's texts, 178
  Indo-African, 142, 152
"An Invisible Woman" (Mukherjee), 63
Iraq, 2, 10, 34
  attacks on, 64
Iraq war, 149, 164

J

JanMohamed, Abdul R., 104
  "The Economy of the Manichean Allegory," 188
Jasmine (Mukherjee), 69–72, 84
  "authentic" American identity, 68
Jayawardena, Kumari, 35–36
Jesus is Indian (Sam), 135–36, 149–50
Joshi, Rama, 31
Juletane (Warner-Vieyra), 19, 115–23
Jussawalla, Feroza, 65–66

K

Kafka, Phillipa, 4
  On the Outside Looking In(dian), 14
Kali, 40, 69
Kaplan, Caren, 14, 16, 24–25, 164, 174
  "Politics of Location as Transnational Feminist Practice," 13
Karodia, Farida, 6, 48, 149, 155, 160
  "Crossmatch," 135, 154

Katrak, Ketu H., "Decolonizing Culture," 175
Kenya, 145
Khanna, Tarun, 21
Kingston, Maxine Hong, *The Woman Warrior*, 185
Kipling's "White Man's Burden," 30

L

Lady Chatterley's Lover (Lawrence), 129
Lal, Vinay, 22, 25–26, 55
  Empire of Knowledge, 20–21, 56
language, 2, 16, 19, 140. *See also* names of individual languages
  male-dominated language, 5, 50
  means of spiritual subjugation, 18, 170
  new language, 49
  of postcolonial female writers, 51
  Westernized discursive systems, 105
Lawrence, D.H., *Lady Chatterley's Lover*, 129
leaving "oppressive" home space, 154, 193–94, 198. *See also* "escape" through education and "expansion"
Lelyveld, David, 184, 188
lesbianism, 166–68
liberal humanism, 34
Liddle, Joanne, 31
"Lifting the Veil," xi
liminal spaces, 126, 130, 138, 160, 198
Lionnet, Françoise, 197
"Local Sites/Global Contexts" (Gopinath), 166
London, 145, 148, 155–58, 194
Loomba, Ania, 6, 37
Loreto House Convent School, 63, 79
love, 81, 107, 150, 153, 174, 182
  Radha for Krishna (divine love), 100
love, concept of
  associated with fallen woman, 93
love, romance, and courtship
  problematic for Indian women, 93–94
Love Under the Banyan Tree, 156, 158
lover, role of, 86, 95

224   REPRESENTATION AND RESISTANCE

M

Macherey, Pierre, 25
madness, 15, 73, 76, 79, 90, 117–19, 138, 170–71, 199. *See also* mental breakdown
    abortion as, 74
    aftermath of colonialism, 172
    Alexander's use of, 177
    cultural and psychological, 19
    murder, 78
    in *Parama* (film), 98, 100, 102
    representations of violence, 133
madness and sexual ambiguity, 169
madness in postcolonial texts, 48–50, 58
madness or deviancy, 20, 26
"Madras on Rainy Days" (Ali), 190
Madras on Rainy Days (Ali), 190, 192
The Madwoman in the Attic (Gilbert), 50
Maira, Sunaina Marr, 166
male-dominated language, 5, 50
male domination, 192–93. *See also* patriarchy
male literary tradition, 104
Mama, Amina, 15, 53
Manhattan Music (Alexander), 178, 183
Manichean allegory, 104–5, 192
market liberalism, 10, 18, 21, 62, 88
marriage, 150
    arranged (*See* arranged marriage)
    companionate marriage, 41, 67, 94, 109
    "controversial marriage," 107, 109
    divorce and remarriage, 89
    in Muslim society, 109
    polygamy, 110–13, 117–18, 120
marriage consummation, 191
marriage for convenience, 121
marriage market, 101, 130–31
marriage to younger man, 89, 121
Marxism, 6, 19
mass media, 109
    building solidarity, 148
    community of sentiment, 139, 147
    imaginary spaces, 143
materialism, 153
matrilineal form of family organization, 31

Mayo, Katherine, 32
    Mother India, 32–33
media. *See* mass media
Meer, Ameena, 66
Mehta, Brinda, 172
Mehta, Deepa, 6, 164, 166, 173–74
    complicity with Western ideology, 168
Memmi, Albert, 15
Menon, Nivedita, "Nation *is* tradition," 54–55
mental breakdown, 90, 133. *See also* madness; nervous breakdown
    rejection of Westernization and patriarchal practices, 130
mental colonization, 126
metropolitan centres, 144, 155, 159, 174–75
middle class, 90
middle-class, 47, 95, 110, 138
    postcolonial world, 21
Midnight's Children (Rushdie), 64
migrancy and loss, 116
migration, 155, 178, 181, 184
    deciding for herself, 150
    in order to make a living, 143
Mill, James, 30–31
Miller, James, *The Passion of Michel Foucault*, 98
Minh-ha, Trinh T., 50–51
miscarriage, 119
Mishra, Vijay, 174
Mississippi Masala (film), 135, 141, 146
    hybrid transnational space used for empowerment, 144
    "Indianness" questioned, 142
    Indo-African sexual alliance, 142
    patriarchal control and structure, 142
Mitra, Indrani, 66–67
    "Colonialism," 33
    "I Will Make Bimala One with My Country," 37–38, 41, 138
mixed race sexual relationships, 142, 145–46
    Black and Indian, 142, 152
modern sexualized subjects, 183

modernity, 14, 22, 41, 48, 61, 144
    and the construction of liberated
        sexuality, 168
    cultural hierarchy and oppression, 21
    feminist participation in, 26, 164
    idiom of, 57
    as marker for equality, 175
    Mootoo's support for, 174
    Mukherjee's complicity with, 26
    promise to (post)colonized women, 150

Modernity at Large (Appadurai), 179

modernity/tradition. *See* tradition vs. modernity

Mohanty, Chandra Talpade, 70
    "Under Western Eyes," 175

Mootoo, Shani, 6, 165
    Cereus Blooms at Night, 164, 168, 172
    diaspora of late capital, 174
    "nervous condition" of postcolonial people, 169
    politics of location, 169
    supporting the agenda of modernity, 174

Mother Africa (trope of)
    gendered theory of nationhood and writing, 4, 104

mother-daughter relations, 9

mother-in-law, 10

Mother India (Mayo), 32–33

Motherlands (Nasta), 35–36

"*motherlands, mothercultures, mothertongues*"
    appropriate tropes for re-imaging, 6

Mukherjee, Bharati, 6, 48, 52–53, 62
    affiliation with the West, 65
    alienation from home culture, 62–63, 66, 79, 84
    "Americanness" as liberating, 84
    assimilationist protagonist, 70
    celebration of the U.S., 66
    commodification of Indianness, 73, 82
    complicity with modernist agenda, 26
    conflicted cultural space, 65
    Days and Night in Calcutta, 63–65, 72, 79
    Desirable Daughters, 79–88
    effort to explain Hinduism, 85
    experience as visible minority, 63, 65
    "exuberance" of the immigrant experience, 68
    Indian society as tradition bound, 62
    Indian women as oppressed and brutalized, 70
    "Indianness" as backward and "traditional," 64, 66, 84
    "An Invisible Woman," 63
    Jasmine, 68–72, 84
    Jussawalla's criticism, 66
    Loreto House Convent School, 63
    marriage to Clark Blaise, 63
    protagonists "between roles," 78, 87
    psychic violence, 71
    reductive and easy binaries, 81
    rewriting of "sanctioned suicide," 77
    seeming return to *her* India in *Desirable Daughters*, 86
    stereotyping of Muslims, 84–85
    The Tiger's Daughter, 62, 64–65, 67, 69, 72–73, 82
    token representative of oppressed Indian Womanhood, 21
    treatment of sexuality, 76
    valorization of arranged marriage, 85
    Westernized consciousness, 61, 64–65
    Wife, 61–78, 84

Mukherjee, Meenakshi, 93

multiculturalism, 21, 24, 66, 69, 159, 176

multiple nationalisms, 144

Mumdani, Mahmood, 141

Muslim patriarchal system, 117

Muslim polygamous practices, 122

Muslim woman, 151

myth of liberal West, 192

N

Nair, Mira, 6, 135, 148
    Mississippi Masala, 141

naming lesbianism, 18

Nasta, Susheila, 4, 6–7
    Motherlands, 35–37

"The Nation and its Women" (Chatterjee), 83
Nation and Narration (Bhabha), 159
"Nation *is* tradition" (Menon), 54
nationalism, 6, 8, 21, 26, 43–44, 58
   confusing and ambivalent for the new woman, 29, 42, 138
   debates since 9/11, 23
   and education for women, 35–36, 137
   emergent elite, 35
   essentialism (gender), 37, 137
   femininity adjusted in accordance, 39
   modern notions of sexual equality, 40
   "new woman," 29, 35, 37, 41–42, 114, 138
   no change in material or social position of women, 138
   and purity of Indian woman, 44, 46
   reinforced patriarchal repression of women, 5, 39, 42, 137
   seen as predominantly male enterprise, 103
   selective modernization of colonized woman, 41–42
   Western universalism idioms, 20
   woman as goddess or mother, 36, 39–40
   women must not become essentially Westernized, 44
   women's participation in, 8, 37, 46–47, 104
   women's struggle for gender equality and, 47
"The Nationalist Resolution of the Women's Question" (Chatterjee), 43
"native informants," 24, 26
Négritude movement
   further oppression of African women, 104
Négritude poetry, 3
   Manichean allegory of gender, 4
Nehru, Jawaharlal, *The Discovery of India*, 41
neo-liberalism, 2, 54–56
neocolonialism, 14, 18, 26, 174

nervous breakdown, 91, 100, 118, 187. *See also* madness; mental breakdown
"nervous condition," 16, 26, 129, 132, 170
Nervous Conditions (Dangarembga), 125–34
   Flora Veit-Wild's interpretation, 126, 129, 132
nervous subjectivities, 18, 58, 100
new music
   fusion of culture of East and West, 148
"new woman," 29, 35, 37, 41–42, 83, 138
   "educated" and transformed wives and mothers, 114
   within the Muslim African culture, 106
   of nationalist discourse, 179
   spiritual qualities, 42, 154
New World. *See also* Global North; United States
   possibilities for reconstruction of identity, 69
New World Order, 113, 173
Newell, Stephanie, 4, 105
Ngugi wa Thiong'o, 16–18, 25, 170
Nigeria, 12
9/11. *See* post-9/11 world
nostalgia, 116, 172
NRIs (non-resident Indians), 174

O

Obiechina, Emmanuel, 109, 112
obligation to bear children, 9–10
"occult instability," 49
Ogunyemi, Chikwenye Okonjo, 4, 11–12, 22, 26
On the Outside Looking In(dian) (Kafka), 14
Orientalists, 32, 64, 67, 193, 198
Our Feet Walk the Sky (Ali), 190
out-of-body experiences, 133
overappropriation, 180, 187
Oyêwùmí, Oyèrónké, 4, 12–13

Index   *227*

P

Parama (film), 89–102
    Arora's critique, 91–92, 100
    "bedroom" scenes between woman and husband, 97
    commercial success, 90
    companionate marriage, 93
    controversial, 90
    crisis, 98
    madness, 98, 100, 102
    oppressed Indian woman and Indian patriarchy, 89
    Radha Subramanyam's view of, 91–92, 95, 102
    reception in India, 89
    sexually aware woman in domestic space, 102
    sexually explicit scenes, 90, 95
    work outside home, 100–101
The Passion of Michel Foucault (Miller), 98
Patel, Sujata, 46–47
paternalism, 6, 88
patriarchal discourse, 50
patriarchal ideology, 122
patriarchy, 10, 120, 125, 131, 142
    in companionate marriage, 109
    control of female sexuality, 38, 41
    Indo-Caribbean, 172
    with its practice of polygamy, 118
    Muslim patriarchal system, 117
    new partriarchy advocated by nationalism, 39
    romanticizes women as the Great Mother, 4
    supported by colonial enterprise, 126, 128
    violence against women, 9
Pereira, Charmaine, 7
Petersen, Kirsten Holst, 174, 179
Petty, Sheila J., 3–4
petty-bourgeoisie literature, 16–17
pluralism, 160
plurality, 22
politics of location, 13–15, 102, 105, 163, 169, 176, 197
"Politics of Location as Transnational Feminist Practice" (Kaplan), 13
polygamy, 110–13, 117–18, 120
post-9/11 world, 10, 23, 54, 159, 163, 174, 192
postcolonial African feminism, 120
postcolonial female writers and artists
    entrapping cycle, 7
    idioms of modernity, 1
    misread and misinterpreted, 48–49, 53
    need to redream, 9
    as "secular, liberated," 71
    Western patriarchal conventions, 50
    writing about "oppressed third world woman," 187
    writing madness, 50, 52 (*See also* madness)
postcolonial feminism, 12, 50
    different from international and transnational feminism, 10
postcolonial feminists
    hybrid identity, 52
    "Third Space" for rearticulation, 52
Postcolonial Studies, 19
postcolonial transnational feminism, 11, 22, 56
postcolonial/transnational/multicultural/diasporic Indian women, 23
postcolonial/transnational/multicultural feminism, 3, 12–15, 23–24
postcolonial women's texts, 5
    ambiguity and conflict, 40, 42, 47
    recasting female subjectivity and agency, 125
    writing madness and nervous conditions, 49
postmodern feminism, 150
postmodernity, 16
postnational political order, 20, 161, 199
Pratt, Mary Louise, 49
pregnancy, 113, 118, 121, 145–46, 156
    in *Wife*, 73–74
"prior hegemony," 75
"Projected Memory" (Hirsch), 178
"Promised Land," 192
prostitute metaphor, 105
psychic violence, 71

"psychological violence of the classroom," 18
purdah, xii, 2, 33, 46

R

Race Classification and Group Area Acts of South Africa, 153
"race redoubling," 15
racism, 15, 126, 147, 152, 175, 192
    U.S., 160, 192
Ray, Satyajit, *Devi: The Goddess,* 19, 39
refusing to eat, 129. *See also* anorexia; madness
regulatory power of ideology, 125
"rejection of motherhood," 9. *See also* abortion
relocation to West, 154, 171, 193–94, 198
resistance, 19–20, 129, 133
    cultural constructions of gender identity, 138
    in form of madness, 138 (*See also* madness)
    against patriarchal ideology, 77
return to homeland, 116–17
Rhodesia, 126
Rich, Adrienne, 58
Richard, Cliff, "Summer Holiday," 148
Rodowick, David N., 96
romantic love, 72, 97, 109, 111–12, 117–18
    in modern West Africa, 109
    supports patriarchal institutions, 110
A Room of One's Own (Woolf), 13
Roy, Anindyo, 65–66
Rushdie, Salman, 52
    "imaginary homeland," 136
    Midnight's Children, 64

S

Sam, Agnes, 6, 160
    "A Bag of Sweets," 151
    Jesus is Indian, 135–36, 149–50
    "The Well-Loved Woman," 151

Samuelson, Meg, 9
San Francisco, 158
Sarkar, Tanika, 41, 45
Sartre, Jean-Paul, 126
sati, 69
    Mukherjee's treatment of, 70–71
satyagraha (civil disobedience, non-cooperation), 46
science, 19
Seidel, Michael, 122
Sen, Aparna, 6, 26, 48, 198
    divorce and remarriage, 89
    Parama, 89–102
Senghor, Léopold Sédar, 3, 105
sexual abuse, 181, 187
sexual identity, 98
    Indian society, 95–96
    no space for, 97
sexual liberation, 26, 38, 76, 81, 84–86, 95, 113, 168
sexual repression, 95–97, 130, 179
sexuality, 9, 15, 23, 94–96, 101, 182–83. *See also burqa, purdah,* and the veil
    illicit sexual relations, 145
    Mayo's concern with, 32–33
The Shock of Arrival (Alexander), 95, 178, 180, 189
Shohat, Ella, 24, 176
silence, 119
"silence of madness," 98
silences of a text, 25
Silverman, Kaja, 178
sisterhood, 10. *See also* community of women
So Long a Letter (Bâ), 103–14
    marriage and romantic love, 110
social reform movement in India, 36
South Africa, 170
South African Indian population, 140, 149
    arrived as indentured labourers, 136
    post-apartheid affluence, 21, 157
    suppressed history, 136
South African Writings in English (Chetty), 136, 153
South Asian diaspora. *See* Indian diaspora

South Asian gay community in San Francisco, 158
    racial oppression and marginalization, 160
spinning wheel, 46–47
Spivak, Gayatri Chakraborty, 11
    "Can the Subaltern Speak?", 30, 77, 193
stereotype of the "independent woman," 102
Stratton, Florence, 3–4, 105
    Contemporary African Literature and the Politics of Gender, 104
Sturgess, Charlotte, 116
Subramanyam, Radha, 91–92, 95, 102
suicide, 76–77, 90, 99, 118
Summer Holiday (film), 148
"superior" self-identity of the East, 43
sustainable justice, 199
suttee, 30
swadeshi (development of indigenous economy), 47
swaraj (self-rule), 47
Syal, Meera, 145

T

Tagore, Rabindranath, *The Home and the World*, 19, 37, 41
Taliban, xii
technology and multimedia. *See also* mass media
    impact on identity formation, 139
"Third Space," 87, 91, 100, 144, 149, 169, 179, 198
Third World diasporic sensibilities, 140
"Third World Feminists," so-called
    disseminating distortions in Western academy, 7
Third World subjects, 2
Third World Women, 71, 178–79, 185–87. *See also* African woman; Indian woman
    arranged marriages and abusive husbands, 183
    triple oppression (gender, colonialism, male-dominated language), 5

Third World women
    Caribbean women writers, 116
Tiffin, Helen, 116
The Tiger's Daughter (Mukherjee), 64–65, 69, 72–73
    author's misgivings about India, 82
    reflections of author's experience, 67
tradition *vs.* modernity, 24, 38, 74, 125
    ideological crisis, 107
traditional ceremonies of "cleansing," 131. *See also* Female Genital Mutilation (FGM)
traditional cultural and familial practices modified by modern Western thinking, 43
    selective acceptance, 11
transgression, 98–99, 121
transgressive women, 90
    shame upon families, 194
transnational diaspora, 154, 159
    changes in thinking, 142
    conflict and ambiguities, 61, 79
    construction of identity, 79
    Indian women leave "oppressive home culture," 144
    new cultural forms and new hybrid identities, 143
transnational feminism, 10, 15
transnationalism, 24, 174
travel as transformation, 174
trope of Mother Africa, 4, 104
trope of the tribe, 159, 203n2

U

Uganda, 140, 170
"Under Western Eyes" (Mohanty), 175
United Kingdom, 144
    Asians categorized as black, 146
    Black Caribbeans, 146
    legal actions against Indians who force daughters to marry, 147
    suttee abolished, 146
United States, 54, 140. *See also* Global North; West

divisions among minority
    communities, 142
imperialism, 10
liberating for women, 54
Orientalists, 193
racism toward minorities, 160, 192
universalism, 18–19

V

veil, xii, 2, 34–35
Veit-Wild, Flora, 126, 129, 132
    Writing Madness, 51
violence, 58, 62, 70, 161, 172, 199
    cyclical violence theory, 169–70
    in Mukherjee's work, 69, 77–78
    psychic violence, 71
    "psychological violence of the classroom," 18
    racism and, 175, 192
violence against women, 9, 131, 145
    blaming the woman, 146
violence inherent in construction of the Self, 68–69

W

Walcott, Derek, 52
Wallerstein, Immanuel, 18–21, 57–58
War on Terror, 64
Warner-Vieyra, Myriam, 6, 48
    critique of polygamy, 117, 122
    Juletane, 19, 115–23
    reinforces patriarchal ideology, 122
"The Well-Loved Woman" (Sam), 151
West. *See also* Global North; United States
    liberating for women, 54
    as a liberatory space, 172
    myth of the liberal West, 192
    reality of minority and gay oppression, 172–73
Western academy, 5–7, 14, 19, 24, 56–57, 175, 178
    status to cultural workers/brokers in diaspora, 188
    token representatives of oppressed Indian Womanhood, 21

Western audience, 13, 16, 21, 24, 32, 61, 70, 73–74, 97, 164–66, 170, 176–78, 192, 194–95
Western-educated women, 1, 43, 48, 122
    clashing with expectations of a patriarchal society, 112
    limited choices, 113
    still defined by relationships with males, 129–30
Western-educated women writers, 25, 30
Western education, 29, 63, 110. *See also* education for women
    barrier to woman's role as wife and mother, 4
    to bring choices, liberation, and positive change, 107, 131
    ideology of liberal humanism, 34
    impact on construction of gender identity, 103
    imposed by colonial administrators, 106
    pitfalls of, 107–8
    produced anxiety within colonized culture, 106
    shame of Indianness, 140
    status for men (not for women), 129
"Western hegemonies," 164
Western ideology, 168
Western knowledge systems, 25
Western Romantic tradition, 109
Western universalism, 18–19
Westernization of woman's body
    threat to national identity, 125
white man saving brown woman from brown man, 30, 193
"White Man's Burden," 30
white women, 32
Wife (Mukherjee), 62, 71, 84
    dislocation and psychic violence, 61–78
"woman question," 35
The Woman Warrior (Kingston), 185
women
    African (*See* African woman)
    domestic and spiritual realm, 39
    Indian (*See* Indian woman)
    kept in domestic roles, 128

religious duties and family life and ties, 39
traditional cultural practices in the domestic sphere, 4
use of painful means to acquire privileges and power, 132
women as bearers of national culture, 36–37, 151
women as Mother Africa, 4, 104
women of colour
   triple oppression, 5
women well jumping, 177, 185
women's community, 120, 133, 173. *See also* sisterhood
   within Indian patriarchal structures, 101, 149
   reimagining, 123
"women's question"
   debates over social reforms in Bengal, 83
Women's Studies, 19
Women's War of 1929–30, 104
Woolf, Virginia, A *Room of One's Own*, 13
work outside home, 90, 100–101, 156
working classes, 17
"world system theory," 57
World Trade Center attack, 149. *See also* post-9/11 world
   sparked violence against Sikhs and South Asians, 160
Wretched of the Earth (Fanon), 48, 126, 169
Writing Madness (Veit-Wild), 51

Z

Zeleza Paul, 55
zenana, 41–42
Zimbabwe, 126, 170. *See also* Rhodesia

www.ingramcontent.com/pod-product-compliance
Lightning Source LLC
Chambersburg PA
CBHW052059300426
44117CB00013B/2196